Democracy Is You

Democracy Is You

A Guide to Citizen Action

RICHARD WAVERLY POSTON

Director
Bureau of Community Development
University of Washington
Seattle

HARPER & BROTHERS • PUBLISHERS • NEW YORK

21700

To My Mother Who Inspired Me

And To The People Of
BATTLE GROUND—WHITE SALMON—BINGEN—TROUT-
LAKE—GLENWOOD—BELFAIR—TOLEDO
WINLOCK—HAZEL DELL

Who Helped Make This
Guide Possible

Contents

Preface

IN 1944 THERE BEGAN A THREE-YEAR EXPERIMENT KNOWN AS "THE
Montana Study," financed primarily by the Rockefeller Foundation
and carried out through the University of Montana, at the instiga-
tion of Ernest O. Melby, now dean of education at New York
University.

Founder of the project, and the man who developed it, who
worked out its philosophy, who directed it, and who witnessed its
tragic demise was Baker Brownell, professor of philosophy at
Northwestern University. Melby is one of America's great deans,
Brownell one of her great teachers, and the father of a method of
community development which has the potential to bring a rebirth
of spirit in America and eliminate war and starvation from the
earth. But there are only a few who know that.

In 1946 I became obsessed by the potential energy for human
progress which the Montana Study had to offer. It was in most
respects an infant thing, it had yet to be fully developed, and still
has. But it was new, and like all new inventions it had yet to be
elaborated on and worked out to its full capacity.

In 1950 Harper & Brothers published *Small Town Renaissance,*
which was the product of my own efforts to tell what I had learned
from four years of careful study of the Montana project. This was
a description of the dramatic events that had taken place, with an
indication of what could happen if the forces locked up in the potential of this project were really set loose in the communities of
America. Later came Brownell's *The Human Community* and *The
College and the Community.* These dealt with the philosophy of
community life and the present relationship of the college to that
life.

In the summer of 1950 Raymond B. Allen, then president of the
University of Washington, heard of what had happened in Montana
and because of his own great vision saw at once the potential of a
magnificent idea which had only to be carried out to the full limits
of its capacity. Here in embryonic form was a program that could
strengthen and enrich America, community by community. Through

this program the resources of a great state university could be mo-
bilized to help the men and women who support it gain the motivation, the incentive, and the knowledge to solve their own problems
for themselves, to inject new life into the ideals which built a nation.
Here was a potential which if put to work in local communities
could generate a force and a vitality that could bring new hope to
the future of all the world.

And so in the State of Washington we began where Baker Brownell had left off in Montana. The first job was to write a guide for
community self-study which could be used anywhere, for this was
the basic method of the program. This I entitled *Group Study Guide
for Community Development*, and it was used in six different community areas in mimeographed form. By actual use we learned from
the communities where it needed more detail, elaboration, and
change. After two community study groups, one in the Mount Adams area centered in White Salmon and Bingen on the Columbia,
and one in Battle Ground in southwestern Washington, supplements
were added to the guide. Finally, after two years of continuous use
in these and other communities, the present volume has evolved,
and is, I believe, now in a form which can be successfully applied
in a wide variety of community locales.

In the Bureau of Community Development at the University of
Washington, this is the guide that is used in the initial phase of the
community development program. Following this guide, but making
adjustments wherever a particular local situation demands, the people make an intensive and systematic study of life in their own
community in an effort to learn how they may improve it—culturally, economically, socially, and spiritually. We of the Bureau of
Community Development act as consultants and help guide the
community study. We endeavor to bring in additional services
which are requested as a result of the study, and to do what we can
to help the community help itself.

The potential returns in human achievement are virtually unlimited. This we have found as eyewitnesses of the new birth in community life that already has taken place. Yet the potential has
hardly been tapped. It now remains only to be released and applied
wherever men yearn for a better life.

And so this book has been written in the hope that the method

of community development which Baker Brownell first began in
Montana may now be applied in communities throughout America
wherever men would again take their destiny into their own hands
and mold it for themselves, and that state universities and colleges
across the nation will recognize this as their opportunity for new
vistas of service.

RICHARD WAVERLY POSTON

Seattle, Washington
June 16, 1952

Part I

Philosophy

Community Action:
The Great Need

AMERICAN DEMOCRACY—THE WAY OF LIVING THAT BUILT A NATION, gave to men a tradition of freedom, reshaped a world, and conditioned the thinking of generations—today stands on trial. No longer can it remain taken for granted. No longer can it be considered secure, solid, firm. Instead, it struggles for survival.

This, then, is the question: Can the principle of a democratic society with its tradition of freedom succeed in the modern world?

The answer to that question will depend upon the action of people within their communities. For without thought, action, and participation by the people in their own community life no democratic society can long exist. No centralized institution, no organization or association, be it private or public, political or academic, can make the processes of democracy a working method in human society. Democracy as a social force springs only from the people in their communities. It cannot function through actions that are devised or superimposed from above. Yet this has become the method of the age in which we live.

Child of the Industrial Revolution, ours is an age of unrestrained technology, of achievement which has brought material success in a spectacular degree; success which has exceeded even the wildest dreams of our American founders.

This is the age in which we have mastered the principles of mathematics, of physics, of chemistry, and of electricity. We have written these principles into books and we have built schools in which we could teach them to our children so that they could learn what we have been told are the fundamental tools of living. With these tools we have made machines that have brought riches to mankind, made living easier, and housework simpler. And by these means we have released ourselves from the drudgery and the backbreaking labor that chained our grandmothers to the farmhouse.

From it all we have built up a system of business and finance

3

which has produced millions of jobs and added more tools to make life easier. We have developed vast systems of credit which now make it possible to enjoy next year's income this year, while we are still paying for what we enjoyed last year. We have heaped structure upon structure of new laws and government. And we have thus progressed into what is referred to as modern civilization. In the race for advancement our schools and universities have been transformed into great mills where graduates are mass produced, where subject matters have been systematized and stored into vast libraries for the scholar. And by this means we have developed the practice of specialization in which the student can devote a lifetime to becoming an expert in the most minute particle of human knowledge.

And so with our newly made tools of knowledge and mass technology we have succeeded spectacularly in remaking the social and cultural fabric of America, and of a good deal of the rest of the world.

But in the process we have made a costly mistake. We have made our technology, our knowledge, and our material goods the ends in life instead of the means by which to create something even more important than the tools. And for this we have paid dearly.

During the great depression of the thirties, the winds swept eastward across the high plains of Mid-America and black clouds of silt moved toward the Atlantic. News writers called it the "Dust Bowl." But the true story of that tragic era was written on the ground. Man, with his technology, had converted the grasslands into a living hell. Homes were abandoned, houses stripped of paint, village church windows boarded over, and streets deserted. Where towns had thrived and thousand-dollar combines had mowed the wheat there was desolation. Man had not been wise enough to use his technology for human values.

Here in graphic form were the human consequences of man's failure to control and adjust the technological creation which he had made. This is a part of the story of what we have lost. The whole story of two world wars is a story of what we have lost. The Korean War is another. And in the threat of a new war which may blast millions from the face of the earth and crush all democratic processes in one last failure, the vast story of human loss from an age of industrialized technological society continues to unfold.

Now we have built the most expensive system of formal education in all history. We are turning out more degrees than at any other time within the memory of man. Our libraries are bulging with recorded knowledge, and we have had to invent the microfilm because we no longer have even space enough to store our records of research. Yet with all our accumulated intelligence and specialized knowledge, human beings grow more frustrated, problems of society multiply, and the mess in the world grows worse.

This is the age in which we live, a bit lopsided perhaps, but it is there gnawing at the sinews of American democracy. It has not come about from democratic processes. It has come from a technology that has shaped and fashioned a new kind of society, a society in which democracy cannot live unless there is developed a modern community setting which will permit it to function.

Perhaps the idea of this community setting can best be gained from a glimpse into our past.

There was a time in America when democracy operated in an atmosphere of town meetings, small communities, and face-to-face relationships. Social science was in the act of living. Cooperation and group discussion, civic responsibility and community pride, did not have to be taught. They were a part of life. It was a simple life —intimately human, warm, personal.

When there was a local problem to be solved the people knew that unless they got busy and solved it for themselves it would not be solved. Instinctively they knew that if the job was to be done they must do it together. Families and groups of families pulled and worked together to provide what they needed. And whatever they needed they created for themselves. The principles of work, thrift, responsibility, initiative, were the natural spiritual products of a rich community life. There was a natural framework for the exchange of ideas and of human spirit, a fertile environment for democratic processes. It was a natural breeding ground for such qualities as leadership, civic integrity, and statesmanship. There were weaknesses, inconsistencies, and undemocratic practices then as now. But it was in this general atmosphere of community life that the American tradition was born, and in which it grew and thrived and made this the land of freedom that it is.

But with the coming of the Industrial Revolution and the development of top-down mass methods community life began to dry up. The small town began to decay. Millions were massed together in urban mobs, and sprawling cities grew up by machine methods with virtually no inner development of true community life. Families lost much of their social significance. Many of the jobs that parents and children once performed in the home were taken over by specialists who had been mass produced from the classroom assembly lines. Human values were lost in a maze of punch cards and number systems which were devoid of flesh and blood. Neighborhood life in any meaningful sense, the environment which had nurtured initiative, civic integrity, and social responsibility, began to grow sterile. The control which men had once exercised over their own lives gradually slipped away into the distant offices of a centralized and impersonal society.

Giant organizations, private and governmental, came into being, far ranging in scope but without roots in the community where men lived. Great pressure groups rose up across the land and cut across community lines, breaking the local neighborhood into segments, each cut off and walled apart from the other. Bigness, commercialism, professionalism, scholarship, efficiency, became the gods of worship and the control over men's lives continued to grow more and more centralized in powers that were far removed from the individual in his community and in which he had little, if any, voice.

Slowly but steadily the new technology with its mass methods gnawed deeper and deeper into the foundations of community life. Like a great parasite it sucked away the strength of neighborhood society until men and women by the millions lost their motivation for community responsibility. An attitude of what's-the-use-anyway spread like a plague across America. Many lost confidence even in their own ability. The majority became bystanders in public affairs, and in all parts of a great nation men and women had assumed an attitude of leaning on someone else.

As community wholeness and integrity continued to decline, America began to lose something of moral and spiritual fiber.

The legislative process became largely a system of specialized pressures all competing for the legislative favor, while the voice of the individual was smothered further and further beneath top-level strategy. Community action of the people had changed largely to a kind of action which was determined from the top down by national organizations, impersonalized institutions, and great trade and professional combinations. And today in an all too realistic sense millions of Americans no longer have a genuine say in the affairs of their own destiny.

Millions are pieces of men living a kind of existence from payday to payday in a great mass of anonymous and socially isolated human fragments. That spirit of neighborhood identity and true participation in community life activities has diminished until millions live side by side without speaking to each other, without caring what happens to the family across the street. Crime, delinquency, frustration, broken homes, a fear of something that men cannot define have grown to tremendous proportions, and it has been estimated that one out of every twenty Americans will spend a portion of his life in a mental institution. These are the symptoms of a society out of adjustment to the technology that created it.

The natural community in which human values flourished and which was conducive to democratic processes is almost gone. It has been crushed by the rising crescendo from a world of knowledge, machinery, and science, to which we have been unable to adjust ourselves in order to preserve the very human values which our technology and knowledge were designed to serve. Man has become the slave to his own mechanical and intellectual creation which now threatens to destroy him in one last mighty blast.

And so the whole mode of American life has been altered. Vast material advantages have been gained. But in towns and cities throughout America democratic living and self-expression have gone.

Vital community life is something creative. It is integrated. It is an organic whole. It is personal, cooperative, and mutually stimulating. People exchange their services, their thoughts, their ideas. They feel responsible for one another. They take part together in many different activities. They work, they play, they visit together. There is a sense of belonging in an atmosphere of neighborliness and understanding, a spirit of unity and of community solidarity.

But the era in which we live has tended to make us a nation of spectators. We have somehow acquired the habit of letting someone else shape our lives for us. Someone else—the expert, the professional—handles our economy, our culture, our politics, tells us how to raise our children, how to do our community planning, and in large measure does our thinking for us. This is all a part of the decline in community vitality. And slowly, but just as surely as the grinding movement of the glacier, it is sapping the life strength from our American heritage. It is destroying the democratic processes. It is leaving our Republic weak and flabby; it is making us a hypocrite before a world in which we are attempting to demonstrate the strength of our American ideals.

The vitality of democracy in America cannot be measured in dollars and cents, shiny automobiles, bathtubs, machines, and libraries full of knowledge. It cannot be measured in terms of efficiency. Democracy is spiritual in nature. It is a basic process, a method of communicating, of exchanging thoughts, ideas, joys, sorrows, and human feelings. It is freedom to live, to choose, to be responsible. It is a process by which free people in a free society are in communication with one another and together mold and control their own destiny at the neighborhood or community level. It is intangible, yet real and concrete. It cannot be sold to the rest of the world, or even to our own people, unless we can learn to practice it in a more realistic way than we are now practicing it.

Democracy in the American tradition will function only when it functions inside the local communities of which America is made up. It can be a vigorous and dynamic force nationally and internationally only if it is vigorous and dynamic in the home-town community, in the village and rural crossroads, in the city neighborhood and small town, in the places where people live.

A free democratic society at the higher levels—state, regional, national—is but a myth unless the initiative, the controls, the ideals, and the direction come clear and uninterrupted from the people in their home communities. This is where it must be practiced, this is where it must have meaning in the personal everyday lives of men and women if it is to be practiced and have meaning anywhere.

Obviously, we cannot turn back the clock to the early American village, and would not do so if we could. But unless we begin to take more action than we are taking today toward adjusting ourselves to the technological age in such a way as to make our knowledge work *for* human values and community life, instead of allowing it to destroy them, then America will continue to limp along on but a small fraction of the power of which she is capable, and we will continue to lack the moral influence so desperately needed in the world today.

No single factor is more important to the future of America and to the world at large than is the local community. From it come our ideals, our integrity, our moral strength, our leadership; and these qualities will be no stronger in the American people than are the communities in which they live. For it is the community and the environment found in it that will largely make us what we are. If our communities are strong, America will be strong. If they are weak, America will be weak.

This is the critical problem.

Its solution will not be easy. To reverse the spiral of democratic decay we must first recreate a social environment which is conducive to human values and democratic vitality. This means that the community must regain its organic integrity, its wholeness, its self-expression, and to an important degree its self-control. It means, in short, that community life must be redeveloped. For without wholeness and completeness of community life there can be no democratic society.

Democracy is a process in which people are free to exchange ideas in a direct personal manner, to communicate with one another mentally and spiritually, and thereby to work out their own common destiny. If this process is blocked by policies and regulations that are determined from above, by institutions and organizations that are controlled from afar, by the separation of functions, by professional and specialized planners, by religious, social, or economic barriers, or if it is blocked by any other barrier real or imaginary, then democracy cannot function.

A free democratic society requires a certain environment in which to live. This is an environment of wholeness and social completeness, of stability, of self-control, of mutual sympathy and cooperation, of understanding and tolerance among heterogeneous interests.

This environment may exist inside the local community, but if it does not exist there it cannot exist anywhere.

In America there are still the resources—human and physical—with which to build such a community environment. They are in the skills, the knowledge, the very creation which has made the technological age. The job now is to make use of the freedom, the intelligence, and the resources that we have for the rebuilding of community life in order to preserve human values.

In the trend toward specialization we have fallen into the habit of breaking up the community into a vast collection of carefully arranged compartments, each walled off and separated from the others. One is labeled business, another is agriculture, another is education, another is health, another is recreation, another is government, another is social service, another is religion, another is the home. The list is almost endless. Each of these compartments has become a special world in which there are further subdivisions. Then there are the organizational, special interest, and occupational groupings.

Operating on or within these compartments are the fixed and formalized disciplines, each seemingly an end in itself. Physical science with its specialized departments functions in its orbit. Biological science with its departments is in another orbit. Social science and another batch of departments occupy still another orbit. Philosophy, religion, the humanities, business administration, public planning, all have their carefully defined orbits.

There is the myriad of specialized agencies, institutions, organizations, associations, which reach down from the top and in some disconnected way operate on one of the so-called areas of the community.

It is the bringing together of all these functions, compartments, areas, and specializations into one integrated whole in a community setting that must be accomplished if American democratic society is to survive in the modern world. This can be done by people of all interests and of all groups working together inside the community itself, and that is the only place where it can be done.

Science—physical, biological, and social—may be utilized to enrich total community life rather than for special purposes without regard to total community values. Each phase and aspect of the community—its business, its agriculture, its educational system, its health services, its governmental facilities, its religious institutions— all may be developed not as specialized functions unto themselves, but as essential parts of the whole which are related in some vital way to all other parts of the community.

By making use of all the resources we have—human and otherwise —to bring together, to integrate, to enrich, and to strengthen all phases of the total life of the community we can create a modern environment in which it will be natural for people of all interests, groups, and beliefs to communicate mentally and spiritually with one another. Only then can our society adjust itself to the techno- logical age in which we live. When this is done in local communities throughout all America the full power of democracy will be re- leased, and America will recapture its human values and moral strength.

Thus, America may again have a natural social framework in which democracy can function. Here the individual may regain his sense of belonging, his sense of personal importance as an integrated and contributing member of society. He may be creative, inde- pendent, reliant. Civic responsibility, initiative, and leadership may once more become the natural by-product of life itself. Here there may be a natural motivation for citizen alertness. Through active participation in community life men and women may once more exercise a genuine say in their own destiny. The grass roots may again come to life. To some this may seem like an idealistic dream. It isn't. It has happened already in certain communities. It can hap- pen in others.

The development of community life in modern America will re- awaken and revitalize democratic processes. It will also provide the social foundation from which America can rise to new heights as a free society, from which the principles of human rights and repre- sentative government may regain their vitality, and from which our Republic may renew her moral influence in the world family of na- tions. But the critical point in the national fabric is the local com- munity. For unless democracy can survive there it cannot survive anywhere.

This is the broad purpose of the community study outlined in this guide. It is a program in community development through which a group of people may sit down together to study life in their own community in order to find out for themselves how they might enrich and improve it.

Though action projects may be launched by the community study group, the group itself is not intended as a permanent direct-action body for reasons described in Part II of the guide. However, community action that will help to improve the quality of community life is the central objective of this study plan. Exactly what that action will be, just when and how it will come about is a matter which cannot be prescribed. This is a matter for the people themselves to decide. It is also for them to decide whether they want action, or whether they don't. The program outlined in this guide is no panacea—not a magic formula. It will not work by itself.

Neither can it be predicted what progress the community may expect from the study. Other communities have made much progress, but that was determined by those communities. Who, other than the individual himself, can say when human values have been gained? Community unity and solidarity, a felt need which is self-inspired, the ability and desire to think imaginatively and creatively, an inner urge for community action, the ability to work and pull together—these are the aims of this study. But this achievement will be determined by the people themselves. This is basic. And it is upon this democratic principle that the future of America will rise or fall.

Part II

Mechanics of Procedure

1

Purpose and Intent

THIS IS A GUIDE INTENDED FOR THE USE OF A COMMUNITY STUDY GROUP. It is designed to help organize and carry out a study of the total life of a community for the purpose of bringing about greater understanding and full community cooperation and development.

It is not intended as a pat formula to be applied without change in every community. But it is hoped that it will provide material assistance in organizing group effort in an orderly and logical fashion so that all segments of the community may be ultimately brought together in a well-coordinated plan of over-all action. This has been the result in other communities where the procedure here outlined has been followed.

Obviously it is impossible to design one guide which will fit exactly all the specific conditions of all communities. All communities, like all human beings, are different. For this reason each community group will be aware of certain points that should be added to the guide in order to cover every specific local situation. Likewise, certain questions will be raised in the guide which do not apply to this or that particular local situation. In such cases the leaders of the group should make any alterations that may be necessary.

But just as all communities differ, they are also alike in many ways. There are, just as in all forms of life, certain basic principles and patterns of action that apply to all communities regardless of their specific differences. It is from these fundamental principles and patterns of community life that this guide has evolved.

The guide is designed for communities of a few hundred people up to places of several thousand. It is impossible to draw an exact limitation with respect to the size of the community, but in general the term "community" is used here to imply a neighborhood area in which there may be common communal ties and functions, where there may be a variety of interests and mutual services, where people may learn to know each other as individuals, and where they may have some personal measure of control over their own communal destiny. These conditions are possible in a small community. They may be possible in a local neighborhood area of a large city.

Part III of the guide is arranged in fifteen sections with material in each section for one or more weekly discussions of the study group. The over-all plan is that each step in the study should build into the step that follows until a comprehensive self-analysis has been completed of all aspects of the community life. Hundreds of questions are asked which will in turn suggest many others. In searching out the answers to these questions, the members of the study group will systematically ferret out local strengths and weaknesses, point up in their own minds community problems, and devise for themselves ways of solving them. Special surveys are provided for in the guide, and sample questionnaires for the collection of needed facts and information are included.

This guide, then, is a plan of community self-study in which the members of the study group are asked to strip away all the preconceived notions about their community and look at it honestly and realistically for what it actually is. Only through intelligent understanding of conditions as they are can the citizens of any community begin to solve their own problems and create for themselves the kind of community in which they would most like to live.

The number of weeks necessary to complete the study will depend upon the group. Usually the study group finds the work so engrossing that the question is not how long to keep going but when to stop. In most communities where the program has been carried out the basic study outlined in the guide has been only the first step in a long-range plan of action that has become an established part of the life of the community. However, the length of time necessary to complete the study here outlined will average about twenty-two weeks.

In summary, this material is designed for use by a community study group to aid the members of that group and others in the community:

1. To make an over-all self-analysis of life in their own locality to gain a better understanding of what makes their community what it is.

2. To become better acquainted with one another as human beings and to gain a greater insight into others' points of view in order to develop a more realistic spirit of human brotherhood, tolerance, and understanding throughout the community.

3. To identify the local problems which are real, to become keenly aware of them, and to understand why they exist.

4. To collect all facts and information that have a bearing on these problems and on the basis of the facts work out intelligent and appropriate solutions.

5. To develop from the study a sound plan of community action necessary for the full development of its resources, and to create within the community that spirit of unity and citizen alertness which is needed to make the action program a permanent, ongoing process.

If this kind of effort can be made sincerely and honestly by the people of every local community throughout America, the full power of democracy can and will be released.

2

Who Should Take Part

THE COMMUNITY STUDY GROUP SHOULD BE AS REPRESENTATIVE OF THE entire community as possible. It should include people from every local organization. It should also include people who do not belong to any particular organization and ordinarily do not take part in community activities. It should include those from all occupational groups, including housewives. It should include rich and poor, educated and uneducated, male and female, young and old, people who are management and people who are labor. It should include people from all churches, all creeds and classes, and from all shades of political opinion. It should include the most influential and the least influential. It should not in any sense be exclusive, but should include everybody and anybody who is concerned about the future of America and is willing to do his share in this combined effort to make his own community a better, more satisfying, and more prosperous place in which to live.

The study can and should include as many people as may be interested. The more the merrier! And the more who take part the more effective will be the final results. However, the effects of the study may spread far beyond the group itself. A small group of dedicated people can work wonders. Size need be no crucial problem.

3

First Study, Then Action

ALTHOUGH CITIZEN ACTION GEARED TOWARD THE IMPROVEMENT AND full development of the community is here a prime objective, the community study group is not primarily an *action* body. The study group is, just as its name implies, a *study* group.

Community action comes from a need or a series of needs which must be recognized and *felt* by the people themselves. When these needs are felt strongly enough by enough people, and when there is established at the same time a community spirit of unity and solidarity, and an attitude of self-confidence on the part of the people in their own ability to go ahead with a definite plan, then constructive action will follow as a natural process.

The process of arriving at the proper point where action is ready to begin, particularly if it is to become an established pattern of life in the community, is primarily a process of self-discovery and self-education. By this process people learn first to ask themselves the right questions and to seek the right answers. They learn to understand themselves and each other. They learn to appreciate the other fellow's problems, and to understand why their neighbor takes the point of view he does. They alert themselves to their own needs, their possibilities and their limitations. They learn, in short, to *know* their own community, to know why certain problems have come about, and to understand why this solution is so important to the future of America.

In the normal process of making the study they will begin to knit themselves together in a more integrated common life. Gradually they will begin to build a stronger, more united spirit, a stronger attitude of neighborliness, and an atmosphere in which community action and progress grow naturally.

As these qualities of community spirit, of human understanding, self-confidence, alertness, and the will to go forward, are building up through the process of group study and discussion, the various committees of the study group are collecting the facts and necessary information upon which a sound plan of action can be built and carried out. If all members of the group do their share in the discussion process, there will come a point where the community is ready and able to mobilize its total resources—human and physical—for concerted action. This means a kind of action that does not collapse because it was started prematurely, or that began "half cocked" in a sudden flush of temporary enthusiasm which has been so common in our American communities.

Community action for a specific tangible project, such as lighting the local ball park, is a simple matter. But the enthusiasm generated by the promoters of such a project is frequently exhausted with the completion of the project. The community then settles back into the rut and apathy that today plague American communities.

The kind of action envisioned in the community study group is a fundamental change in the whole cultural and spiritual fabric of community life. This change may mean lights for the local ball park; it may mean a good many other tangible action projects. But it also means much more. It means a richer cultural and spiritual life. It means long-range planning for the community's physical facilities. It means an expanding economy that spells new jobs and greater economic stability. It means a healthier and more satisfying environment conducive to vital human living. It means better adjusted people and a better adjusted community. It means a basic revitalization of the democratic way of life and its permanent growth throughout the community.

If this kind of action is to be built into the life and habits of the community it must spring first, as does all human action, from accepted ideas and feelings. They must be ideas that are practical. They must be based on vision, imagination, and enthusiasm which come into being inside the community and which are a product of its own initiative and sincerity.

To launch such thoughts and ideas into action, or to launch a kind of ongoing program of action from which such thoughts and ideas will grow and become a natural part of the community life, there needs to be a definite and integrated plan at once short range and long range in nature and which has behind it sufficient group feeling or desire to put it into concrete operation. This kind of community planning and action will come basically from long, arduous, objective, and systematic study by the people themselves. The thousands of defunct planning bodies—state, regional, and local— the uncounted numbers of community projects gone bust, monuments to good intentions, are the mute reminders of those who meant well, but failed to recognize this principle of the use of the community study group.

The first objective of the community study group, then, is study: to learn the nature of local conditions as they actually are. The second objective is to analyze, weigh, and discuss these conditions, and to work out honest conclusions as to the inner nature of the problems posed. The third objective is to develop from these discussions and conclusions a concrete plan of action which will embrace all local interests and all groups in the community. And the final objective is to see that this plan is set into operation.

4

The Conduct of Meetings

IN THE SPIRIT OF AN OLD-FASHIONED AMERICAN TOWN MEETING THIS
democratic group of men and women known as the community
study group will sit down together once each week for a series of
meetings to study, analyze, and discuss the life and problems of
their own community in an effort to gain a better understanding of
the place in which they live and to find out for themselves how
they can make it better. Meanwhile, outside the regular weekly
meetings, various committees will work collecting the facts and
information needed for intelligent discussion and actual planning.

The whole tone of the proceedings should be one of informality.
The more informal the better. There should be no formal memberships. There should be no dues. Participants should try to become
as well acquainted as possible, and as soon as they feel free to do
so should make an effort to call each other by first names. Leaders
should be regarded simply as leaders, not as officers in the usual
formal organizational sense. There should be none of the formality
that often exists in established community organizations. Parlia-
mentary procedure should be avoided as a general rule, and used
only where it is necessary to bring things to a head. All members
should feel free to interrupt, ask questions, or introduce ideas and
points of view at any time they see fit. Frankness, objectivity, and
human courtesy should be the common practice. Free discussion
and full spontaneous participation by all individuals present is the
general procedure.

One definite rule, however, should be adhered to. This is the matter of attendance. Each part of the guide and each phase of the
study are built upon those that go before and in turn prepare the
way for those yet to come. For this reason much of the value of the
study will depend upon a reasonable continuity of attendance at

the weekly meetings by all members and upon going through the whole program in the order outlined in the study guide. This will make it possible to build each week's discussion on the basis of the previous weeks and gradually to build up an integrated pattern in which all phases and aspects of community life—its social structure, its economy, its cultural, educational, and spiritual developments— are seen in proper relationship to one another.

Therefore, in order to achieve the greatest degree of success, all those taking part in the program should make a "ladies' and gentlemen's agreement" to attend regularly every meeting in the series if at all possible. Some people will, of course, have a legitimate reason for missing a meeting now and then, but the reason should be very legitimate! The importance of this point cannot be overstated.

Another principle that should become a part of the community study group should be a definite starting and closing time for each regular meeting. This will be more difficult to achieve at the first few meetings than it will be as the study gets further under way. But as soon as possible it should become a habit of procedure. This point is essential because some people will not want to keep coming if they find they are going to be kept up so late that they will not like working the next day. If the members of the group like to "hang around," as they probably will after the meeting has been adjourned, that is as it should be. Indeed, much of the value of the study is the talk it stimulates outside the regular meetings. But the regular meeting should be adjourned on time. It is better to stop while people still want to continue than to go on until they have exhausted themselves.

The plan of operation for each weekly meeting is as follows:

1. The group assembles in a large room of the local school building (or in some other appropriate building), and the general chairman calls the meeting to order. The secretary presents the report on last week's meeting. This report may or may not be read aloud, but in any event each member of the group should receive a copy to read.

Whatever general announcements may be necessary are called for at this time, and each committee chairman is called on for a brief progress report.

2. The general chairman announces the subject of discussion for the

evening, and whatever committee report may be due is presented at this time.

3. The study group then divides up into discussion groups, or "buzz sessions," of from twelve to twenty persons each. Each of these small groups goes into a different room of the building to discuss the subject of the evening. All the buzz sessions discuss the same questions or the same subject; they simply do it in different rooms. Each one of them has its own discussion leader, and a recorder to keep notes on what is said.

4. After the discussion period is completed for the evening, the buzz sessions reassemble in the general assembly.

5. After the study group has reconvened in its general assembly, the buzz session recorders seat themselves around a table at the front of the room, somewhat in the form of a panel, and the general chairman leads them in a discussion of what was said in the various buzz sessions. Each recorder reports on the discussion and conclusions reached in his or her buzz session. This reporting should be kept brief, concise, and to the point, and reach a definite conclusion. Duplication should be held to a minimum. The general chairman might proceed by calling on the recorder for "Group One" to report on the first question, then asking the other recorders if their groups agreed or disagreed, or if they have anything to add to the report from the first group. The general chairman then asks the recorder of "Group Two" to report on the next point, and so on around until all points have been covered.

6. The general chairman then gives a brief summary of all the recorders' reports, points out the areas of agreement and disagreement, emphasizes the problems posed and the recommendations for action, and pulls together the loose ends of the discussion.

Comments from the general assembly are always welcome either during the time the recorders are giving their reports or at the time the general chairman gives the final summary for the evening.

7. The meeting adjourns.

The breakdown of the general assembly into the small buzz sessions is accomplished easily by having the members present count off around the room, "1-2-3-4-5-6, 1-2-3-4-5-6," and so on until each person in the meeting has called out a number. All the "ones" become members of "Buzz Group One" and go into a room together, all "twos" go into another room, "threes" into another room, and so on until the whole study group is divided up into small buzz sessions for the discussion of the evening.

The number of buzz sessions into which the study group should be divided will depend upon how many people are present at the meeting. No buzz session should be much over twenty persons in size, and a group of twelve or fifteen is preferable.

The discussion leaders and recorders should not be included in the count, and in order to avoid confusion they may sit together in the front of the room or step aside when the counting is ready to begin.

The purpose of dividing the study group into buzz sessions is that in a large assembly true group discussion is impossible. Many people are shy or hesitant about speaking up in front of a large assembly, and unless the buzz session technique is followed most of the people who attend never get a chance to say anything.

One of the prime objectives of the community study group is to encourage *everybody* to take an active part in the discussions. Ideas and opinions should be communicated freely and there should be plenty of opportunity for each person attending the meetings to say anything that he may feel like saying. Lively, active, dynamic discussions in which everyone can and does participate should be sought after by every practical means. By use of the buzz session technique everyone is given this opportunity to take an active part in the discussions, yet no one is excluded because it is not necessary to limit the size of the study group.

These buzz sessions will not consist of the same persons every week, but because of the system of counting off will change in personnel from week to week. The more the people in the study group rotate from one buzz session to another the better. For this reason it is often found advantageous to begin the counting off from different corners of the room. This rotating from one buzz session to another will help to get everyone acquainted. Another suggestion for the purpose of getting acquainted is to have each person at the meetings wear a slip of paper with his name written on it, as is customary at conventions.

The discussion leaders and the recorders should, however, be the same persons throughout the study. This will give the greatest possible continuity to the work and will make it possible to know at all times who is to be responsible for the necessary leadership. This also makes it possible to get as discussion leaders and recorders the people who are best qualified to perform these jobs.

Once the buzz sessions are assembled in their respective meeting places the procedure in each session is simply a process of reading and group discussion. Each participant opens his study guide to the section being covered that evening and the leader starts by reading aloud from the background for discussion or by giving an oral summary of what it says. Others in the group may interrupt to make comments or they may be asked to help out with the reading and summarizing. This continues until the first question for discussion is reached, at which point the leader reads the question and the group discusses it. After there has been sufficient discussion for the group to reach a conclusion on this question the discussion leader then reads the next question and the discussion continues. Members of the group may interrupt at any point in the reading to raise questions, to agree or disagree, or to inject any comments they may care to make. Also, the questions asked in the guide will give rise to other questions either from the leader or from other members of the group. By this process the group will round out its thinking, build up its discussion, and come to its own conclusions. Meanwhile the recorder keeps notes on the questions raised, the problems posed, the points made, the conclusions reached, and the recommendations for action or for further investigation.

5

Organization

AS ALREADY INDICATED, THE ORGANIZATION OF THE STUDY GROUP should be as simple and informal as possible. It should in no event have an organizational structure in the tight formal sense of an established club. However, in order to conduct the study in a logical and systematic manner and to get things done it is necessary that a certain amount of organizational structure be established. This structure is of utmost importance to the success of the group.

All leaders and committee chairmen should be chosen with extreme care in order to make certain that those chosen are persons whose ability and background make them well suited for the job they are to do. Each leader must be counted upon to carry out his or her responsibilities to the fullest. The quality of leadership will make the difference between success and failure of the group. This is a cardinal principle. *The necessity of getting the right leaders in the right jobs cannot be overemphasized.*

The leaders needed for the study will include:

1. A *general chairman* to open and close each meeting and to act in the capacity of an over-all leader of the group. This person should be one who is deeply community-minded and alert to the full meaning of good citizenship. He (or she) should be a person of considerable social vision who has a great deal of organizational ability, a faculty for persuading other people to do things, and a keen sensitivity to other people's feelings and reactions. The general chairman should not be a controversial figure in the community but should be a person who is generally accepted by everybody. The general chairman should also be the kind of person who will follow through, who is efficient, prompt, and knows how to get things done. A special guide for the general chairman is given in Part IV.

2. A *secretary* to keep notes on the meetings and maintain a permanent file of all records and reports of the study group. The secretary should be a good "note taker" and should be adept at writing notes up in a style that will make interesting reading. The secretary should have a certain amount of organizational skill and the basic personal qualities of community-mindedness, energy, and a strong desire to see things happen. The secretary is more than a mere "minute taker," and might be better described as an "executive secretary." A description of the secretary's duties is given in Part IV.

3. An *advisory committee* of six or eight persons equally divided between men and women to meet with the general chairman and secretary whenever a situation arises during the course of the study which seems to make such a meeting advisable. The first job of the advisory committee is to assist the general chairman and secretary in the appointment of the various committees which are to collect the facts and detailed information necessary to conduct the study. These committees are listed be-

low and a special outline is given for each of them in Part IV. The general chairman and secretary and the chairmen of all other committees should attend the meetings of the advisory committee, and the general chairman should preside. A full report should be kept on the proceedings of these meetings for inclusion in the secretary's weekly reports to the regular meetings of the entire study group. Each member of the advisory committee should be a leader in the community who has a deep personal interest in the success of the study and the progress and development of the community.

4. A *secretarial committee* to assist with the clerical work of the secretary. These people should be able to type and run a mimeograph, and be willing to devote a certain amount of time for these purposes. The fact that their jobs are somewhat mechanical in nature makes them no less important. Unless the mechanics of the study group are properly attended to, the work will bog down and the over-all effort will be seriously impaired. The secretary acts as chairman of this committee.

5. A group of *discussion leaders* to lead the discussions in the various buzz sessions. There should be one discussion leader for each buzz session. In choosing these leaders it should be borne in mind that group discussion is the basic procedure of the community study program, and that the success of a discussion depends largely on the leader of the group. A description of the duties and responsibilities of discussion leaders is given in Part IV.

6. A group of *recorders* to keep notes on the discussions in the various buzz sessions and to assist the discussion leaders. The recorders also summarize and report to the general assembly of the study group on the discussions and conclusions of their respective buzz sessions at the close of each regular weekly meeting. Again, these people occupy key positions in the study group program and should be chosen with the greatest possible care. A description of the recorders' responsibilities is given in Part IV.

Organization of the study calls also for the appointment of a number of special research committees which meet outside the regular weekly meetings of the study group. These committees conduct the actual surveys and investigations that are needed by the group for a complete analysis and discussion of community life, and a detailed outline is provided for each one of them in Part IV of the study guide. These committees are in a sense the lifeblood of the study. It is their job to go out and collect the facts and details which are necessary not only as a basis for intelligent discussion but for purposes of actual planning and community action. These committees should begin their work immediately upon the formation of the study group and should be prepared to assume leadership and supply needed facts and information whenever the group discussions move into their fields of specific interest.

A point is designated in the study guide when the final report and recommendations of each of these committees is due for presentation to the study group. Periodically, however, up to the time their final reports are submitted, each committee should make a brief progress report to the study group. As many members of the study group as possible should serve on at least one of these committees.

BOUNDARY COMMITTEE

One of the first problems of the study group will be to determine what constitutes the community. What physical or geographical area does it include? How far out does it extend in each direction? Probably the community as a whole is a good deal more extensive in area than the actual city limits of the town proper. But just how much more extensive? This is a question that must be answered and agreed upon at the outset so that each committee will be working on the same physical area and so that all members of the group will be talking about the same area when various factors about the community come up for discussion. This is the purpose of the Boundary Committee, and this committee will be the first to report.

POPULATION COMMITTEE

The group will also need to have a great deal of basic information and statistics about the people who live in the community. How many people are there? What are the various groupings as to age, sex, occupation, and marital status? What is the rate of population increase or decrease, the birth and death rates, the housing situation, etc.? This kind of information will not only be necessary for purposes of intelligent discussion but will form a factual basis for a good deal of the planning and action that will come later. This is the purpose of the Population Committee.

COMMUNITY ORGANIZATIONS COMMITTEE

In order to understand the social structure of the community and to look at some of the basic factors that influence its vitality, it will be necessary to know something about its organizational life. What kind of established organizations does it have? What are the purposes of these organizations? How many people take part in them? And how many don't? These and many other questions will be analyzed by the Community Organizations Committee.

CHURCH COMMITTEE

Another important aspect in the life of every community is its religious institutions, its churches. To a considerable extent the vitality of the community can be measured by the vitality of its churches. This important feature of community life will be covered by the Church Committee.

GOVERNMENT COMMITTEE

One of the most important of all American institutions is the institution of local government. The numerous ways in which this aspect of community life affects the community are, of course, obvious. Many Americans are becoming more and more concerned with the apathy of citizens toward government. In order to develop the full capacity of human life in any community it is important that the problems of local and county government be studied and well understood by the people themselves. Research into this important area of community life and the problems or needs it presents will be the job of the Government Committee.

SOCIAL AGENCIES COMMITTEE

Another kind of institution which operates in most modern communities is the organized social agency. Usually there are several of them, some public and some volunteer. Some of them may not have an office in the community, but may operate from an office located in another town. These agencies include such organizations as the Welfare Department, the Y.W.C.A., the American Red Cross, homes for the aged, and a wide range of many others. In many ways the work of these social agencies, as well as the organizations themselves, reflects the needs and problems of the community. This aspect of community life is covered by the Social Agencies Committee.

LIBRARY COMMITTEE

No modern community is complete without adequate library services. The library should be a center of information and enlightenment for all the people. For this purpose the study group should include a Library Committee.

The work of the committees mentioned thus far will be largely completed when their reports have been submitted to the study group. Some of them may be asked to carry out additional research or to draw up specific plans for action after their report has been discussed in the study group. However, the actual work to be done by these committees is not likely to continue to any great extent after their final reports are brought in. Thus, the members who serve on these committees will in most cases be released for work on one of the other committees set forth below.

The committees which follow should be regarded in the nature of *standing committees* whose functions will continue throughout the period of the community study. In terms of the amount of work to be done these will be the largest committees of the study program.

ECONOMIC DEVELOPMENT COMMITTEE

It is obvious that no community can develop or maintain the most vital kind of community life without a stable and expanding economy. The opportunities for earning a living and the extent to which these opportunities are increasing or decreasing will have a major impact on every other phase of community life. If the community is unable to produce enough job opportunities to enable its people to support themselves adequately, then there can be no stability in anything. The economy is basic to all else. For this purpose the study guide provides for an Economic Development Committee. This committee is divided into three subcommittees: (1) *Trades and Services*, (2) *Industries*, and (3) *Agriculture*. (In a community where there is no agricultural activity, and no opportunity for any, the Agricultural Subcommitttee will, of course, be omitted.)

BEAUTIFICATION COMMITTEE

There is an old saying that "When a community *looks* progressive it *is* progressive." The physical appearance, the over-all beauty, the orderly arrangement and layout of material things, will have a great deal to do with the actual quality of community life. It will affect deeply, though perhaps indirectly, the whole process of a community's development. Certainly it will have considerable influence on whether the community is looked upon by strangers as a desirable place in which to live, and by the local residents as well. The collection of facts on this important aspect of the community will be the job of the Beautification Committee.

EDUCATION COMMITTEE

Perhaps no aspect of community life has attracted greater interest and concern from the American people than that area which deals with education and the public schools. Certainly there can be no doubt that the public schools and the use that is made of them will leave a deep impression for better or for worse on the life of every community. Moreover, not all of a community's educational system should be confined to the teaching of children. Of equal importance are the educational opportunities that are designed to serve adults. Much of a community's educational system is informal in nature and exists outside the regular school program. The educational aspects of community life may have many ramifications and be far reaching in influence upon the entire citizenry. The matter of community education will therefore absorb a great deal of attention in the study group, and the Education Committee will be the means through which the necessary facts and information for this purpose will be collected and assembled.

HEALTH COMMITTEE

The most valuable resource of every community is the people who live there, and for this reason much attention will be devoted in the study program to the health and well-being of the people themselves. This means health in its very broadest sense: physical health, mental health, social and moral health. Detailed investigation into this phase of community life will be the responsibility of the Health Committee.

RECREATION COMMITTEE

Another aspect of major significance to the life of the community is what people, young and old, do with the hours they aren't at work or in school. America is becoming more and more a nation of habitual spectators. Fewer and fewer people take any active part even in the creation of their own recreation. Instead, they are willing to pay someone else to do their entertaining for them while they sit by and watch. Much of the richness of America's heritage and culture is unknown to many Americans, and there is getting to be less and less opportunity for the majority of the people to do anything of a creative nature. This trend toward passive spectatorship is having a seriously adverse effect on the vitality of democracy and community life, and is only partly expressed in the now often heard comment, "There just isn't anything to do in this town." This important aspect of community life will be covered by the Recreation Committee.

HISTORY COMMITTEE

Just as experience can be the teacher of all individuals, local history offers a valuable lesson for all modern communities. By examining the events of his own life and his reactions to these events an individual may learn to understand himself better and thereby gain greater self-confidence. The same principle of self-analysis from a historical point of view applies to the community. From a knowledge of their own community history the people may find many important suggestions for future action. They should gain a deeper and more objective understanding of how and why certain problems of the present came into being. They should develop greater community pride and a richer appreciation of their own cultural heritage. Thus life in the community may become more interesting and more worthwhile. Investigation into this aspect of community life is the job of the History Committee.

PUBLICITY COMMITTEE

It is of utmost importance that all citizens in the community have a clear understanding of the purpose and objectives of the community study from the moment it begins, and that they be kept constantly informed as to its findings and progress. It is therefore essential that the group have from the outset an effective Publicity Committee. This is one of the key committees in the program.

In summary, the committees needed for the community study program are:

1. Boundary Committee
2. Population Committee
3. Community Organizations Committee
4. Church Committee
5. Government Committee
6. Social Agencies Committee
7. Library Committee
8. Economic Development Committee
   (a) Subcommittee on Trades and Services
   (b) Subcommittee on Industry
   (c) Subcommittee on Agriculture
9. Beautification Committee
10. Education Committee
11. Health Committee
12. Recreation Committee
13. History Committee
14. Publicity Committee

There will be a certain amount of overlapping among these committees, but in many natural ways all of them are interrelated. This refers to the fact that community life is an organic whole and any program that seeks to develop community life must deal with it as such. For this reason it is not uncommon to find two or more of the committees bringing in similar recommendations for action. In any case, the work of all these committees will be brought together in an integrated pattern through the instrument of the community study group.

6

Physical Facilities, Supplies and Equipment

THE COMMUNITY STUDY GROUP WILL NEED, FIRST OF ALL, A SUITABLE place to hold its regular weekly meetings. If possible these meetings should always be held in the same place so that people will get accustomed to the location. Probably this will be in the school, but not necessarily.

It will be necessary to have one large room where the whole group can assemble, and enough smaller rooms to accommodate all the several buzz sessions. It is, of course, desirable that all these rooms be in the same building.

The physical arrangement of the meeting rooms will have an important bearing in creating the proper atmosphere for successful meetings.

THE LARGE MEETING ROOM

The large meeting room for the general assembly of the community study group should be large enough to accommodate everybody who might wish to take part. The most desirable situation is to have a room which just fits the size of the group. A room which is too small tends to create an overcrowded and therefore uncomfortable situation, but a room that is too large tends to create an atmosphere of being lost in space. A large group which would give people the feeling of strength in numbers can actually feel small and weak in numbers if the meeting is held in a half-filled auditorium.

Unless the group becomes too large to make it practical, the ideal situation is to have the people in the general assembly of the study group seated around tables in such a way that all of them, or at least most of them, can face each other. This arrangement is much better than the traditional seating arrangement where people can see only the backs of each other's heads and are thus separated from the people in front of them. People are always more comfortable if they can have a table in front of them on which to spread out their papers or rest their elbows.

Everything possible should be done to create an atmosphere of informality and to make for comfort and good-fellowship. Smoking should be permissible if at all possible, and ash trays should be provided. Many people who have the smoking habit become fidgety and anxious to get away if they are not permitted to relax and smoke when they feel like it.

It is also a good idea to have the large meeting room located close to a kitchen so that the group may have coffee or other refreshments served if the people desire. Some community study groups have found that drinking coffee or tea while listening to the recorders give their final summaries in the general assembly after the buzz sessions have reconvened contributes to the informality and comfort of the meeting. The more informal people feel the more natural they feel, and the better the discussion. All this contributes to the vitality and success of the study.

At the front of the large room there should be a table for the general chairman and secretary, and for the recorders to sit around while giving their reports after they have returned fom the buzz sessions.

If the study group gets large, as it does in many communities, it is a good idea to use a public address system with a table microphone that the general chairman and recorders can pass back and forth as the summary is given on the discussions of the buzz sessions. This makes it possible for everyone in the room to hear easily, and makes it easier for the recorders to talk. This also makes it a simple matter to make tape recordings of the meetings for use by the Publicity Committee. These recordings make valuable records for future depository in the community library. Such recordings are, of course, not necessary, but if equipment is available for making them they may be used for many desirable purposes. These tape recordings always make good radio program material. They might also be used in the programs of various local organizations.

At the front of the room there should be a large blackboard that can be seen easily by everyone in the meeting. Or, if an overhead viewgraph [1] is available, this is even better. The blackboard, or the viewgraph if one is available, may be used for various notes and drawings during the general assembly at the opening of the study group meeting; and during the time the recorders are reporting for their buzz sessions in the closing part of the meeting the highlights of their remarks may be recorded for everyone in the room to see. This makes it possible for the study group to hear and see the recorders' summaries at the same time. It also adds an extra touch of interest to the meetings.

The writing of the recorders' statements on a blackboard or viewgraph also makes it possible to make a quick visual comparison of the discussions in the various buzz sessions, and to put down a quick summary of the problems posed and the recommendations for action.

The Small Meeting Rooms

The small meeting rooms for the buzz sessions should be located as close to the large meeting room as possible. This will enable the general assembly to break up into buzz sessions and to reconvene after the buzz session with a minimum loss of time. Buzz sessions should not meet in the same room. Each one should have its own room so that they will not disturb one another and so that as cozy and private an atmosphere as possible can be created in each session.

The ideal arrangement for these small discussion groups, or buzz sessions, is to have the members seated around a table. This provides by far the most suitable climate for lively give-and-take discussion, and every effort should be made to make this arrangement possible. If no tables are available, perhaps it will be possible for the participants to sit in a circle. In schoolrooms where there are movable armchairs or desks this arrangement in a circle is satisfactory. The main thing is to set up the room so that all members of the buzz session are facing each other and can thereby see the expressions on others' faces. This always makes people feel more a part of the group. It contributes greatly to informality, to active participation,

---

[1] An overhead viewgraph is a piece of audio-visual equipment such as is used in bowling alleys by means of which handwriting done with a wax pencil is flashed simultaneously on a screen overhead.

and is the natural arrangement for group discussion. There is no expression on the back of a person's head, and the atmosphere of a meeting is usually rather stiff when everyone has his back turned to most of the others present.

If there are no rooms to be had where members of the buzz sessions can meet face to face, then it will probably be necessary to use the traditional schoolroom with the rows of unmovable desks. But this should be done only as a last resort, and if this becomes necessary the discussion leader should see to it that everyone sits as close together as possible at the front of the room.

In each buzz session room there should be a blackboard with an eraser and plenty of chalk.

Care should be taken at all times to see that heat and ventilation are as they should be, and if possible smoking should be permitted in the buzz sessions as well as in the general assembly.

Secretarial Supplies

Each week the secretary's report of the study meeting should be mimeographed so that a copy may be distributed to each member of the group at the following meeting. Also, all committee reports should be mimeographed and distributed to the members of the group at the time these reports come up for discussion. The copies of these various reports, including the secretary's reports, will also be of valuable use to the Publicity Committee. When the study is complete, all reports of the entire proceedings of the group from start to finish may be bound into a single volume with enough copies for distribution to all persons who have taken part in the study. Copies of this report of proceedings will also be of value for distribution to other interested persons and organizations.

Equipment and supplies needed for the conduct of the community study will therefore include the use of a typewriter and mimeograph, and plenty of paper and other mimeograph supplies.

Study Guide

Each person taking part in the community study should have a copy of the study guide. The guide will be the manual for each person and each committee in the study group. In it is material for each regular weekly meeting, including informational background and questions for discussion in the buzz sessions. There are also special outlines in Part IV for the general chairman, the secretary, the discussion leaders, the recorders, and for each of the various committees. It would be of considerable advantage if every person in the group would read in advance of each meeting the material in the guide which will be discussed that evening. Each person in the group should have his own copy and bring it with him to every meeting so that he will have it for use in the discussions. This applies also to members of the same family because they will probably be in different buzz sessions.

7

Cost of the Community Study

THE COST OF MAKING THE COMMUNITY STUDY WILL BE VERY LOW. IT will amount only to the cost of paper and a few supplies, and to whatever expense the Publicity Committee may wish to incur. The equipment mentioned above is usually already available in most communities. The method of financing these costs varies from community to community, and in many cases much of it is borne by the local public school. One method of financing which is not recommended is the practice of collecting from local businessmen. The primary purpose of this program is to strengthen democracy and community life. It is a program from which everyone in the community will profit, and for this reason all organizations and individuals should be given an opportunity to share in the expense.

The only other expense of making the study is the cost of the individual study guides which each member of the group should purchase for himself.

8

How to Get Started

THE KIND OF ACTION NECESSARY TO GET THE COMMUNITY STUDY PRO-
gram established will, of course, be different in each community.
The first move toward getting started may come from a local organization or institution or from any group of public-spirited citizens
who see a need for the program in their community. It may be
spearheaded by the local press, or by the radio station if there is
one. It may be initiated by the school administrator, by a minister,
or by any other individual citizen who is concerned about the well-
being of his community. One person may discuss the idea with others who will share his enthusiasm and become interested in helping
to get the program started.

Great care should be taken at the start, however, to avoid the possibility of having the program labeled as a project of any one group,
organization, or institution. The community study group should not
at any time be looked upon as a school program, a church program,
a program of the local planning commission, or as the program of
any particular institution or organization. Any one of these groups
may well assume leadership in helping to get it established, and all
of them may be solidly behind it, indeed should be, but from the
earliest beginnings it should be made clear that the community
study group is to be a program of the whole community and nothing
less than that. It should also be made clear that the community
study group is not to be a permanent organization in the usual organizational sense, but that it is just what the name says, a community study, which will be completed within a reasonable period
of time.

And so the community study group is a project not of any one
organization but of the entire community. Obviously, this does not
mean that every citizen in the community has to participate actively

in the study in order to make it successful, though it is hoped that as many people as possible will take part. It is also obvious that as a practical matter somebody, or some particular organization or institution, must make the first move to get other people and other organizations interested, and to get the program started.

In general it is best to begin by talking up the idea to a few community leaders representing various interests until a small group of interested people has been established. This small group may then assume the responsibility of an informal steering committee, and the community study group is built up from this nucleus of interested people.

Once this nucleus of interested people has been formed, the next steps toward organization may be somewhat as follows:

1. Draw up a list of every organization and institution in the community. List all major occupational and business groups, social, religious, and economic groups in the community. This list should provide a specific idea as to the various people who ought to be contacted in order to get a good cross section of the whole community.

2. Make *personal contact* with as many people as possible in each of these groupings, explain the program to them and invite their assistance in helping to get it started. Do not at this point invite people by sending out written invitations unless the mailing is made to *everyone* in the community. Invitations sent to a selected list are bound to result in some people feeling left out, and the moment this happens a handicap has been created which later must be overcome.

3. Publicize the idea of the program through whatever media of public information there may be in the community. Chances are that the newspaper editor will be much interested and will do a great deal to help spearhead the idea.

4. Get as many people as possible talking about the idea. Have it discussed in the various civic-minded organizations and get them to help push it. Talk it over with the members of the local government, the school board and school administration, church leaders, businessmen, social agencies, and other community workers. If there is any kind of planning body, talk it over with them. A council of presidents of the various organizations, or any comparable group, would be an especially good place to discuss the idea.

5. After the idea has been discussed sufficiently around the community to have enlisted an enthusiastic degree of public interest in going ahead, plans should begin for the calling of a public meeting at which time the

program may be discussed and the actual organization of the community study group may begin. Care should be taken at this point not to call the organizational meeting prematurely. Until there is good evidence that there is a strong nucleus of community interest in taking hold of the program and going ahead the organizational meeting should not be called.

6. Plans for this meeting should begin well in advance so as to leave plenty of time to publicize it, and to complete other important steps in the preparation.

7. Read and thoroughly digest the entire study guide, giving special note to the philosophy and organizational mechanics which have been described up to this point, so that the program can be clearly outlined and explained to all persons who attend the organizational meeting.

8. A good deal of advance thought should be given to the matter of who would make a good general chairman for the community study group, and who would be willing to accept the job if it was offered. It would be well to get two or three persons in mind and to sound them out for this purpose. The same kind of advance thought should be given to the job of secretary, and several people should be sounded out for this purpose.

Nothing will do more damage to the organizational meeting of a community study group than to have several persons decline a nomination. And to get people in the various posts of leadership who are not suited for the jobs, or who are unwilling or unable to put forth the necessary effort, is perhaps the worst handicap the study group can have. Indeed, it is virtually impossible to conduct the program successfully without competent local leadership.

9. Check in advance of the organizational meeting to make certain that suitable arrangements can be made for the meeting rooms of the study group, both for the general assembly and for the buzz sessions, and that necessary equipment for the study is available.

Also make certain in advance of the organizational meeting that enough study guides will be available, either that evening or shortly thereafter, so that each participant will be able to secure his own individual copy.

10. Now comes the public meeting, open to everybody who is interested in strengthening democracy and his own community. The community study group is organized.

At this time the philosophy of the program and the form of organization for the community study group is explained and time allowed for questions and free open discussion.

Probably a member of the informal preorganizational steering committee will act as temporary chairman, but at the organizational meeting a general chairman for the community study group should be chosen, and from that point on should assume leadership of the meeting. Next, the group should choose a secretary, after this the Advisory Committee should be chosen, and the Boundary Committee should be appointed. The Boundary Committee's report will be due at the first regular meeting of the study group. Also at this time a regular night should be designated for the weekly meeting.

The various other committees should be listed on the blackboard and sheets of paper circulated for each person to list his name, address, and telephone number, and to indicate on which committee he would like to serve.

It is preferable that the appointment of discussion leaders and recorders, and of the various other committee members and committee chairmen, not be made at this organizational meeting. To do so would drag out the meeting through half the night, and in a large gathering it is difficult to get people placed in the committee for which they are best suited. The job of getting the right people in the right jobs, or the square pegs in the square holes, is a difficult one at best and can usually be done more accurately in a smaller meeting.

The job of setting up the committees and selecting the discussion leaders and recorders should therefore be entrusted to the Advisory Committee and the general chairman and secretary.

11. On the day following the organizational meeting the Advisory Committee should meet with the general chairman and secretary and complete the organization of the study group by setting up the committees and selecting the discussion leaders and recorders. For this purpose they should make use of the list of names and preferences for committees given at the organizational meeting the night before, and should give special consideration to the duties and responsibilities as outlined in the study guide.

The schedule of meetings and committee reports is given in sections in Part III of the study guide. One or more weekly meetings will be needed to cover the material outlined in each section.

Part III

Meetings and Discussions

1

Organization of the
Community Study Group

THE PREORGANIZATIONAL WORK AS OUTLINED IN PART II OF THE STUDY
guide having been accomplished, an open public meeting is called
for the purpose of actually organizing and launching the community
study group.

Some of the items in the agenda of this organizational meeting
might include the following:

1. Meeting called to order by a temporary chairman.

2. A description of the preorganizational work which has been carried
on up to this point, and a statement of the purpose of this meeting.

3. An explanation of the philosophy and purpose of the community
study program.

4. An explanation of the organizational and operational mechanics of
the community study group as outlined in Part II of the study guide.

5. Questions from the floor with adequate time for general discussion.

6. A description of the various leaders and committees needed for the
conduct of the community study, and a listing of them on the blackboard.

7. Sheets of paper may be circulated for each person's name, address,
and telephone number. This will provide a record of who attended the
meeting. Ask each person to indicate under his name the committee on
which he would like to serve.

8. The selection of the general chairman.

9. The selection of the secretary.

10. The selection of the Advisory Committee.

11. The selection of the Boundary Committee.

12. Settle on which night the community study group will hold its
regular weekly meetings.

13. Set a time on the following day for the Advisory Committee, general chairman, and secretary to meet and complete the appointment of
discussion leaders, recorders, and chairmen and members of all other
committees.

45

14. The study guides should be distributed at this time, or an announcement made that the guides will be available from the secretary at the close of the meeting.

15. An oral statement on the work to be covered in next week's meeting as outlined in the next section of the study guide.

16. Message from the general chairman and secretary.

ORDER OF COMMITTEE REPORTS

The Boundary Committee reports at the opening of the meeting on Section 2, The Character of Our Community.

The Population Committee report is due for the discussion on Section 3, The People of Our Community.

The Community Organizations Committee report is due for the discussion on Section 5, The Organizations of Our Community.

The Church Committee report is due for the discussion on Section 6, The Churches of Our Community.

The Government Committee report is due for the discussion on Section 7, The Government of Our Community.

The Social Agencies Committee report is due for the discussion on Section 8, The Social Agencies of Our Community.

The report from the Economic Development Committee is due for the discussion on Section 9, The Economy of Our Community.

The report from the Beautification Committee is due for the discussion on Section 10, The Appearance of Our Community.

The reports from the Education Committee and the Library Committee are due for the discussion on Section 11, The Education of Our Community.

The report from the Health Committee is due for the discussion on Section 12, The Health of Our Community.

The report from the Recreation Committee is due for the discussion on Section 13, The Recreation of Our Community.

The report from the History Committee is due for the discussion on Section 14, The History of Our Community.

In Part IV of the study guide there is a special outline for each one of these committees. Special outlines are also given in Part IV for the general chairman, the secretary, the discussion leaders, the recorders, and for the Publicity Committee.

Immediately upon appointment all committees should read and digest their respective outlines in Part IV, and the section in Part III which pertains to their particular subject, and then begin work. The committee chairmen should not delay calling the first meetings of their committees. Each committee will need all the time given it in order to get its report ready by the time the study group reaches that section in the guide at which the report is to be discussed. The importance of having the committee reports ready on time cannot be emphasized too much. The committees are the fact finders of the community study. If they do not function promptly, the success of the over-all effort will be seriously impaired.

2

The Character of Our Community

WHAT IS THIS GROUP ALL ABOUT ANYWAY?

THIS IS NOT JUST ANOTHER ORGANIZATION. WE ARE SIMPLY A GROUP of citizens who are interested in making an honest study of our community in an effort to find out how it can become a better place in which to live.

Our methods for doing this are going to be simple. They are not complicated, or new. Basically this is just a modern version of the old town meeting in which anyone can speak up on whatever he might be thinking about his own town. Our procedure is open, forthright discussion on how we feel about life in our community as it is today, and how by working together we might improve it.

To do this we need to be straight with ourselves and straight with each other. We are not here to win an argument or shove our ideas down anybody's throat. This is a give-and-take proposition.

This means that we are going to think constructively and together, and perhaps find out that as individuals we can be wrong. We will search out the facts, and on the basis of the study we will state problems, draw conclusions, and recommend whatever seems to be the best course of action for improvement.

This is a study of life in our community which we will make for ourselves and which will go forward on the American principle that frank and open discussion in an atmosphere of tolerance and good faith is the best way to get at the facts and work out our own destiny.

At times this may be a little painful. We aren't here to pull punches, dodge issues, or cover up the truth. Our discussions will be sincere and good natured. But they will be honest. If they aren't, then we had better not begin. We are putting our community on the couch and analyzing it for what it actually is. This will be our method of learning for ourselves exactly what has to be done if we are to achieve real, honest-to-goodness progress.

In the group there will be all kinds of people from all segments of our community. They will represent different ideas, different backgrounds, and different personal interests. Some of them may be in conflict. But all of them will have one thing in common—the community in which they live and its importance to us all.

This is truly democracy in action. It is our honest effort to take our destiny in our own hands and mold it for ourselves. It is an effort in which everybody is wanted and everybody's ideas are welcome. If people will always do this in the communities of America, democracy will always live and grow stronger.

BACKGROUND FOR DISCUSSION ON THE REPORT FROM THE BOUNDARY COMMITTEE

Communities have a certain layout or physical design, which can be plotted and located on a map. In some instances this comes from definite planning and advance layout of streets, parks, business areas and industrial zones. But in most cases this design simply grows up through the years along natural lines of human activity. Frequently it begins at a crossroads or a natural point of service and grows up in whatever pattern circumstances happen to dictate.

This often leads to unfortunate problems which arise because in the beginning there is not enough advance planning. Clustered about a central basing point are the stores, shops, and firms where people do their shopping and conduct most of the business transactions that are so important a part of their community life. Here, or not far away, are the schools, churches, the seat of municipal government, a library, and other centers of community services. In larger towns these services may be fairly well distributed throughout the whole area, but in small communities they tend to be located more toward the center.

Social and cultural services and the business houses along Main Street draw the community together into a common physical center from which radiate the residential streets and neighborhood groupings where people live. This center, plus the residential areas of relatively closely built homes, form what may be thought of physically as the *town proper*. In incorporated places the town proper is limited by legal boundaries which separate it from the outlying areas beyond.

But in a broader sense this part called the town is not the entire community. Spreading out in one or more directions are the neighborhood districts which gradually taper off into the broad surrounding countryside. Because of proximity of location or naturally established lines of communication and various kinds of mutual service, the people in these outlying areas are just as much a part of the whole community as those who live in the town proper.

Reaching out to a vaguely defined geographical limit there are families, some of them on farms, who feel more closely attached to this town than they do to any other.

In this broader, and probably truer, sense the total community includes far more people than just those who live in town. The people who live in the outlying areas of the community are of importance to the town center, just as the town center is of great importance to the outlying areas. If the community is to develop the richest kind of life and the greatest possible degree of stability, it is essential that this entire natural community be developed as a whole. The people in town and the people out of town should learn to know and understand each other and to work together for the good of the entire community. If they learn to face and deal cooperatively with community problems whether these problems are in town or out of town, to learn why these problems arose, and if they develop a sense of common loyalty throughout the whole, then they will have a stronger, more satisfying, and more prosperous community. Otherwise it is doubtful that the community can ever reach its full potential for the richest kind of human life, either in town or out of town.

Thus, for purposes of this study, the *total community* should be thought of as including all persons, in and out of town, who feel that they belong to this community, or that this is their "home town."

For this reason it is necessary at the outset that the study group decide definitely what area constitutes our community, and that this area then be drawn out on a large-scale map, copies of which can be made available to each committee of the group.

This area should then be thought of as our community for purposes of all discussions, surveys, and analysis undertaken during this study, and for purposes of whatever action program the community wishes to initiate as a result of the study.

At some point on each road leading away from the town center there is a line where people cease to feel that they belong to our community and begin to feel that they belong to the next community down the road. This line may be considered the natural boundary of our community. In most cases it is not a sharp dividing line like a national boundary, but is more of a transition zone. But some point on each road leading away from the center should be determined as the community boundary line.

In open country communities where there is no real town center these boundaries may be located in the outermost areas of the district without reference to a town center.

At this time the Boundary Committee should submit its report for discussion and approval, or amendment by the group.

BACKGROUND FOR THE COMMUNITY CHARACTERISTICS SURVEY

Every community has its own peculiar character or way of doing things that makes it different from all other communities. This character is a mixture of many things. In a sense it is the sum total of all the characteristics of all the people who live in the community. This makes it a tricky thing to get at. It is intangible in nature, it cannot be seen, it is difficult to measure. To discuss it is like trying to grab hold of smoke. But it is this character that in large measure will determine the whole destiny and progress of the community. In the same way that impulses of emotion and thought shape the actions of an individual, the collective thoughts and emotions of the people as a whole will shape the actions of the community.

Evidences of a community's character may be seen in the arrangement of the town, the appearance of streets and grounds, the architecture of buildings, the nature of the businesses and industries, and in the actions and social behavior of the people.

There is a certain pattern of thoughts, attitudes, customs, habits, values, ideals, and ways of looking at things that grows up with the people and over a period of generations becomes established in the basic character of the community. This character is not static, for just as the community and the people in it change, so too does the community's character change. The change may be slow and not readily noticed, but it goes on. If people are willing to examine the character of their community and understand it, they can, by determined effort, mold it largely to suit themselves.

The ultimate purpose of this study is to strengthen and promote the vitality of democratic processes and to improve the quality of community life. This purpose is based on the belief that the local community is essential to the American ideals of democratic living and self-government. Therefore, if our community has in it certain basic characteristics that tend to prevent or retard community development and democratic action it is our purpose to uncover these characteristics and bring them into the open where they can be examined, analyzed, and understood in order that we the people may devise intelligent means of eliminating or changing them.

Our immediate purpose in this section of the study guide, then, is to examine and discuss some of the intangible qualities in the basic character of our own community with a view toward gaining a better understanding of this character as it actually exists at the present time. This will call for a great deal of honesty and sincerity from each member of the group. It is not always easy for people to look at themselves as they actually are. Yet this is the place to begin.

Some of the qualities that help to mold the character of a community are the kinds of values that the people who live there consider the most important things in life. This refers to what we often call a person's "sense of values."

This sense of values will have great influence on a person's thoughts, actions, and whole mode of living, and will in turn affect greatly the actions and ways of doing things of the community. However, inasmuch as each individual is in part a product of community life, his own sense of values will not only affect the community, the community will greatly affect him. It is a two-way process in which each individual affects the character of his community and the community affects the character of the individual.

If the community is indifferent to its own problems, the people are likely to be of that character too, and by their personal actions they will contribute toward making the community still more indifferent.

If there are several groups in the community whose values differ sharply, as there often are, or are in open conflict with one another, as often is the case, the chances are that until something is done to develop better communication of thought among these groups they will not be able to understand one another and work together in harmony and coordination for the achievement of community goals.

The sense of values held by the community as a whole, or by certain groups in the community, is often not what people in the community think it is. An individual is not always influenced by what other people think is important, but by what he *thinks* they think. These misunderstandings are of great significance not only to the individual but to the community, for it is entirely possible that the progress of a whole community may be held back only because of a misunderstanding.

The attitudes which various groups and organizations have toward each other from the standpoint of prestige, social status, and class distinction also are significant factors in the character of the community. These attitudes are perhaps some of the greatest blocks to democratic vitality in any community. And here again there is often widespread misunderstanding.

It is true, of course, that many people do have a feeling of social superiority, but in many instances such feelings are wholly imaginary in the minds of those who feel left out or looked down upon.

Nevertheless, an imagined idea that certain groups feel superior will make others in the community just as resentful as though such attitudes actually existed. Obviously, where such misunderstandings prevail, democratic processes are impossible and community progress is retarded.

The nature of relationships that exist between the people in the town proper and those who live in the outlying countryside, also the kind of relationships that exist among neighboring communities, is significant. The extent to which the people feel a spirit of community loyalty, the way they react to change and to new ideas, their attitudes toward strangers and newcomers, the things people like most about their community and the things they dislike about it—all this will have a significant bearing on the character of the community, the quality of life that develops, and the ability of the people to mold their own destiny.

Procedure for Making the Community Characteristics Survey

The main job to be accomplished at the first meeting on this section of the study guide is to begin an analysis of some of the important characteristics of our community. Open discussion in which everyone is encouraged to speak out on what he thinks is the regular procedure of the community study group. However, this meeting is the exception to that procedure.

Instead of holding a discussion, each member of the group is asked at this meeting to write out on sheets of paper his answers to a series of questions which appear below and which pertain to some of the characteristics of our community. The answers to these questions should be given in as frank and pointed a manner as possible. No punches should be pulled, no thoughts withheld. Everyone is asked to write down exactly what he thinks, no matter what. The more honest the answers the more meaningful the survey.

No one is to sign his name to the answer sheets. All answers will be anonymous. No one is to peek, and no one should allow the person next to him (including husband or wife) to see what answers he writes down. Secrecy is of utmost importance; otherwise some people might not answer the questions exactly as they feel.

After the group has finished, the papers should be collected by the general chairman, and the meeting adjourned.

Before the next weekly meeting, which will also be on this section of the guide, the answer sheets to the questions given below are to be tabulated and consolidated into a single written report. This report on the Community Characteristics Survey is to be mimeographed and copies distributed to all members of the study group at the meeting next week. Thus, the report on the Community Characteristics Survey, containing what the whole group said anonymously about itself and the character of our community, will serve as the subject for discussion in the buzz sessions at the next regular meeting.

THE COMMUNITY CHARACTERISTICS SURVEY

Following is a list of questions designed to help analyze the character of our community. Each member of the study group is asked to read each question in full, then write out his frank and honest answer on a blank sheet of paper.

Be sure you number your answers to correspond with the number of the question being answered. Do not sign your name. Say exactly what you think.

QUESTION (1). What values do *you personally* consider the most important in life? Read through the list of values given below, then write out this same list in the order you think it should be arranged, adding any other values that you think ought to be included.

    Financial success
    Value and location of home
    Possession of material goods
    Length of residence in the community
    The kind of work one does
    The friends one has
    Family background
    Personal pleasure
    Making a home and raising a family
    Nationality
    Education
    Taking part in community affairs
    Leadership in the community
    Being informed on public issues
    Cultural development

Being tolerant of others
Leading a Christian life

QUESTION (II). *In your opinion* what values are considered most important by people in this community as a whole? Arrange the same list used for Question (I) in the order that you think it would rate in the community as a whole.

QUESTION (III). What organizations give people the most prestige in this community? List organizations in order of importance.

QUESTION (IV). Most communities have their various levels of class distinction or social position. These levels we might call "social layers." For example, the sort of thing people have in mind when they speak of the "right or wrong side of the tracks." How would you describe the social layers in this community? Are they based on wealth, family background, race and nationality, length of residence in the community, leadership in certain organizations, a combination of several factors, or what?

QUESTION (V). How easy is it in this community to move from one social layer to another?

QUESTION (VI): In your opinion, what are the most important annual events in this community? List the events, who sponsors them, and who takes part.

QUESTION (VII). Are there any factions or groups in this community who generally disagree with each other, or who have conflicting ideas on how things should be done? If so, describe these factions and state who and what they represent.

QUESTION (VIII). In this community, what is the general attitude of the people who live in town toward those in the outlying areas of the community? Do the people in town have any feelings of being superior? Do they have any feelings of being inferior?

QUESTION (IX). What is the general attitude of the people who live out of town toward those who live in town? Do the people out of town have any feelings of being superior? Do they have any feelings of being inferior?

QUESTION (X). Have any special community problems grown up between the people who live in town and those who live out of town? If so, give specific examples.

QUESTION (XI). How well does this community get along with its neighboring communities? Are there any points of important disagreement? List any special problems that may exist.

QUESTION (XII). To what extent would you say there is a spirit of unity and community loyalty in this community? Is there room for improvement?

QUESTION (XIII). Do people in this community hesitate to speak out openly in public meetings on what they honestly think about local affairs and conditions? If so, why?

QUESTION (XIV). How easy is it for newcomers to become established and feel at home in this community? Or, how long must a person live here before he is no longer considered a newcomer?

QUESTION (XV). What things do you *like most* about this community?

QUESTION (XVI). What things do you *dislike most* about this community?

QUESTION (XVII). What do you consider the outstanding needs of this community?

This completes the first phase of the analysis of our community. Please turn in your answer sheets to the general chairman. At the meeting next week we will discuss the tabulated report of the answers from the study group as a whole.

3

The People of Our Community

BACKGROUND FOR DISCUSSION

A COMMUNITY HAS A CERTAIN PHYSICAL DESIGN THAT CAN BE CHARTED on a map, and with the aid of our Boundary Committee we have agreed upon the area that constitutes our community. We have found that this boundary extends considerably beyond the town proper and includes a great deal of the surrounding countryside. This is the area in which people feel a common community of interests. Within this total area all interests and all people are interdependent for the full development of a rich and satisfying community life. Therefore, people from all parts of this area should be encouraged to take an active part in the work of this study group.

But a community has more than just a physical design that can be described by streets, roads, and other physical features. It also has a *functional design.* It is this functional design—the economic, social, cultural, and spiritual qualities of the community—that will absorb most of our attention during this study.

One important key to the kind of life a community will develop is this: What qualities of individual character and personality do the people in the community consider most important, or what in their minds are the most priceless values in life? What are the patterns of thought, habit, and custom that influence the way people act toward one another, and that thus tend to shape the life and actions of the community as a whole? These are some of the significant qualities of community life that we discussed in Section 2.

We said that the sum total of all these varied attitudes and human values goes into the basic character of the community. We found that because this character is intangible in nature it is one of the most difficult things to analyze about community life. Yet it is of utmost importance, for this character is a significant part of the structure, or functional design, of every community and in large measure will determine its entire destiny and future.

We said, too, that in many ways a community may be compared to an individual. It may have zest, drive, and ambition. Or it may be lethargic, inert, and suffer from a kind of community hardening of the arteries. And other human traits enter the picture. Community action may be actually blocked simply because of a group attitude which is wholly imaginary. Unless these false ideas can be corrected, community development may be impossible.

These, in summary, are some of the things we discussed in Section 2. Suffice to say here: These intangible qualities of a community's character are deeply woven into the whole social structure of the community. We have devoted a good deal of time in an effort to make an honest appraisal of this character in order that we might better understand each other and our community as it actually is. From this appraisal we should now have some important clues to some of the basic needs and problems of our community with which we will be dealing in our future action.

In our community each part—the economy, the educational system, the physical appearance, the health, etc.—is dependent upon every other part. The community, like all forms of life, is a whole. All members, aspects, and parts are interdependent and interrelated. If one part is defective the whole community will be affected; just as in the human body if a kidney breaks down the whole body will be affected.

For these, and many other, reasons the best kind of community developmest doesn't just happen. People have to want a better community. They must believe in their own ability, and they must be willing to exert their own energy for what they want.

But even the most sincere people will not get far unless they are willing to expend their own time to collect the facts they need to understand exactly what kind of community they have to work with. This kind of fact gathering is not going to be easy. It means that somebody, and in this case that means us, is going to have to do a lot of footwork and a lot of digging. This is why we have our research committees.

Then, after the facts have been assembled, the people must be willing to study them, interpret them, what problems they pose, decide what action should be taken, and then take it. Determination, a willingness to pull and work together, and absolute honesty in facing up to whatever the facts may indicate are the keys to success. No community problem can be solved unless the people are willing to admit that it exists. This may hurt. It may be embarrassing. It may take time and long-continued effort, it may require some swallowing of false prides and prejudices, but it is the only sure road to full community development. It is also the road to an alert citizenry and a vital, living democracy.

We have already considered our community's physical design. In discussing the character of our community we began to look at its functional design. We are now ready to examine some other aspects of this structure and to see what other problems we may discover.

In the report of our Population Committee we have before us some basic facts about the people of our community. It is now the job of the buzz sessions to examine these facts, agree or disagree with them, determine what they indicate about the kind of community we have, and decide what action they indicate for purposes of building a better community.

Questions for the Buzz Sessions

Question (i): How many people and how many families are there in our community? How many of them live in town? How many live out of town? (See report of Population Committee.)

A. What are some of the significant factors indicated by these figures about the population of our community? Think about them in terms of business, education, health, cultural and recreational activities, friendliness and neighborliness and understanding of each other.

B. In what ways are the people in town and those out of town dependent upon each other?

C. At the present time do these two groups include each other in their planning as much as they should? Do they have any trouble getting together?

D. Does this suggest any problems? If so, what problems? What ought to be done about them?

Question (ii): Is the population of our community increasing or decreasing, and at what rate? Or is it remaining about the same? (See report of Population Committee.)

A. What does this tell us about the present prospects for the future of our community?

B. Does it pose any problems? If so, what problems?

C. In what ways is this population trend an asset or a liability to our community?

D. Does this indicate any needed action?

Question (iii): What sections of our community are undergoing the greatest amount of population growth at the present time? Which sections are undergoing the least amount of growth? (See report of Population Committee.)

A. Do these facts indicate any needs in terms of planning for the future? If so, what needs?

B. Does this present any problems, (a) in the sections where there is the least amount of growth, (b) in the sections that are expanding? If so, what problems?

C. Does it indicate a migration within the community? Does this present any problems? If so, what problems?

D. What recommendations can the group make as to possible ways of solving these problems?

Question (iv): How do the annual birth and death rates in our community compare with the rate of growth in population? What are the trends of birth and death rates in our community?

A. What does this tell us about the migration of people in or out of our community?

B. Does it present any problems?

QUESTION (v): What does the report of the Population Committee show in regard to the number of families that have left our community for good in the past ten years, and those who intend to leave? What reasons are given for this movement out? Can the members of this group think of any other reasons?

A. Does this pose any community problems that are in need of solution? Are there any recommendations for action?

QUESTION (vi): Again, looking at the report of the Population Committee, what percentage of the local high school graduates have left our community to stay within the past ten years? Why have they left? What percentage of the young people now juniors and seniors in high school plan to leave for good when they graduate? Why?

A. What effect does this have on the age levels of our population? Are we becoming a community of older people?

B. What effect does this have on the starting of new families in our community?

C. What effect does it have on the prospects for future community leaders? What effect does it have on the number of present community leaders?

D. Does all this pose any problems for our community? If so, what recommendations can this group make as to possible means of solving them?

QUESTION (vii): What percentage of the people in our community have been here less than five years, from six to ten years, from eleven to fifteen years, from sixteen to twenty years, and twenty years or longer? What percentage of our families were started here? (See report of Population Committee.)

A. What does the length of residence, or the rate of population turnover, mean to our community in terms of richness and stability of community life? What does it mean in terms of community progress? Does this present any needs in our community?

QUESTION (viii): Look at the various age groups of our population as given in the Population Committee's report. How many people are there in each of the various age levels?

> under 1 year old
> 1 year old
> 2 years old
> 3 years old

    4 years old
    5 years old
    6 to 12 years old
    13 to 17 years old
    18 to 20 years old
    21 to 29 years old
    30 to 39 years old
    40 to 49 years old
    50 to 59 years old
    60 to 64 years old
    65 years old and over

A. Do we seem to be short in any particular age group?

B. Are we becoming overbalanced toward any particular age group?

C. How do these figures relate to the rate of our population growth as discussed above? To the birth and death rates? To the rate of movement out? To length of residence and population turnover?

D. What problems do these figures on the age groups of our community suggest in regard to education and school planning? In regard to community health and the need for health services? In regard to the need for recreation? In regard to the welfare loads of our community and future prospects? In regard to local business activity and future prospects for expansion?

E. What significance does all this have in terms of community progress and current prospects for the future of our community?

F. Does all this suggest any action or long range planning that ought to be going on in our community?

QUESTION (IX): What does the report of the Population Committee show in regard to the classification of people in our community by sex?

A. What is the ratio of males to females?

B. What is the ratio of single adult males to single adult females?

C. Does this indicate any community problems? If so, what might we do about these problems?

QUESTION (x): Do the figures on marriage and divorce rates as given in the report of the Population Committee indicate any special problems for our community? If so, what ought to be done about them?

QUESTION (XI): Again looking at the Population Committee's report, how many employable persons are there in our community? Males? Females? (Think of "employable persons" as people who are employed either by themselves or by someone else, or who would be employed if they could find a job.) What percentage of the total population do these employable persons represent?

A. What percentage of these people are employed full time? Part time? Seasonally?

B. What percentage of our employed people work in our community, and what percentage work in some other community? What effect does this have on community life?

C. What percentage of our people are unemployed? What are the principal reasons for this unemployment? Does this vary from season to season? Why? How does it affect local business prosperity? How does it affect our churches? Our homes? Our mental and physical health? Our schools? The ability of our community to hold its young people? The age level of our population? The cost of public assistance? The vitality of community life and democracy in America?

D. How many people in our community work for themselves, and how many work for someone else? What is the percentage of each of these two groups? Is there a good balance between these two groups? Does this pose any problems for our community?

E. How do the various economic activities (agriculture, industry, trade and commerce, and professional services) rank in our community? Is there a good balance among these activities in our community, or do we tend to "put all our eggs in one basket"? How is this related to the matter of seasonal unemployment? Does all this pose any problems for our community? If so, what should we do about them?

F. The Population Committee has listed in its report all the various occupational skills found in our community, and has indicated which of these skills are *not now* being used. Could any of these unused skills be put to work for purposes of creating new business or industrial activities in our community, on either a small or large scale?

G. Is any of our local labor force union organized? If so, in what unions, and what percentage of the labor force does this represent? (See report of Population Committee.)

H. What are some of the important roles played by labor, and by management, in the life of our community? Are they interested in the progress of the whole community? Do these two groups understand each other as well as they should in our community? Does the general public in our community understand the objectives of these groups as well as it should? If not, how might better understanding be created?

QUESTION (XII): What various nationalities and racial groups are represented in our community? (See report of Population Committee.)

A. What are some of the valuable qualities that these groups have contributed to the life of our community?

B. Do all these groups get along with one another as well as they should? Do they understand each other and properly appreciate each other? If not, what recommendations can the members of this group make for purposes of creating a better understanding and improved relations?

QUESTION (XIII): What percentage of the people in our community were born in our community? In America? In this state? From what other states did our people come? (See report of Population Committee.)

A. Are we a good mixture of people from various cultures and backgrounds?

B. What does this mixture add to the quality of our community life?

QUESTION (XIV): Look at the information given in the report of the Population Committee as to the educational attainment of our local population.

A. What does this tell us about the kind of community we have? Does it present any problems? If so, what problems? What action should be taken to help solve them?

B. Should our community be concerned about education for adults as well as education for children?

C. What effect does the continuing effort of adults to keep themselves educated have on the lives of our children?

QUESTION (XV): What percentage of the eligible voters in our community (persons 21 years of age or older) are *not* registered to vote? What percentage of the eligible voters in our community *did not* vote in the last election? In previous elections? (See report of Population Committee.)

A. What does this tell us about the citizen alertness of our community? Does this present any problems? If so, what might we do about them?

QUESTION (XVI): Read carefully the information given in the report of the Population Committee in regard to housing in our community.

A. Do these facts on housing indicate any needs in our community? If so, what needs?

B. What significance do these needs have in terms of community improvement and economic development? In terms of community health? Mental hygiene? Education? Delinquency? Cultural development? Recreation? Property values and tax base? The general quality of community life?

C. How might these needs be met? What specific kind of community action can the members of this group recommend?

QUESTION (XVII): To sum up, make a list of the community needs and problems that have been revealed by the population survey, and the kind of community action projects that this group would recommend to help solve them.

4

The Social Development of Our Community

A COMMUNITY HAS A CERTAIN LIFE CYCLE. IT IS FOUNDED, IT IS SET-tled, it reaches a certain level of maturity, and it deteriorates. It may, however, by the actions of its people prolong indefinitely its period of maturity. For the extent to which a community has matured may have little bearing on its age.

Many communities, such as the early western ghost towns, were founded suddenly, lived through a period of rapid expansion, and then declined almost as suddenly as they had begun. When the gold was mined out the town disappeared. These communities never reached maturity; they never really grew up. Other towns that we now consider old are still relatively immature and are just barely managing to hang on.

Other towns experience a gradual or even rapid growth and at some point in their life achieve a quality of community maturity. This quality of maturity comes in varying degrees and as long as it is maintained the life of those living in the community is attractive, healthy, and reasonably prosperous.

In the mature community there is an air of self-confidence, a determined belief among the people that broad goals of community development can be achieved. There is a willingness to work together, and a seasoned ability to face local problems honestly and constructively without undue emotion and unnecessary conflict and hurt feelings. It is this quality of maturity toward which all communities should aspire. Indeed, the extent to which the communities of America are able to achieve this quality of maturity will make the difference between the success or failure of the American tradition.

Our own community necessarily fits into some stage of this life cycle. Just where our community fits into this life cycle, and the direction we are going, is in our hands. For the point to be emphasized is that we, the people who live here, can largely determine for ourselves the future of our community.

But to do this we must be willing to examine, and to admit with ruthless honesty, the stage of maturity that our community is in at the present time. This does not mean harping on our weaknesses or being petty or critical just to find fault. It does mean an honest, constructive effort to look at ourselves as we actually are in order to discover for ourselves what improvements need to be made. This is never an easy process. Self-analysis is by its very nature a painful process. Certainly it requires courage, understanding, and a whole lot of talk and discussion. Still, this is the place to begin.

Look a bit closer at that word "maturity." In the case of an individual it is usually applied to one who is able and willing to stand on his own two feet, examine facts, recognize his own limitations, and follow whatever seems to be the right course of action whether he likes it or not. In general he is the kind of person who has learned to face life realistically and make decisions for himself. Through his own actions he keeps to a minimum the situations in which he is unable to manage his own affairs. He thinks in an objective, logical manner and is not afraid to admit when he is wrong. He feels a strong sense of responsibility to his family, his fellow man, and to himself. Through a process of continuous adjustment to his environment he becomes what is often called a "well-balanced" individual. Probably in this sense few of us ever reach complete maturity. The same is true of communities, but it is a goal toward which every community may strive, and to some degree is within the reach of all of them.

The relative maturity of a community may be broadly determined by the nature of its social structure, or by the willingness and ability of its citizens to face realistically their own limitations and difficulties, to recognize common problems, and to work cooperatively and harmoniously toward solving them. Community maturity, then, becomes a matter of continuous adjustment to current situations, and is achieved only by the alertness and wise, progressive planning of its people.

In our previous discussions we said that every community has a certain pattern or "physical design," and we talked about this aspect of our own community. We discussed the report from our Boundary Committee, and we settled on the geographical area which for purposes of this study we have identified as our community. This boundary, together with the physical features inside, makes up the physical design of our community. Through our Beautification Committee we will be much interested in this physical design, and later on we will discuss the report and recommendations from that committee.

Our concern now is with the functional design, or the social structure, which we began discussing with our community characteristics survey, and which we looked at again in discussing our population survey.

Obviously, one of the major factors that helps to determine the social structure, and therefore the level of maturity, of every community is the nature of the families that live in it. These families are the primary units from which our community is built. They are its backbone, its human material. From them come many of the ideals, the habits of behavior, the aspirations, the wants, and the prevailing attitudes of our people which largely determine whether the community is going forward or backward.

The family is the means by which our community grows or declines, by which its character, its ideals, its entire social structure, are transmitted from generation to generation. Anything that weakens our families, such as divorce, substandard housing, inability to earn a living, a lack of communication, and a host of other factors, weakens our entire community. In short, the family, as an integrated part of community life, is the basic form of human organization.

When the drift of young people away from the community becomes excessive (see report of the Population Committee) and older age groups become out of balance with younger age groups, when there is little or nothing to hold families together, then family life has been weakened and the future of the community is in serious jeopardy.

This does not mean that all of a community's youth must stay in the community in order to build a stable community life. It does mean that when a community can no longer offer an attractive life to the majority of its youth, and can no longer provide an incentive for starting new families, that community is dying at the growing point. New families may move in, but when the mobility grows beyond what would be a reasonable shift in population, then the very mobility, the constant coming and going is in itself a factor which contributes to the deterioration of community life. In a community where many of the people have little or no sense of permanence in their home there will be little incentive to build a strong community.

Certainly it should be obvious to everyone that a strong sense of family life and permanence of residence are essential to the development of a rich community life, and are therefore fundamental to the success of democratic processes. But let us consider some of the things that have been happening to family life in America.

Perhaps at no time in our national history has there been as much change in the character of American family life as in the past two or three generations. Some of the more important of these changes have been the marked reduction in the size of most families, the separation of family members, and a loss in the sense of importance which the members of the family once felt toward each other.

Today more young people are living away from home, and the work that people do is carried on outside the family circle more than ever before. For most Americans there is virtually no relationship between work life and family life. These two lives are, as it were, worlds apart which have no knowledge of each other. The father is frequently so drained out by the work he does away from home that he has little energy left for his wife and children. The family knows little about what goes on at the father's work, and he has little knowledge of what happens at home. His children may board a school bus which carries them to a distant place entirely outside the area of the home and which has no functional connection with the community in which the family lives.

The family farm, once the center of life and work for most American families, now functions as a unit of livelihood for no more than a small percentage of the nation's families. Today people are far less dependent on the family than they used to be. Indeed, under modern living conditions a family may even be a liability.

Someone has said that a family the size of those in grandfather's day could no longer be supported by an income. It would take an endowment!

As a result of these and related factors, many families are now much less closely knit than they used to be. With this change many of the intangible values of family function and solidarity once considered important in the building of character, leadership, and democratic idealism seem to be disappearing from the American community.

These basic changes in American living, and the consequent decline of the family as a closely knit unit, are largely the result of the Industrial Revolution which brought us into the modern technological age. In this age a host of factors tends to draw people away from the family circle. Thus the family grows smaller and less significant, it produces less and less for itself. It performs fewer and fewer of even the household services. These trends are having their effect on the vitality of community life; they are eating away much of the internal fabric from which our American Republic once drew strength.

Another change in American family life has come about from the increasing tendency for mothers to work for wages outside the home. As families have produced fewer and fewer of the material things they use, as costs of living have climbed, more and more families have found the mother's earnings essential to make ends meet. In many cases the mother's earnings are not essential, but she and her husband have grown reluctant to do without them. Thus, even the function of caring for children in the home is often performed by persons from outside the family.

All these changes in family life are deeply involved in what has been perhaps the greatest single influence on the American community—the growth of the giant city. This is something of what Louis B. Lundborg, vice-president of the Bank of America, had in mind when he said recently, "The deterioration of community life throughout America is a serious problem, too little understood and even less appreciated. The clean-up-and-get-out history is only half the story. I have a feeling that the obverse side of the coin, the condition of the sprawling cities that have grown up in California and elsewhere without becoming communities, is a related problem that has just as many dangers."

The objective at this point is not to lament what has happened to "the good old days." The practical question here is simply this: How can we recover the best from the past and at the same time retain and make the best use of the modern advantages that we have gained?

Or, how can we take our modern technology in hand and make it work for us instead of against us? This is the question which goes to the heart of an age in which we have learned to split the atom but have not learned to live with it. The question could be asked in many different ways, but the issue remains the same. Can we in our local communities adjust the use of our modern technological knowledge to the strengthening of human values and rich community living? This is perhaps the most difficult and complex question that today faces America. The whole future of a free democratic society will depend on our ability to work out a satisfactory answer at the local community level.

The place to begin that job is here, in this group, in this community.

We have been discussing the importance of the family unit as a fundamental part of the human community. However, no matter how well the family unit might be knit together, a collection of disconnected, isolated families would not create a rich community life. It is only when these families are tied together in a network of active, personal, and well-rounded interfamily relationships that true community life can develop. Many communities think that their families are in close contact with one another, but upon close examination it is found that in the community as a whole there is actually little interfamily communication.

Even in the small community important local problems are often unknown to the majority of the people. The community is often broken into segments or factions; organizational life is specialized and divided into groups that often have little relation to each other. Many people are not acquainted with each other as whole persons, and care less.

Thus one of the important measures of the vitality of community life is the extent to which this network of family relationships has developed throughout the community as a whole. This interrelationship of people in the community as a whole will also have a real bearing upon the quality of family life. The influence of the family upon the community is not, then, a one-way proposition. The community exerts its influence on the family, and the consequent changes in family life again influence the community. It is a kind of circle process.

This organizational structure will have much to do with determining the destiny and maturity of every community. It is an intangible, to be sure, but this structure will influence the life and maturity of a community just as thought processes influence the life and maturity of an individual.

Some of the organizational relationships of community life develop through marriage between families. Others develop through the business service that a member of one family performs for the members of another family. Whether these business relations contribute to a rich community life will depend on how and in what attitude the service is rendered, and whether or not both parties find the relationship satisfactory.

If, for example, a shopkeeper makes his customer "mad" or if the customer is habitually nasty to do business with, the relationship between these two families will probably not contribute to a desirable kind of community life. Certainly it will not help to promote harmony and a healthy community spirit.

Other relationships of families in the organizational network of community life are in cooperative activities, such as the development of a community improvement program. Others are in church, in organizational meetings. Some are formal, some are informal. Groups get together to sing, to put on a play, to take part in sporting events, or to have a party. Housewives visit each other for a cup of coffee or call on someone who has just moved into the community. Friendships come into being. Clubs are organized. Men get together to compare gardening information, to go hunting, or to play cards. People stand around street corners and talk. There are also other relationships: vice, crime, juvenile delinquency, hidden activities.

This network of community relationships also exerts a powerful influence in molding the character and habits of the growing child. If these relationships are direct, wholesome, and significant, people learn to know and understand each other. They develop a feeling of responsibility for each other, a sense of unity and community spirit. Community institutions become securely established, people are not afraid to express themselves and are not easily offended when someone differs with them. The community grows adept at and enjoys constructive conversation and open group discussion. By these and other means people enter into a good network of active communications with one another and keep themselves well posted on local affairs. Leadership develops in the normal course of events. The community grows up. It matures. And it becomes a rich and satisfying place in which to live.

Let us now examine the maturity of our own community.

QUESTIONS FOR THE BUZZ SESSIONS

Following is a kind of test designed to help point up some of the social strengths and weaknesses in our own community. There are twenty questions on which we may rate our community as Excellent, Good, Fair, or Poor.

These ratings will, of course, not be entirely accurate, but will represent the group's best opinions. Likewise, the measures given in the test represent somewhat idealistic standards which probably don't exist in any community. However, they should help in a fairly specific way to indicate some of the areas of community life where we are in the greatest need of improvement. They should also suggest some important points for consideration in the planning of future action.

In taking this test, the discussion leaders should read each question aloud while the other members of the group follow in their own copies of the study guide. Ample time should be allowed for group discussion on each question, and the discussion leader should then call for a vote on the rating to be given. Every member of the group should express his frank and honest feelings even though he is in the minority, and every member should vote on the rating for each question.

QUESTION (I): The families in our community engage in informal visits with each other. (Consider frequency and proportion of the families involved.)

Excellent .... Good .... Fair .... Poor ....

QUESTION (II): All segments of our community get together for group meetings of one kind or another. None of our families stay out of community affairs, or are left out.

Excellent .... Good .... Fair .... Poor ....

QUESTION (III): In our community people have no fear about openly expressing their honest opinions. Ideas are exchanged freely and frankly.

Excellent .... Good .... Fair .... Poor ....

QUESTION (IV): People in our community are not easily offended when someone differs with them.

Excellent .... Good .... Fair .... Poor ....

QUESTION (V): Our community is adept at and enjoys constructive conversation and open group discussion.

Excellent .... Good .... Fair .... Poor ....

QUESTION (VI): People in our community keep well posted on local happenings and goings-on.

Excellent .... Good .... Fair .... Poor ....

QUESTION (VII): Everybody in our community reads the local newspaper.

Excellent .... Good .... Fair .... Poor ....

QUESTION (VIII): On the whole, people in our community are alert to the problems and needs of the community and are always willing to take the time and trouble to search them out and recognize them for what they are.

Excellent .... Good .... Fair .... Poor ....

QUESTION (IX): In our community people are always willing to capitalize on all possible opportunities to improve family and community life, as evidenced by a widespread willingness and ability to work together.

Excellent .... Good .... Fair .... Poor ....

QUESTION (X): Ours is a community of unity and solidarity. All groups and organizations are community minded. There are no conflicting factions or pressure groups, no chronic bickering. In personal and intergroup relations our community avoids such elements as suspicion, jealousy, and hostility that tend to prevent people from working together.

Excellent .... Good .... Fair .... Poor ....

QUESTION (XI): In our community there is no resistance to constructive change.

Excellent .... Good .... Fair .... Poor ....

QUESTION (XII): Our community is free of such things as malicious gossip, personal nosiness, and other such petty annoyances.

Excellent .... Good .... Fair .... Poor ....

QUESTION (XIII): It cannot be justly said that our community is hidebound. Newcomers are always readily accepted and made to feel at home.

Excellent .... Good .... Fair .... Poor ....

QUESTION (XIV): Ours is a friendly community. It has a genuine spirit of neighborliness.

Excellent .... Good .... Fair .... Poor ....

QUESTION (XV): Our community always looks upon civic leadership as a matter of community service, never as a means of self-esteem or political prestige.

Excellent .... Good .... Fair .... Poor ....

QUESTION (XVI): Our community is blessed by an abundant supply of good community leaders; people who are practical, have plenty of creative imagination, and are willing to sacrifice their own time and energy to get things done for the general community welfare.

Excellent .... Good .... Fair .... Poor ....

QUESTION (XVII): As a people, our community is always willing to get behind its leaders and contribute its share of the responsibility to a community project. Whenever there is a job to be done for the community almost nobody is willing to sit back and let others do all the work.

Excellent .... Good .... Fair .... Poor ....

QUESTION (XVIII): The citizens of our community have a strong sense of pride and loyalty to their community. Community loyalty transcends the loyalty to any one organization.

Excellent .... Good .... Fair .... Poor ....

QUESTION (XIX): This community has a well-developed sense of appreciation for its own cultural heritage. Local historical and cultural matters are always of general interest. Historical landmarks are well taken care of. There are well-developed local traditions that have meaning to the people. There is a good general knowledge of community and regional folklore. These things are a source of pride and inspiration, but they in no way impede progress or prevent the community from having vision for the future.

Excellent .... Good .... Fair .... Poor ....

QUESTION (XX): Ours is a community of well-kept buildings, grounds, and streets. It has many flowers and shrubs. People enjoy gardening. They have a good taste for architecture and landscaping. Anybody should enjoy coming here because of the attractive appearance and over-all beauty of the community. (This question does not consider the natural scenery, such as mountains, etc., which the community had no part in making.)

Excellent .... Good .... Fair .... Poor ....

For each Excellent the community should receive 5 points, 3 points for each Good, 1 point for each Fair, and 0 for each Poor. One hundred would be the best possible score. The important thing, however, is not the over-all rating, but the points on which the community was rated Fair or Poor.

The group should make a list of all points on which it rated the community Fair or Poor, and then devote a few moments of extra discussion to each of these points. On each point, why was the community rated low? For what specific reasons was it rated low? Give examples. What recommendations for action can the group make that would help to bring the rating up on each of these low points? Give specific suggestions.

5

The Organizations of Our Community

BACKGROUND FOR DISCUSSION

THERE IS ALWAYS SOME QUESTION AS TO WHERE A PROGRAM OF COMmunity development ought to begin. Many such programs have been started as projects in economic development. Others have directed their efforts toward city planning, the building of schools, the solution of health problems, or they have been organized for some other specific purpose. However, the point of view suggested in this study guide is that a thoughtful consideration of the broad picture of community life as a whole, the intangible human factors that make the community what it is, and that lie behind all specific community problems, is the best place to begin a sound program of community development. Moreover, the prime concern of this study is the development of community *life*.

Thus we have considered the strength of the family structure, the extent to which families are in communication with one another throughout the community as a whole, to which they participate in, and are informed on community affairs. These, we have said, are some of the basic measures of the quality of community life.

To sum up: The structure of human relations in the community will have an immense bearing on the ability of the people to work together, to recognize and face up realistically to local problems. It will affect the community's ability to analyze itself, to develop an alert citizenry, to direct its own destiny, and to improve its own life. If this basic human structure is thoroughly understood, then it should be much easier to achieve community-wide action toward any specific goal.

If the structure of human relations is such that many of the community's families tend to keep to themselves, if there is an atmosphere of suspicion and jealousy, if community relationships are such that people are afraid to speak out on their honest views, if families are divided into active pressure groups and conflicting interests, if certain people feel unable to act according to their own best judgment because someone else controls what they must or must not do, then obviously something needs to be done about the existing social structure before the best kind of community-wide action can be successfully initiated.

This does not mean that all conflict or differences of opinion must be done away with. Conflict is a part of growth. Democracy is kept alive by differences of opinion. But where there is intolerance of opposing beliefs, a basic unwillingness to listen to the other fellow's argument, where friction has become chronic or approaches the point of bickering, then community progress is definitely limited and many problems must go unsolved.

These are some of the important tests that tell whether a community is growing or declining. No form of life ever stands still, and this includes the community. Every community must go forward or it must go backward, and when a community becomes so satisfied with itself that it fails to recognize any problems, that community is slipping.

Thoughts, actions, and attitudes of the people shape the community's social structure. The people are in turn shaped by it.

With these considerations of the social structure in mind, let us now examine what might be thought of as one of the more formal aspects of this structure, the community organizations.

In a community where the social structure is healthy, most people will place their loyalty to the whole community first, and their loyalty to any one group or organization second.

There are, then, two ways of looking at a club or organization. One is when the organization becomes an end in itself, the other is when the organization is viewed only as a means of achieving the broader goal of enriched living, or a vigorous and democratic community life. Probably the acid test of an organization is this: Are its members willing to subordinate a goal of their own special interest to the larger goals of the community as a whole?

To the degree that community organizations are poorly developed and established patterns of communication are lacking among them, to the extent that the various organizations are uninformed about each other's purposes and activities, and there is an atmosphere of misunderstanding, to that degree will people ignore community needs, assume attitudes of indifference or hostility, and resist any change that might mean community progress.

Most communities have many groups and organizations, but often these organizations overlap in leadership, in membership, in purpose and function. A dozen organizations travel along parallel tracks, all striving for similar goals. But they always pull separately. They never pull together. Often the lack of common planning becomes so acute that the various organizations actually weaken each other. In the end the whole community suffers.

Frequently it is found that people have spread their energies so thin in trying to join so many organizations that they have no energy left for the community. In these communities life is no longer whole. It has been broken down into so many segments that community-wide effort is virtually impossible. Both leaders and followers are so much absorbed by special fragmentary interests that loyalty to the community as a whole exists only in limited degrees, or perhaps not at all. Each organization is almost walled off from the others and within these narrow limits each seems to think that its own special goals should be considered the goals of the whole community.

Yet even in communities where people are "overorganized" and it is impossible to find a free night in the week, even where people seem to be so busy in organizational work they just can't take on anything else—even in these communities—it is not uncommon to find that a substantial proportion of the total population, sometimes even the majority, does not belong to any organization, never attends a meeting of any kind, and has no sense of community service. A few people are nearly meeting themselves to death, 5 or 10 per cent are carrying the entire load, and the majority are content to let them do it. Under these conditions it is difficult to achieve citizen alertness and cooperation for real progress on a community-wide scale. Too many people are dragging their feet.

However, the fault may not be entirely with those who seemingly aren't interested. It may be that some of those who complain the most about being overworked are actually so eager to assume the role of leadership that others who may also have ability are in effect frozen out. Almost every community has people with ability whose services are never utilized.

But there is nothing more deadening to the vitality of community life and democracy in America than apathy.

QUESTIONS FOR THE BUZZ SESSIONS

QUESTION (I): How many organizations are there in our community? (See report of Community Organizations Committee.)

A. How many of these are adult organizations?

B. How many of them are juvenile organizations?

C. What is the ratio of adult organizations to the number of adult persons in our community?

D. How does this ratio compare with the number of memberships per organization?

QUESTION (II): What is the total number of memberships in all the adult organizations combined? (See report of Community Organizations Committee.)

A. What percentage of the adult population does the total number of adult organizational memberships represent?

B. How many actual people does this total number of organizational memberships represent? What percentage are these people of the total adult population?

C. How many adult persons in our community do not belong to any community organization? What percentage are these people of the total adult population?

D. How many adults in our community hold membership in more than one organization? Classify the adults who are members of organizations by the number of memberships held.

QUESTION (III): Of the total number of organizational memberships in our community, how many of them could be classified as inactive? (See report of Community Organizations Committee.)

A. What percentage of the total memberships are inactive? What percentage are active?

B. Make an estimate as to the number and percentage of the people who hold organizational memberships in our community, but who are largely inactive in organizational affairs.

C. Classify the adult organizations in our community according to the per cent of their average attendance at meetings.

D. Considering all the organizations together, what percentage of the total number of memberships are in average attendance at organizational meetings?

E. On a scale of 10, assuming that zero is very inactive and ten is very active, classify the adult organizations in our community according to their degree of activity.

QUESTION (IV): Make a calendar of organizational meetings in our community. (See report of Community Organizations Committee.)

A. How many organizations meet on the same day?

B. How many meet at the same time?

C. Arrange the days of the week in order of the number of organizational meetings held on them.

D. Which day is the heaviest for meetings? Which day is the most free of meetings?

E. Do organizational functions ever conflict with one another in our community? Does this present a community problem? If so, can the members of this group think of any recommendations for solving it?

QUESTION (V): What is the total number of organizational offices (including committee chairmanships) in all the organizations in our community combined? (See report of Community Organizations Committee.)

A. How many different people hold these offices?

B. How many of these officers and committee chairmen could be classified as inactive? (A person might hold office in two organizations. If he is active in one and inactive in the other, this would count as one inactive officer.)

C. Do the same people usually do most of the work? Why?

QUESTION (VI): Does all this information concerning the organizations of our community present any community problems?

A. If so, what problems?

B. What recommendations can the members of this group suggest for solving these problems?

QUESTION (VII): Does this group have any recommendations for achieving a more widespread degree of participation in the organizations of our community?

QUESTION (VIII): Classify the adult organizations in our community by the type of their membership, i.e., occupational, age, sex, etc. (See report of Community Organizations Committee.)

A. Are there any segments or groups in our community that are not now included in one or more of these various organizations?

B. Is there a need in our community for any adult organizations that we do not now have? If so, what new organizations are needed? Why?

QUESTION (IX): Classify the number of adult organizations in our community according to their general purpose. (See report of Community Organizations Committee.)

A. How many of them have similar purposes?

B. What does the number of organizations that have similar purposes mean in terms of community unity and progress?

C. Do the organizations in our community actually set up joint community projects in which all pool their energies to get a specific job done?

D. Is this kind of cooperative effort an established practice on the part of most of the organizations, or does it happen only once in a while?

E. Could there be more of this kind of cooperative effort than there is at the present time? If so, what would it mean to the organizations? To the community? To the development of human relations?

F. In some communities this kind of cooperation has become a matter of regular community effort through the formation of some kind of organizational council that acts as a kind of coordinating or mobilizing body. Is there a need for such a council in our community? If so, how might it be established? What might this group do to help get it started? Are there any specific recommendations on this point?

QUESTION (X): Do we have any organizations in our community that are in conflict with one another, either openly or otherwise?

A. If so, what is the nature of this conflict and the reasons for it?

B. Is there any good reason why it should continue?

C. By what means might this conflict be solved?

QUESTION (XI): What is the total number of memberships in all of the juvenile organizations in our community? (See report of Community Organizations Committee.)

A. What percentage of the juvenile population do these memberships represent?

B. How many actual people does this number of juvenile organizational memberships represent? What percentage are these people of the total juvenile population old enough to belong to organizations?

C. How many juveniles in our community old enough to belong to organizations do not now belong to any? What percentage are these people of the total juvenile population of organizational age?

D. How many juveniles in our community hold membership in more than one organization? Classify the juveniles who are members of organizations by the number of memberships held.

QUESTION (XII): Of the total number of juvenile memberships in our community, how many of them could be classified as inactive? (See report of Community Organizations Committee.)

A. What percentage of these memberships are inactive? What percentage are active?

B. Classify the juvenile organizations according to the per cent of their total memberships in average attendance at meetings.

C. Considering all the juvenile organizations together, what percentage of the total number of memberships are in average attendance at organizational meetings?

D. On a scale of 10, assuming that zero is very inactive and ten is very active, classify the juvenile organizations in our community according to their degree of activity.

QUESTION (XIII): What problems are there in our community as regards juvenile organizations? Are there any groups that are not being properly served or any groups that are left out? Are juvenile organizational programs adequate? Is there a need for leadership? Is there a need for other organizations? What effect might all this have on the rate of juvenile delinquency? On the social growth of young people? If there are any problems concerning the juvenile organizations of our community, what specific recommendations can be made for the solution of such problems?

QUESTION (XIV): To sum up: Make a list of the weak points and strong points in our community life that have been brought out in this discussion of our local organizations.

A. What needs have been identified?
B. What recommendations are there for action necessary to meet these needs?

6

The Churches of Our Community

BACKGROUND FOR DISCUSSION

IN DISCUSSING THE SOCIAL STRUCTURE OF OUR COMMUNITY WE HAVE considered the family in its integrated relationship to other families as the basic form of human organization. We have looked at the community's organizational life, its clubs, its associations, its various group relations. These are all vital parts of the culture in which we live and have a major influence on its development.

We now need to consider another phase of this social structure which for our purposes may be thought of simply as the institutional life of our community. Certainly the future and richness of every community are tied directly to the state of development and the effectiveness of its institutions.

Throughout this study we are thinking of the total community, of its significance to man, and of how we can make our own community better. It is the community itself, not any one of its parts, that commands our primary interest. From this point of view each aspect of community life is of utmost importance and must come in for careful examination. For in some significant way each part of the community helps to shape the quality of the whole and therefore has profound influence on the individual lives of the people who live there.

There is perhaps no institution in American history that has done more to inspire noble aspirations in the minds of men and women, to foster human good will and the brotherhood of man than the local church.

It was a fervent belief in religious ideals, and in the freedom to express them, that brought the first settlers to American shores. It was the church that became the cornerstone in these early communities, and that largely made them what they were. It became the common meeting place for pioneer families. It served as a center for worship, sociability, communication, service, and education.

Religion and our kind of democracy have gone hand in hand. From the church we have derived much of our heritage. And in many respects the stability, the spiritual vigor of community life can be measured by the vitality of the local church.

Yet today the average church does not exercise so vigorous an influence for community well-being as it might. In certain respects the church has become another example of the tendency of Americans to become passive spectators instead of aggressive participants.

In many places there is a feeling that the church is not so much a part of the community as it could or perhaps should be; that it has tended to remain aloof and keep out of the full stream of community life. Such feelings may or may not be justified. Yet they exist. Only aggressive and positive action on the part of the church can change this feeling. Probably the existence of such feelings is not entirely the fault of the church. Part of the reason may be that more people do not participate, or have not taken an active enough interest to learn for themselves just what activities the church is engaged in.

Like all institutions, the church is no better than the people wish to make it. The community gets from its churches just what the people want it to get. And this, fundamentally, is the main point of our discussion.

Our purpose here is not to argue the relative merits of religious creeds, nor is it to sit in judgment on the churches and the religious beliefs they foster. Our purpose is that of the community, to look at local churches with the same eye for understanding and improvement that we are using to examine other basic factors that help to make our community what it is.

As a group of citizens concerned with the future of our community we should look at the churches as one important part of our total community life. We are interested in the extent to which the local churches have geared their activities into the life of the community and in the possibilities for greater participation by the people. We are interested in the churches for what they can do to enrich our community life and thereby help strengthen the moral fiber of America.

The activities of most modern churches enter into many phases of community life. There is a wide variety of programs for youth and adults. In certain instances churches have taken official stands on political issues. Many churches support and operate hospitals, schools, homes for the aged and infirm, and other charitable organizations. But our concern here is the church in our own community, the extent to which it is actively willing to take a vigorous part in local improvement, and in the solution of community problems.

Just as any other group of organizations becomes ineffective when they split themselves into fragmentary efforts, the churches grow weak and ineffectual when they are unable to cooperate and work together. Unless there is close communication among individuals there will be indifference or misunderstanding. The churches are no exception. And, just as in any community institution or organization, as long as church members confine their activities and interests to the church alone they will have little influence on the community as a whole.

QUESTIONS FOR THE BUZZ SESSIONS

QUESTION (I): How many churches are there in our community?
A. Which ones are they?

QUESTION (II): What is the membership of each of the churches in our community? (See report of Church Committee.)

A. What is the average attendance at the regular worship service in each church?

B. What percentage is this average attendance of the total membership in each church?

QUESTION (III): Added up, what is the total church membership in our community? (See report of Church Committee.)

A. What is the total average attendance at principal worship services?

B. What percentage of the population in our community are church members? What percentage are not?

C. On the average, what percentage of the population in our community attends church? What percentage does not?

D. How does this information on church membership and attendance in our community compare with the situation ten years ago? Twenty years ago? Forty years ago?

E. Is the church in our community growing or declining in its influence on community life?

F. Does all this present any community problems? If so, what problems, and what ought to be done about them?

QUESTION (IV): In the opinion of this group is church attendance in our community as high as it should be? If not, why isn't it? What specific recommendations can be made for increasing church attendance in our community?

QUESTION (V): Examine the list of programs and activities of the churches in our community as compiled by the Church Committee.

A. To what extent is the community aware of these programs?

B. Do these programs include any activities specifically designed to assist in community improvement and the solution of local problems? If so, what are they? Could any additional activities of this kind be suggested? What would be the churches' reaction to these suggestions?

C. Are there any specific things that the churches of our community could do in addition to what they are already doing to help serve the needs of children and young people?

D. Does our community ever seek assistance from its churches in specific projects for community improvement or for the solution of community problems? Is this kind of assistance sought as often as it should be? Are the churches willing to accept such requests for assistance? Does all this suggest any action that ought to be taken in our community, either by the churches or by the community?

QUESTION (VI): Do the churches in our community ever set up joint community projects in which all pool their energies to get a specific job done?

A. Is this kind of cooperative effort an established practice, or does it happen only once in a while?

B. Could there be more of this kind of cooperative effort than there is at the present time? If so, what would it mean to the churches? To the community? To the development of religious ideals?

C. Does our community have a council of churches or a ministerial association? If so, is it active? What are its functions?

D. If there is no such council or association, should one be established?

QUESTION (VII): What is the present condition of church property in our community?

A. Does it add to the physical beauty of the community, or does it look run-down and ill-kept?
B. Does it need painting, fixing-up, or landscaping?
C. Are the present church buildings in our community suited to the needs of the community?
D. Is there need for improvement in our church buildings in order adequately to meet the needs of the community?
E. Are the church buildings in our community made sufficiently available for the people's use? Are they used as much as they should be?
F. Does all this suggest any opportunity for increased participation by the churches in community affairs, or by the community in church affairs?

QUESTION (VIII): To sum up: What conclusions can be reached as to:

A. The significance of the local church to community life?
B. How our community might gain greater value from its churches than it does at the present time?

7

The Government of Our Community

BACKGROUND FOR DISCUSSION

CERTAINLY ONE OF THE MOST IMPORTANT INSTITUTIONS IN THE LIFE OF every community is the institution of government. Every American has the right to be free, but with that freedom goes the responsibility to exercise an active interest in the affairs of government, to keep informed on political issues, and to vote.

To discharge these responsibilities is the bare minimum of active American citizenship. Yet millions do not even bother to vote, and it might be asked how many of those who do vote know what they are voting for? Apathy, indifference to the policies and practices that govern our lives can be our undoing. This is one of the great dangers to American self-government.

If the people of America should ever lose control of their government, or if government should abuse its powers, it will be the people's fault. We are the government only if we choose to make the government our responsibility. Certainly the development of an alert, reasoning, responsible citizenry is one of the most important aspects of community development. For the development of good citizenship must begin at home.

In our study thus far we have examined our social structure. We have looked at the local church as an important community institution, and in due course we will analyze all phases and aspects of life in our community. We have said that a weakness in any part of community life will affect the whole. From the viewpoint of the total interests of the community, we turn now to an examination of the institution of government.

QUESTIONS FOR THE BUZZ SESSIONS

QUESTION (I): Examine the organizational structure of the municipal government in our community, and read the description of its form and functions as prepared by the Government Committee. Are there any points that any member of the group does not understand or would like to have discussed concerning:

A. The form of the organizational structure?
B. The duties and responsibilities of each department and office?
C. The cost of each department and office to the taxpayer, and the method of financing?
D. The way that the holder of each office is chosen and the term of office?
E. The experience and background that a candidate should have to perform effectively in the various municipal offices?
F. Any other points?

QUESTION (II): Are there any additional needs for municipal services and facilities in our community?

A. If so, what are they?
B. How might they be obtained?
C. How might they be financed?

QUESTION (III): Are there any needed changes or improvements in the way any of the departments in our local government are operating at the present time?

A. Does anyone disagree? Remember, there are two sides to every story. Be sure to get both sides so that all points can be intelligently understood.
B. Does anyone in the group feel that the system of our local government, or the organizational structure itself, could be improved upon? If so, by what specific changes? Why? How do the others in the group feel about this?
C. What agreements can the group settle on as to things liked and things disliked about the functions of municipal government in our community? List any problems that have been posed, and the suggested solutions.

QUESTION (IV): Examine the organizational structure of the local county government, and read the description of its form and functions as prepared by the Government Committee. Are there any points that any member of the group does not understand or would like to have discussed concerning:

A. The form of the organizational structure?
B. The duties and responsibilities of each department and office?
C. The cost of each department to the taxpayer, and the method of financing?
D. The way that the holder of each office is chosen and the term of office?
E. The experience and background that a candidate should have to perform effectively in the various county offices?
F. Any other points?

QUESTION (V): Are there any additional needs for county services or facilities in our community?

A. If so, what are they?
B. How might they be obtained?
C. How might they be financed?

QUESTION (VI): Are there any needed changes or improvements in the way any of the departments in our county government are operating at the present time?

A. Does anyone disagree?
B. Does anyone in the group feel that the system of our county government, or the organizational structure itself, could be improved upon?

If so, by what specific changes? Why? How do the others in the group feel about this?

C. What agreements can the group settle on as to things liked and things disliked about the functions of our county government? List any problems that have been posed, and the suggested solutions.

QUESTION (VII): What percentage of the eligible voters in our community (persons 21 years of age or older) are *not* registered to vote? What percentage of the eligible voters in our community *did not* vote in the last election? In previous elections? (See report of Population Committee, and notes on the discussion of this same question from Section 3. The discussion leaders should each have a copy of the answer to this question and a record of the discussion on it from Section 3, and should read that material aloud at this point.) Are there any further recommendations concerning this question beyond what was suggested during the discussion on Section 3?

QUESTION (VIII): What is the general attitude of people in our community toward holding local, county, or other political offices?

A. Are most people in our community willing to run for, or accept, such offices? Why?

B. Does this pose any problems?

C. What effect does it have on the vitality of self-government in our community?

QUESTION (IX): Does our community have any effective, nonpartisan, organized group through which local citizens are informed of the facts concerning candidates, political issues, governmental operations, the conduct of public officials, etc.?

QUESTION (X): Does our community have any effective, nonpartisan, organized group through which we as a community can make known our wishes concerning the problems and needs of our local area?

QUESTION (XI): If our community does not have any organized groups to do the jobs indicated under Questions IX and X above, should such organizations be created?

A. If so, how?

B. By whom?

C. Are there any recommendations for action?

8

The Social Agencies of Our Community

BACKGROUND FOR DISCUSSION

THE COMPLEXITIES OF THE MODERN ERA HAVE BROUGHT WITH THEM many human needs which the simpler social services of an earlier age are now unable to meet. Thus we have witnessed the growth of the modern social agency specializing in the administration to the human ills and needs of our time, and in the care of people to whom society now feels an obligation. Many valuable human resources would be lost were it not for the work of these agencies.

The modern social agency, both private and public, has therefore become an institution in the community's social structure. Its functions are many and varied and it offers a service to the wealthy as well as the impoverished. No longer is it simply an institution for charity.

The importance of the modern social agency to family and community life can scarcely be overestimated. It is, in turn, an expression of the community's needs and problems, and has become a matter which should be of concern to every locality. Many people who are now lost to society in our penal and mental institutions could be saved for productive citizenship if we were able to provide the proper social services. Others are thrown onto public relief because the community has failed to develop its economy properly. The cost of modern social service runs into billions annually. This is a reflection of the human problems of our time, and there is every indication that the needs for this kind of service are becoming greater instead of less. Deeply involved in these needs is the future of democracy and the American tradition of self-reliance.

89

It is not uncommon to find people complaining about the operation of social agencies even though they actually know almost nothing about the problems these agencies are up against. Every
community would do well to find out just what problems these
agencies have to deal with, and thereby gain a better understanding
of their functions. The community might also examine itself in an
effort to identify its own problems from the standpoint of social
service and try to work out positive methods of dealing with them.
The development of adequate social service and rehabilitation and
the solution of the basic human problems which these needs reflect
are of vital importance to community development in the modern
age.

QUESTIONS FOR THE BUZZ SESSIONS

QUESTION (I): Read the report of the Social Agencies Committee.
A. What community needs and problems does it pose?
B. What positive action might we as a community take to meet these
   needs?
C. What organizations could help?
D. Would more adult education, especially for parents, be of assistance?

QUESTION (II): Are there any suggestions for improvement in the
operation of any of the social agencies listed by the Social Agencies
Committee?
A. Are there any misunderstandings toward these agencies that this discussion might help to clarify?
B. What obligations does the community have financially to these
   agencies?

QUESTION (III): What is the current welfare load in our community?
(See report of Social Agencies Committee.)
A. Is this load rising or falling?
B. What are the various causes for this load?
C. What can we as a community do in a positive way to remove the
   causes?
D. What are the current laws and policies of administration governing
   public assistance in our state? Are these laws and policies satisfac-
   tory? If not, what improvements might be suggested?

QUESTION (IV): Who is responsible for the social ills of the individual
—the individual or the community?
A. What might we as a community do to help reduce the frequency of
   these ills?

QUESTION (v): Does our community have a council of social agencies?
A. If it does, what is the function of this council?
B. If it doesn't, is such a council needed?
C. Are there any recommendations for action?

9

The Economy of Our Community

BACKGROUND FOR DISCUSSION (FIRST MEETING)

EVERY COMMUNITY WILL ULTIMATELY RISE OR FALL WITH ITS ECOnomic base.

The people, the social structure, the homes, churches, schools, health services, government, recreational facilities, all depend upon the local economy for support. Unless expanding opportunities can be created for the people to earn a living they will either move away or be forced into dependence upon public support. In either case serious social problems will follow and the community will decline.

But the development of a sound and expanding economy is equally dependent upon many other aspects of community life. Local governmental services and municipal facilities, vigorous churches, a good school system and well-developed educational services, adequate health services, abundant opportunity for recreation and the enjoyment of life, a healthy social structure, an alert, progressive citizenry—all are essential to the development of a sound and expanding economy.

True community life, as we have said during this study, is an organic whole and must be looked upon in that light if sound community development is to be achieved. No single part of it, including the economy, can be isolated from the rest of the community and developed by itself.

Many people and agencies interested in conservation and economic development have failed to recognize this fact and for that reason have failed to accomplish their purpose, or in their lopsided and specialized success have done more harm than good by creating social problems which far outweigh the advantages of their economic development.

Everyone must have a certain amount of money, but most people also have other values which they must be able to satisfy in the community. Unless all these values can be satisfied, economic and otherwise, there can be no real growth and stability in community life, and in the long run democracy and the American tradition will disappear.

Economic development is involved in educational and social processes, in attitudes of mind. A community cannot, for example, develop the most from its soil and other natural resources unless certain attitudes exist in the minds of the people.

Against wasteful or indifferent attitudes of mind, any effort toward economic development is eventually doomed unless these attitudes can be changed. Conflict or a lack of communication between classes and factional groups in the community, a lack of general pride, inability or unwillingness on the part of individuals and groups in the community to cooperate, emotional prejudice, religious or political bickering, the lack of community spirit and solidarity—any of these factors can prevent sound economic development just as effectively as the lack of necessary capital. Thus the basic character of the community which we have discussed, the social structure, the local organizations and institutions, are major determinants in the ability of the community to develop an expanding economy. In our own community there are many examples of the intangible drawbacks to economic growth, and yet in thinking of these examples there should be a great understanding, for there is in all of us a certain narrowness.

Too many people who are interested in the development of new industries and in increasing the volume of business activity either have no concept of these basic facts or at least act as though they haven't. All of us have certain personal interests in the community which are of greater concern to us than to others. But if any of these interests are to be fully developed in the long run it will be only through a total effort to develop the total community.

All this is of deep concern to every community, whether it is growing or whether it is declining.

Many communities at the present time are enjoying a relatively high degree of economic prosperity, yet they fall short of realizing their full potential. At the moment they feel no pinch. They sense no possible break or decline. They are dulled by their seemingly favorable circumstances into a kind of creeping complacency which prevents them from making adequate plans for future expansion. Thus, despite the prosperity of the moment, economic opportunity in these communities is far more limited than it need be. More young people are forced to leave the community than would otherwise be necessary. Family life and the social structure are gradually weakened by the very prosperity, and the community is not only deprived of its full productivity but it is often unable to make the necessary adjustment when changing conditions threaten the prosperity that it has.

Other communities boast of their millionaires, but fail to recognize the poverty which exists on every hand. When only a small proportion of the population enjoys a high standard of living and there is a sharp division into classes of extreme wealth and extreme poverty, or if a substantial number of families are barely able to make ends meet, then there is a hidden conflict and the decadence of community life is inevitable.

This is one of the great dangers to democracy. Today it is seriously weakening American leadership in a world in which we are attempting to demonstrate the strength of our way of life. And it comes at a time when the threat of peace is upon us; the threat that if we are somehow able to make peace in the world millions of our people might be unable to find work.

Almost every community in America has unrecognized opportunities. The problem is to find these opportunities and to develop the spirit of community progress which will make it possible to use them.

During the years since the beginning of World War II American economic expansion has been unprecedented. Yet the fact is that this expansion has not all represented permanent progress.

The major factor in this economic growth has been the mush-rooming of war industries and military spending. Without our great orders for aircraft, atomic materials, and a host of other military goods it is highly possible that the American economy would fall short of an industrial base sufficient to supply enough jobs for the population. A major slump which many economists feared as late as the summer of 1950 failed to develop largely because the Communists invaded South Korea, and the American program of military spending was thus accelerated.

Yet in spite of the military prosperity many of our communities and rural areas continue to decline. Old resources dwindle, new ones lie undeveloped, the demands for certain products disappear. People become more and more mobile, families are without roots, community life is weakened, democratic processes become less and less a reality. Until people are able to create new economic opportunities within the home-town community there is always the possibility that the American economic fabric will be seriously ruptured and a vast depression will ensue; especially should more peaceful relations be achieved among nations.

The first step toward further economic development is to make a detailed inventory of our community's assets and liabilities, or to determine exactly what resources, natural and otherwise, we have to work with from an economic point of view; then to draw up a definite plan for bringing about the best possible utilization of these resources. This inventory will include an actual listing of all local opportunities and the reasons why these opportunities exist, the prospects for successful development, and the economic requirements such as size of investment, equipment, labor, etc., that will be needed for making use of them. It will also be necessary to include in the plan some of the actual steps which are to be taken in bringing these developments about. This kind of detailed investigation and planning is chiefly the job of our Economic Development Committee.

However, it is essential that thought be given to some of the broad factors which, in general, condition the economic potential of every community. Most of the detailed analysis and specific planning must of necessity be left to our Economic Development Committee. But an intelligent understanding by the people as a whole of the broad factors which influence their livelihood and their economic destiny is of vast importance to the success of any long-range planning.

The first of these broad factors is the climate, the soil, the kinds of natural resources that exist within the region where the community is located. This is the physical environment. Enterprises that flourish in one community or in one region of the country are impossible in another. Methods that get results in one area would be unsuccessful if attempted in another area.

If the community is to develop a permanently prosperous economy, the people must learn to appreciate and understand the physical environment in which they live. They must learn to respect it, to take care of what they have, to adjust themselves and the kind of work they do to the conditions which nature has provided.

If they make only a partial adjustment and utilize only part of what they have, then the community cannot realize its full capacity for a high standard of living. If there is complete failure in this adjustment, the community will decline and its people will be forced to move away.

The ghost towns dotted across our cutover timber regions, the abandoned towns where mining operations once flourished, where the main highway once passed, or where the soil has been depleted, furnish mute testimony to this failure of communities to adjust themselves to the physical environment in which they lived. All this is a severe loss to American strength and the democratic processes. Yet there are still people in America who refuse to admit that it ever happened.

When a community is unaware of the resources that it has, if there is lack of sufficient knowledge and incentive to develop them or if there is a deliberate effort on the part of certain people to prevent their development, then the community will fail to achieve the attractive life that would be possible under more enlightened and democratic circumstances.

Likewise, a policy of carelessness and abuse by the general public or of wasteful exploitation of natural resources by certain operators will lead only to decline of the economy and eventual ruination of the community. Examples of this policy in our national history are well known to all of us. Yet every summer thousands of forest fires

are started through carelessness, and the old attitude of clean-up-
and-get-out still persists in many minds and is repeated in every
generation.

The general attitude of the people toward the development and
treatment of their natural resources in large measure determines the
future of every community.

A second important influence on the livelihood of the community
is the cultural background of the people who live there now and of
those who settled the community at the time of its founding. The
founders brought with them certain customs and habits. They
brought certain skills, occupations, tools, and ways of doing things.
They applied their methods to the conditions in which they found
themselves and thereby made certain changes in the environment.
However, the local conditions necessarily exerted a great influence
on the people, and in the process certain changes were brought
about in their traditional ways of doing things and they began to
develop new skills and new tools to work with.

In the course of the community's history people profited from
their mistakes, and each new idea led to still another idea. From
these early patterns of work people acquired a great many habits,
thoughts, and attitudes toward earning a living which they passed
on from father to son, and each generation was influenced to some
extent by the generation that had gone before. Some of these patterns of doing things have been carried down through many generations from other countries and have helped make the community
what it is today. These patterns have blended with the new developments which came with each period in the community's history, and
today are as much a part of it as Main Street. This is one of the
important reasons why communities differ.

Another factor which helps to determine what people do for a
livelihood is the geographical location of their community in relation
to other towns and other regions. The habits and occupations of
the people who live in neighboring towns, the distance to centers of
population, the freight rates and modes of transportation that connect the community with other towns, the extent of competition
with other centers—all these factors are involved in the community's
geographical location with respect to other communities and will
have an important bearing on the extent and nature of the economy.

The so-called fringe community located on the outskirts of the large city is one of the recent developments in the American scene. Here the economy is usually dominated by what goes on in the city. Usually the majority of the people are actually employed in the city and commute to a distant factory or office to work. The place where they work has no connection with the place where they live. Their home town, if they think of it as such, becomes little more than a bedroom.

In these communities it is frequently difficult to develop any real community spirit or sense of community entity. This often leads to severe problems and to outright conflicts in providing necessary facilities, educational services, and in the development of community organizations and institutions. In many of these places people feel no real loyalty either to the community in which they live or to the city in which they work. Many may not even feel a sense of living in the community as such, but regard their location as just a place where they have moved to get away from the city.

Under these conditions true neighborliness is almost nonexistent. It has been simply a process of urbanizing the countryside and in a very important sense community life has yet to be developed. There are thousands of these places in America and in most of them democracy as a living, functioning process is more of a general principle than a reality.

Even worse is the so-called low-cost housing development which is built in mass production style without any regard for human values and community life. Here the sole concern is to make a financial profit by providing four walls and a roof which can be sold to low-income families for a small down payment.

No thought is given to planning which would be conducive to neighborhood and community development. The land which nature took generations to build is wrecked by mass bulldozer attack. Trees, vegetation, even the top soil which might have been used for lawns and gardens, is scraped away. Houses are set in monotonous rows and sold en masse by high-powered, impersonal methods. The buyer, who will spend the rest of his productive life paying much more than the place is worth, feels no personal relation to the seller, whom he probably never met, and neither buyer nor seller cares a hoot about the other. As a consequence most of the occupants are transient and have no intention of staying any longer than their family finances require. Here is one of the great blights on American community life. Its solution is one of the major social problems of our time.

Perhaps the most significant influence on the economy of the modern community has been the development of science and technology. These developments have altered drastically our entire culture, reshaped our methods of doing business, and changed the whole fabric of community life. In many respects these changes have tended to weaken neighborhood and community ties and have thereby destroyed democratic values.

Yet if we are able to make the proper use of these technological developments there is every reason to believe that we can develop a stronger economy and a better community life than we have known at any other time in the history of America. The problem is to take advantage of our technological advances by using them to strengthen and improve community life instead of allowing them to weaken and destroy it.

Much of the solution to this problem lies in improved industrial and labor relations. Much of it depends on an honest effort by industrialists and corporation executives to make their plants and stores a genuine and responsible part of the community in which they are located. All this requires a much greater degree of understanding on the part of local citizens in general toward both labor and management. It requires also a greater recognition by the people who are directly involved in labor and management that they are, first of all, human beings in the community and that as such their best interests will be served only in so far as the best interests of the community are served.

The survival of democracy is not tied to the success of any one segment of the community without regard for the welfare of other segments, but to the success of the community as a whole. Too many large corporate organizations and government plants are merely located in the community physically and provide nothing more than a place of employment for local residents. This is not enough to maintain the quality of community life which is essential to the survival of our American heritage. The solution will require aggressive and cooperative effort on the part of all groups working together for the community welfare. And each group must be willing to make an effort which goes much further than half way.

The development of modern technology has in some respects made production on a small scale less feasible than it used to be. In other ways it has had the opposite influence. It has created many new occupations and many new ways of utilizing raw materials. This means the possibility of more jobs, it means that in communities where the old economy has been exhausted by the depletion of certain resources there may be opportunity for developing an entirely new economy.

This kind of change will present many complex problems. But they are problems which must be met if the community is to continue as a satisfying place in which to live. In dealing with such economic change the people in the community are faced by two basic alternatives. They can move away and leave the home town to gradual decline or they can develop new industries and occupations for themselves, and produce more for home use and local or regional markets.

In many ways people can diversify the work that they do so that their eggs are not all in one basket. This is, of course, no simple process. It will require thought, study, and imagination. It will also require a willingness to work together. But it can be done if the people are willing to use their own brains and depend on their own ability.

The diversification of a community's economy may begin with the production of more things in the home for use in the home. This kind of effort will not only help to build the future economy, it will have a profound effect in making the family more stable and more secure. Home production can become a source of deep personal satisfaction, as in the case of the man who enjoys making furniture for his own home. Home production can also provide children with a greater sense of responsibility and thus contribute to the building of character and good citizenship.

There is also the possibility of producing goods within the community for sale either in the community itself or in the surrounding region. This kind of regional economy has many advantages and can go a long way toward making the home community less dependent upon distant market fluctuations and other factors in the national or international economy over which the community has no control.

Diversified production for local or regional consumption, or industrial decentralization, carried to the full extent of its practical limits will make a substantial contribution toward strengthening the home community, and thus add to the economic security and democratic strength of America.

Modern technology with its inexpensive mechanical devices requiring relatively small amounts of power has in many ways made small-scale manufacturing and diversified production for sale to local and regional markets increasingly practical. There is also the possibility that the smaller community might develop local small-scale manufacturing industries which could become subcontractors for some of the large industrial concerns located in nearby cities. Where conditions of transportation and other economic factors make this kind of effort possible new and varied opportunities should be opened up to many communities.

In times of national emergency this would mean that many families who would otherwise be uprooted and moved into a crowded urban housing project could remain intact in their natural home environment, thus helping to prevent many of the expensive and demoralizing social problems which arose from the heavy concentration of families in the transient housing projects of World War II. From the standpoint of preventing serious psychological and social problems which must sooner or later be paid for, small-scale production within the home community might be far more economical than one would at first suppose. From the standpoint of the atomic age it may be a prerequisite to survival.

There is, of course, a limit as to how far we can go in local production for home or community use, but there is also a limit to how much our democratic traditions can stand the strain of centralized power and control with the consequent dying off of local initiative and community life.

Probably the practical answer lies in an optimum balance between small- and large-scale production. At present, mass methods probably outweigh small-scale production more than is necessary. This inbalance can be corrected in large part if the people in local communities throughout all America begin to use their initiative and their ingenuity in a more intensive effort to create new economic opportunities for themselves in their own home towns. Great funds of knowledge have been accumulated in our universities and tax-supported research centers that could be used for these purposes. We have the inventive resources of the people themselves which is a part of our American heritage. One of the great questions, however, which has not been answered is how to get these two forces together. Or, how can the knowledge of our research centers become accessible to the people in their communities where it can be put to work? Perhaps this study group can help to bridge that gap.

These problems are serious ones. They affect not only our opportunities for a job; they affect our institutions, our homes, our churches, our schools, our community organizations. They affect deeply the quality of our lives, our human values, our families, the entire social structure of our community, and the future of America as a democratic power.

QUESTIONS FOR THE BUZZ SESSIONS

QUESTION (I): What are the general attitudes of the people in our community toward the conservation and development of natural resources?

A. In what ways could these attitudes be described as intelligent? What specific examples can be cited that show constructive and intelligent treatment of our natural resources?

B. In what ways could the attitudes of people in our community toward the conservation and development of natural resources be described as wasteful, ignorant, or indifferent? What specific examples can be cited as evidence of these attitudes?

C. What about local forest practice? How about our soil? Do the majority of local farmers make every effort to use the latest knowledge of good land management? What about local attitudes toward fish and game laws? Is improvement needed? If so, in what specific ways?

D. What has been the history of people's attitudes toward natural resources in our community? What effect has this history had on our economy of today? Does it offer any lessons for the future?

E. How might the attitudes of the people toward the conservation and development of natural resources in our community be improved?

QUESTION (II): Is the economy in our community well diversified, secure, and expanding, or does it tend to be more of an up-and-down kind of economy? Are there any weak spots? If so, what are they?

QUESTION (III): In what ways is our local economy influenced by the physical environment in this area?

A. Are we making the best possible use of our natural resources (climate, soil, topography, water, forests, mineral deposits, etc.)? Give specific examples.

B. Are there any specific ways in which we could make better use of our natural resources?

C. Make a list of all the natural resources in our local area that are being used to a greater or lesser extent at the present time. Which of these resources could be better utilized than is the case at present?

D. Make a list of all the natural resources in our local area that are not being used at all at the present time.

E. Do we make full use of the various agencies, federal, state, and local, that are in a position to give advice or help in the development of our natural resources?

F. Make a list of the various agencies that might be of help in this connection.

QUESTION (IV): What kinds of work skills, preferences, and traits did the people who settled our community bring with them?

A. Has this background had any influence on the development of our local economy? In what ways?

B. Are there any traces in our economy today of these influences? Give examples.

QUESTION (V): What are some of the influences of other areas and neighboring towns on the economy of our community and the type of work that we do?

QUESTION (VI): What has been the effect of modern science and technology on the economy and type of work that people do in our community?

A. In what ways have science and technology tended to limit opportunities in our community?

B. What new opportunities do science and technology offer us that we might take advantage of to improve our local economy?

C. Make a list of all the new businesses, industries, and various economic opportunities that the members of this group think might be possible for development in our community.

D. Are there any new industries that we would not want in our community? If so, what are they? Why wouldn't we want them?

E. Does growth necessarily imply an increase in numbers?

BACKGROUND FOR DISCUSSION (SECOND MEETING)

We have thus far been considering only the broad factors that tend to shape our over-all economy. In general terms we have discussed the physical environment in which we live, the cultural background of our people which has influenced their ways of doing things, the geographical location of our community with respect to neighboring towns and other areas, and the influence of modern technological and scientific advances.

We now need to examine our economic life in more specific terms and to determine in some detail just what opportunities we have for further development. To accomplish this we must first do some careful stocktaking to find out as specifically as possible what our resources are, how they are being used, and from what sources our present income is derived. Once these facts are in hand we will be in a position to sit down and make a definite analysis of exactly what we have to work with and to determine the best possible use that can be made of it. We should then be prepared to map out an effective and definite plan for bringing about the full economic development of our community.

For purposes of analysis, the local economy may be divided into three general headings: (1) agriculture, (2) industry, and (3) trades and services. By examining the economy as it fits into each of these three general headings it will be much easier to determine what we have to work with and to spot the places where there is room for expansion.

If our community is to attain a well-balanced diversified economy which will provide sufficient job opportunities upon which to build a well-rounded kind of community life, there should be some development in each of these three categories. Development in each of them up to the full limits of feasibility will lead to the greatest possible utilization of our natural resources and raw materials. This will enable us to develop the highest possible standard of living for all our people, and to build the strongest possible economic base for our institutions and community life.

If the present economy is overbalanced in any one of these three categories and little attention is being given to the other, it is likely that the community will tend toward instability and underdevelopment. Under these conditions the community will be much less able to withstand the shock of any shift or change in the general economy. Therefore, one of the important measures of economic stability is the extent to which some balance has been achieved among these three areas of economic activity.

A community may utilize its natural resources in some form or another in only one of these categories, or under ideal conditions it may utilize its resources in all three of them. For example: A farmer may grow a certain agricultural product from the basic natural resource, the soil. This product may then be processed in a local industrial plant. It may then be sold through local retail merchants to consumers inside the community. And, through local jobbers or wholesale merchants, the surplus may be sold in areas outside the community, thereby bringing in new money for local circulation. It may also be possible that waste materials from this same product are processed locally into by-products or that the basic raw material is used to make several other products.

This is the fullest and most efficient use that the community can make of its raw materials. A resource that is utilized to this extent will provide far more jobs, more local prosperity, and more taxable wealth than is possible when the raw materials are shipped away for processing elsewhere and consumers' goods are always purchased and shipped in from the outside.

Perhaps it is impossible for our community to utilize all its resources to this extent. But the chances are that we could develop a much fuller utilization than we have in the past. The principle is this: The more fully a resource or raw material can be utilized or processed within the community the more stable and secure will be the life of that community. This means that we should make every possible effort to make multiple use of the resources that we have, we should make plans for salvaging our waste products, and we should put old things to new uses.

Through our Economic Development Committee we will get a list of all the businesses and commercial operations in each of the three categories: Agriculture, industry, and trades and services. This list can then be compared with the natural resources and raw materials that we have, and by this means we should be able to make a complete analysis of the extent to which we are using our resources at the present time, where we can make better use of them, and where there might be an opportunity for further development.

The committee will also determine what raw materials and goods we buy from outside the community and ship in for local use. From this information we may get still more ideas for local production and economic development. These are some of the places where we might look for new possibilities of providing larger payrolls and more employment opportunities at home.

One of the things which is important to most people who work for a living is the opportunity to engage in an occupation that is interesting to them. Too many people find it necessary to make their living in a job that they either dislike or for which at best they have little enthusiasm. Probably there is no community in the country where everybody is doing exactly the thing he would most like to do. But the nearer people can come to finding in their home community an opportunity for the kind of work they enjoy doing the more satisfying and prosperous the community will be. The productive and creative power of our people, the skills and occupational tastes that we have, constitute one of the community's most valuable economic assets.

Every possible effort should be made to provide suitable outlets for these interests by diversifying our economy, increasing the degree of utilization of our resources and raw materials, and by creating wherever possible and desirable new enterprises and commercial operations. This is, of course, a big job. It can be accomplished only if the community makes up its mind to accomplish it.

Let us now look specifically at each of the three economic categories mentioned above. By analyzing the situation as it is at the present time in each one of them we may come up with the kind of factual information which will enable us to chart a definite plan for further development.

Agriculture

The agricultural production of every community is limited by such factors as markets, transportation, topography, soil fertility, amount of available moisture, and the extent to which farmers are using the best known methods of land management. Some of these factors are largely beyond our control, but if the best methods of land management are applied by all of our farmers the effect of these limiting factors can be greatly reduced. This is one way of using our scientific knowledge for getting the most from what we have and thereby increasing the value and productivity of the land on which the future of the community must rest.

Unfortunately, many of America's farmers have not made use of the scientific agricultural knowledge that is available in order to get maximum results. This is not necessarily the farmer's fault. It may be due to circumstances beyond his control or to the fact that no one has yet approached him in a manner that is acceptable to him. However, whatever the reason might be, the result is that the farms in many communities are so badly run down that they are barely supporting their owners, are worth much less than they could be worth, and are producing only a fraction of what they should produce. Many of our farms are being used to grow crops which are not suited to them or which are much less suited to them than something else would be. If this is the case in our community, it may be of great personal value to our farmers, and to the community as a whole, to make a thorough study which will bring out the facts so that recommendations can be made for the right kind of corrective action.

The Economic Development Committee should collect the facts necessary for this purpose. These facts might include figures on the number and size of farms in our community, how many of them are owned and operated by local residents, how many are rented, and how many are owned by people living outside the community. These facts will have an important bearing on farm productivity and on what chances we have of increasing it. The committee will also need certain statistics on farm valuations and on the total farm income and expenditure. By comparing these figures with similar information for other areas we will get some idea as to just where our community stands. We will also need to find out about what proportion of the farm income is spent inside our community, how much of it goes out of the community, and what the money that goes outside the community is spent for. This will give us some definite ideas as to what extent our community is making the most of the income that it has. It should also suggest some of the steps that might help to keep more of it at home, and it might suggest possibilities for new business developments.

It would be helpful to know just how much land there is in our community, what percentage of it is suitable for farming, and what proportion of that which is suitable for farming is actually being farmed. Inquiry might also be made to determine what crops and farm products the land in our community is best suited for, and this information should then be compared with the actual use that is now being made of the land.

This kind of information will help to determine how these lands can be utilized more efficiently, or whether there are any crops or farm products other than those now being produced which could be grown to more profitable advantage. With these facts at hand and a spirit of community progress and democratic cooperation it should be a fairly simple matter to plan intelligently for our own future prosperity.

The Economic Development Committee should consult with the county agent's office and other agricultural agencies to find out whether a professional soil survey and agricultural analysis has ever been made in this community. If such a survey has been made its findings should be useful in helping to determine our major farm production possibilities and limitations. Some of the best information of this kind can, of course, be obtained from some of the farmers themselves.

In many communities professional surveys of this kind have been made at various times but the results never found their way into practical use. This represents a tremendous waste of time, money, and knowledge, and it may be that as a result local farm production is much lower than it need be.

Some effort should be made to determine whether or not the farmers in our community have available to them regular established sources from which they can obtain needed information on the latest research concerning farm life and productivity, and if so, where these sources are located, how they might be used, and the extent to which they are being used at the present time. These are merely suggestions. It is often found that people are not aware of all the help that is available to them, or the agencies and institutions that can give help have not made adequate provisions for getting their information distributed to the people who can make use of it.

In most rural areas there are a great many people who live on small plots of land, or on farms, but who work in a nearby industrial plant or somewhere else off the farm for a portion of their income. This practice may be a matter of choice or it may be because of an inability to get a full year's income from the land. There are many cases where the job in town actually supports the farm, and the land thereby becomes a losing proposition.

It would be a good idea for the Economic Development Committee to find out to what extent this is true in our community, and why, and some effort might then be made to determine what, if anything, can be done about it.

If more of our farms could be developed into full-time incomes or the number of productive farms could be increased, a valuable contribution might be made to the economy of the community. Also it might be that more opportunities can be created for profitable part-time farming to supplement and round out family incomes now obtained from seasonal employment in industrial or other commercial operations. This would help to balance the economy in slack seasons.

Other facts that will prove helpful for purposes of agricultural analysis include information concerning markets and transportation facilities that are available for local farm products, and what possibilities there are for improvement and expansion of these facilities. Sources of farm credit and whether these sources can be expanded is another kind of factual information that the committee should obtain.

Obviously, it is to the best interests of the community to keep as many farm loans as possible within the local area. Otherwise a good deal of the community's income will be drained off in the form of interest payments into distant centers and our community will be made that much poorer. For this same reason we might find it profitable to examine the extent to which local farm products are processed in our community.

All these basic economic factors are of great importance to family stability and community development. But the facts will not be worth the paper they are written on and all the scientific research in the world will not help unless there is developed among the people themselves a spirit of unity and solidarity, and unless there is a bond of active cooperation between the people who live in the rural parts of the community and those who live in town.

This leads right back to the basic character of the community and its social structure which we discussed in the earlier parts of this study. This means that the future of a community's economy is largely in the hands of the people who live there, and in their willingness to put into practice the kind of human relations which are essential to democratic processes and a rich community life.

One of the most important functions of the community's town center is to provide proper and friendly service for its farmers. Through the exchange of mutual services and through social and cultural relationships the town and the surrounding rural area may be tied together into a common community life. Unless this tie is well established the entire community will suffer.

Industry

One of the most profitable ways of bringing about full economic development of the community is to encourage the establishment of new industries or processing plants to utilize raw materials locally instead of shipping them away to be processed elsewhere. By establishing new local industries it is possible that many of the community's resources and raw materials that are now idle and unused can be put to productive use, thereby creating more jobs and making the community's life more secure.

Not all these new industries, indeed none of them for that matter, need to be large establishments. America was built on small businesses and there are many economists today who believe that the future economic strength of the United States lies very much in the extent to which small business maintains its vigor and strength. If the community is willing to take the trouble to analyze carefully its own resources and economic possibilities, to provide *in writing* the kind of facts that cause people to invest money, and then to map out an aggressive plan of action, there is little doubt that industrial companies and other investors can be attracted to come into the community and establish new plants. This kind of effort is, of course, limited by what the community has to offer, but in most communities the people have grown to take their assets so much for granted that they do not see their own possibilities.

The encouragement of plant developments in the community by companies and other people from outside the community is one possibility. A more desirable possibility, and one which usually will lead to a sounder kind of local economy, is to develop local resources from within. In thinking of new industries too many communities think of nothing but trying to get someone from a distance to come in and establish a plant when as a matter of fact the people in the community could develop their own plant with their own brains and their own capital. There are, of course, limits as to how far this policy can be carried, and beyond these limits the community may seek outside help to bring about full economic development, but wherever this policy of economic development from within is carried out to its full practical limits there will be greater inner security and a more democratic community life.

We have already suggested the possibility of small plants in the smaller communities serving as subcontractors for large manufacturing establishments located in nearby cities. This kind of development depends, of course, on the ability to meet competition, on available transportation, on freight rates, on available power, and on an existing labor supply or on the ability to attract new labor from outside the community. The Economic Development Committee should investigate all these possibilities and collect the necessary facts and information.

There is also the question of economic balance. If the community at present is largely dependent on agriculture, the chances are that it has too many eggs in one basket to assure a secure economic future. The business of a one-industry town leaves no cushion to fall back on should hard times adversely affect the one thing it depends on. An economy that is overbalanced in any one direction means, too, that a good many young people who might otherwise stay in their home town to live and raise families will have to seek employment opportunities elsewhere. This loss of human talent, productivity, energy, and creative brainpower is the most serious loss that a community can sustain. Hundreds of communities throughout America are literally dying a slow death for this very reason.

In a study made by the San Francisco Chamber of Commerce in

1950 it was shown that a typical industrial plant employing 150 persons provided at that time an annual payroll of more than $400,000, supported some 1,000 persons, provided for 393 occupied homes and the purchase and maintenance of 320 automobiles. Results of the study indicated further that such a factory supported 24 professional men, 22 schoolrooms, and 33 retail stores providing retail business amounting to $244,000 a year—$92,000 for food, $63,000 for automobiles and fuel, $24,300 for furniture and appliances, $17,550 for lumber and hardware, $8,400 for drugs and sundries, $34,000 for miscellaneous services, and $10,500 for entertainment. Every community may not have the conditions necessary for developing a new plant that would employ 150 people, but these figures should illustrate the significance of a flourishing industry in the community and how many personal pocketbooks and community activities it can reach into.

In our analysis of local industrial possibilities our Economic Development Committee should list each of the various industries that are operating in our community at the present time, the number of persons they employ, and the total annual income which all these industries together provide. We will want to know what raw materials and supplies they use, what products they make, and other kinds of information about them. This will provide the committee with a good supply of facts with which to begin looking for new possibilities. Perhaps our most likely opportunities for future economic development are already partially established and have not occurred to us before. Again, this is the policy that has already been suggested: That the best place to begin is to look for what we already have.

If possible we might plan to step up the use of local raw materials that are already being used by expanding present operations or by creating supplemental ones to take care of waste products and to further refine the manufacturing process.

There may be a mill in the community, for example, which saws logs into rough lumber. If this lumber can be re-manufactured into finished lumber, and if the finished lumber can be made into doors, sash, moldings, cabinets, furniture, and other products, then we will be making more out of what we have and our forest resources will be greatly extended. It may be possible also to utilize sawdust, edgings, chips, bark, and other waste products. If the tree is considered as the raw material in this case, this kind of activity would constitute a much greater utilization of that raw material than would be the case if the logs were merely sawed into rough lumber and shipped elsewhere for further manufacture. There are also many other possibilities in the use of forest residuals, or the material that is left in the woods after logging operations are finished. This kind of intensive utilization will obviously provide more local employment and greater community stability.

In any sound plan for economic development it will also be necessary to know what kind of a labor supply is available, or if more labor would move into the community if new plants were established. And, as in the case of agricultural production, it will be important to assemble a good many facts on available capital, transportation, freight rates, market outlets, and available power.

Here again we should check to find out what governmental agencies, federal, state, or county; or what educational institutions and research centers might be able to provide useful information. If professional survey reports are available they should, of course, be looked up and put to use. These will be some of the jobs for our Economic Development Committee.

Other important factors which have a great deal to do with local industrial development concern the working conditions and wage scales now being paid in the industries that we have. We should check to find out how our community compares in this respect with neighboring towns and other areas with which our community might have to compete for labor.

If there are active unions in our community, we should know what kind of relations exist between them and management. We should know, above all, the attitude of the unions and of management toward our community, and we should give some careful consideration to our community's attitude toward the unions and toward management. For in the final analysis all of us, the unions, members of management, and the general citizenry, have one important thing in common—the community in which we live. The development and enrichment of the community is of such strategic importance to the future of America that it cannot be overemphasized.

QUESTIONS FOR THE BUZZ SESSIONS

Questions for the buzz sessions on this portion of the study should be prepared by the Economic Development Committee. This will make it possible to prepare questions which will bring out discussion on the specific information contained in the committee's report, and on the wishes of the community with respect to the specific information it contains. The community should give careful thought to exactly what kind of economic development it wants.

BACKGROUND FOR DISCUSSION (THIRD MEETING)

Trades and Services

Probably the greatest volume of business in most local communities is in the area of retail trade. Everywhere people are consumers. They demand a certain amount of consumers' goods as a part of their everyday lives. If these demands are not met in the home community, the people will go somewhere else to do their shopping and the community will lose an important part of its potential income. Or, many people will move away entirely.

In the face of modern mass production, standardization of products, large-scale buying, and specialized merchandising practices, the local merchant is handicapped by a degree of competition that he is often unable to overcome.

Indeed, the local merchant who fails to exercise the last ounce of ingenuity that he has and to utilize every legitimate means at his disposal will probably not be able to stay in business. Or he will manage to exist only as something of a hanger-on. The future of community life in America therefore rests in no small part on the shoulders of the local merchant and his ability to maintain a profitable and going business.

The degree of the stability of every community can be measured largely by the stability of its retail stores and shops. Today these businesses must not only meet the competition of lower prices and wider choices outside the community, they must also meet the lure of urban centers, the bright lights, the excitement, the adventure, which Americans have come to attach to the modern urban city.

This is difficult for the small community and rural area. There was a time when it took all day or even a week's travel over rough or muddy roads for the rural family to make it into the city and home again. This has all changed. Today farmers and small-town people can travel with ease to the city, and frequently do, for most of their shopping. These are powerful forces for the home-town merchant to combat. They affect the sale of virtually every retail item from a can of pepper to a piece of farm machinery.

Yet despite these handicaps, the local community has certain advantages. One important advantage is the atmosphere of neighborly relationships, the familiar greeting, the personal recognition of the man behind the counter, or the attendant who meets you at the gas pump.

The local businessman can, if he wishes, offer a kind of personal service that even the most highly trained salesclerk in a distant city cannot equal. The local mechanic can develop a degree of trust that the large departmentalized garage cannot approach. But if he is to stay in business, if he is to remain a cohesive force in his community, the local merchant must recognize his handicaps and adjust himself accordingly. Shopping is a business transaction, and to hold his customers the local merchant must offer what they want with the kind of service they want, and at a fair deal.

The vigor and volume of retail business is without question an essential element in the survival of true community life in America. But the vitality of the community's business life is not dependent upon its merchants alone. Of equal importance are the intangible forces such as community loyalty, a feeling of solidarity and community spirit which may or may not exist in the home community or neighborhood. These are in the attitudes of mind, in the qualities of neighborliness, and in the human relationships that are developed in the community's social structure, which we have discussed.

These qualities are built into and emerge from the community's human organizations and institutions, its churches, its schools, its library, its recreational activities, and all those things that cause people to know, appreciate, enjoy, and in a sense feel responsible for each other. All these things will in turn be affected by the success or failure of the community's local stores and shops.

These are the spiritual qualities of community life in which the democratic processes find their natural environment, in which the American traditions can grow and thrive and endow people with that sense of belonging which traditionally has characterized the American small town, and which is so important to the stability and happiness of the human being.

Unless the community has built these democratic institutions and human relations strong and solid, it will not have that spirit of loyalty and solidarity which enables it to realize its greatest potential—*and which is the greatest financial asset that a local businessman can have.* But the success of the local businessman becomes in turn a part of this community spirit.

If we are to analyze realistically the retail trade of our community with an eye toward increasing it, we are going to have to examine the facts squarely as they are, whether favorable or unfavorable. This is not always easy, but the smart businessman as well as the housewife consumer will welcome it, for the results can lead to a better community for both of them.

One of the methods used by large merchandising organizations in keeping themselves up to date on consumer habits and demands, and in deciding where to locate new stores, is to survey the actual wishes and shopping habits of the people who are potential customers in a given area. The information obtained from a survey of this kind is of tremendous importance from a cold cash point of view because this tells the merchandiser what people buy, where they usually buy it, and why. With these facts in hand the merchandiser is then able to adjust his store layout, his stock, his services, and his merchandising practices in general to the consumers' wishes and is thus better able to attract more customers. The cost of a survey for this purpose commonly runs into thousands of dollars, but the information gained pays for itself many times over.

Despite the value of this kind of information few small merchants can afford the cost of getting it, nor do they have the necessary techniques and facilities for the survey.

In order to assist the merchants in our community by providing them with the same kind of information which many of the large sales organizations use so effectively, and thereby to help increase the volume of retail trade in our community, it is suggested that the Economic Development Committee conduct a survey of the shoppers' buying habits in our local trading area. This will tell us where the people in our community buy, whether locally or elsewhere, and why. It should tell something about the extent to which they buy locally and the extent to which they buy elsewhere, and something about the reasons why they buy certain items in one place and not in another.

From the survey made by the Population Committee we should have a pretty good estimate of the effective buying power in our community. The Economic Development Committee may determine the total retail sales in our community, and by comparing this figure with the effective buying power of our local population, we will then be able to determine about what percentage of the money our community spends for retail goods and services is spent outside the community. The consumers' buying habits survey should tell us why. We will then know what kind of action program is necessary to keep a larger percentage of our retail dollars at home and thereby strengthen the economy of our community. It may be that the merchants will want to contact the university extension service in their state for a special local course in merchandising and salesmanship in order to take advantage of the latest information available in marketing techniques.

These surveys may also give us some good clues to possible new businesses which could be profitably developed in our community, thus adding to the local economy and making our community a more attractive place in which to live and to trade.

A downtown center of thriving business concerns which meet the demands and wishes of the people usually means a thriving community. A dying business or a store that is failing is a community liability. Thus, anything that can be done within the limits of practical economics to help make local businessmen more successful or to help establish successful new ones will contribute substantially to the life of the community.

Some of the common complaints against the businessmen in many communities is that they try to run the town, that they are too independent and aren't willing to put themselves out to meet the wishes and needs of the people.

On the other hand, the businessmen themselves often complain that the people make no effort to understand the businessman's problems, that people go outside the community to save a nickel while spending a dollar for gas.

Probably when such complaints become prevalent there is some truth on both sides. But certainly this situation does not make for a healthy community spirit, or for a thriving local business. If such complaints exist, whether they are true or not, they will get no better by hiding them or denying them, or by grumbling about them in places out of hearing distance of the people concerned. Indeed, this is one of the chief causes for inner community friction and social disorganization. The best and perhaps the only way to handle complaints of this kind is to bring them out in the open for friendly and objective discussion so that they can be talked over and overcome.

With the help of the Economic Development Committee the study group should seek to determine what kind of relations prevail at the present time between local businessmen and the rest of the people in the community. If there are complaints on either side, to what extent are they justified? And what might be done to cure them?

Other factors that will have a direct bearing on the problem of increasing retail trade will include finding out what changes in service would cause people to do more shopping at home. Is local merchandise up to date? Is the selection adequate? What lines would attract more local patronage?

What about the over-all physical appearance of the shopping center? Is it dull and unattractive, do the buildings look run down and in need of paint? Or is it bright and well kept? The answer to these questions may have an important bearing on the way people feel about the whole community and, whether people realize it or not, it may keep a good many dollars out of town. A dilapidated-looking town in New England was swept by a fire that burned out the entire business center. It was then rebuilt into one of the most attractive little towns in the country. Thereafter business stepped up to a new level from which it has never fallen back.

The extent to which local businessmen cooperate with one another to put on special sales and to provide the best all-round shopping center possible will affect deeply the community's volume of retail trade. Adequate parking facilities close to the stores, clean public rest rooms, attractive places to eat and to stay overnight, clean, well-equipped automobile service stations—these and other factors are important considerations.

One of the most important areas of business activity which many communities overlook is the possibility of a good tourist trade. Tourist trade has become a big business, but to get its share of that trade the local community will first have to put its own house in order. Tourists will not stop where facilities are inadequate if they can help it, and most of them will avoid stopping in a town that looks shabby and run down.

In addition to the revenue that the community receives from a good tourist trade, the tourist takes nothing away from the community's basic resources. After the tourist has gone, the scenery is still there for the next tourist to visit.

The study group, through the Economic Development Committee, should make a careful check to determine what tourist attractions there are in the community or in the surrounding area that might cause people to want to visit here. This information may be common knowledge to local residents, but remember, most of the people who might be our tourists probably never heard of it. All tourist attractions in the area should be carefully written up in the final reports of the study group, together with a specific description of any facilities, or the lack of them, that we might have for accommodating travelers.

Among the most important of all community services are those rendered by doctors, dentists, nurses, lawyers, and other professional persons. Not only does the community need enough dentists to provide adequate health services, but every time a housewife leaves town to go to the dentist she probably takes more of her shopping dollars with her. If the community has difficulty in getting or keeping enough professional people to meet its needs, there is a possibility that something about the community makes it less attractive as a place to live in than need be.

Questions for the buzz sessions on this portion of the study should be prepared by the Economic Development Committee from its report on retail trade.

10

The Appearance of Our Community

BACKGROUND FOR DISCUSSION

SOMEONE HAS SAID THAT IF A TOWN LOOKS PROSPEROUS IT IS PROSperous.

Nothing makes a traveler want to go somewhere else faster than a town that looks shabby and generally run down. People are likely to be drawn to places where buildings are neat and kept up, where there are parks, clean lawns, and landscaping. Yet thousands of communities are dingy in appearance and there seems to be little pride or effort on the part of the people to change. Certainly the physical appearance of a community will have an important bearing on possible development and the kind of life that is found in the area.

Crime, delinquency, and disease seem to thrive best in places that are congested and ill kept. The appearance of a town will affect deeply its desirability as a place to live. If the very physical appearance is a reminder of decadence and thwarted ambitions, the community will tend to lose its young people even more than it would otherwise, and new families will hesitate to move in.

The community's appearance may also tell something about the traits and attitudes of the people. Certainly a run-down looking town and countryside does not indicate pride, ambition, and enterprise. Many communities do not seem to realize the importance of a good physical appearance to their own development, yet they are anxious to expand the economy and bring greater prosperity. The valuation and sale of property usually decline when the community begins to take on a dingy, slum-looking appearance. This may affect many things, far more than most people seem to think.

For four years the chamber of commerce in a small western town had tried to get two additional doctors for the community. Several good prospects were enticed to come in and look the place over, but each time the story was the same. The people were wonderful. Possibilities for financial success were good. Clinical facilities were available. But this wasn't a town you would want to live in. Buildings were in need of paint, some looked as if they had never seen paint. Streets needed repairing. Lawns were ill kept. The city hall was run down. Almost nobody who cares about his surroundings wants to move into a community like this if he can help it. Then the town got busy and lifted its face. In less than four months they had the two doctors they had been trying to get for four years. But that wasn't all. In time other people began to move in, several established new payrolls, the citizenry seemed to have come alive. Things happened that had been undreamed of before. A little painting and cleaning up had started a chain reaction.

When people want to rent out a room their first step usually is to put the house in order. This applies also to the community; if people are really serious about developing their community they will first take steps to weed out the eyesores and make it an attractive place in which to live, or in which to stop and tarry awhile.

In other places where community study groups have been organized it has been found that one of the best projects with which to get started on a citizens' action program is one having to do with community beautification.

One of the best examples of this kind of action, and of what it can accomplish in the life of the community, took place in Winlock, Washington, where a community study group was organized late in 1951. They were in the tenth meeting of the series when several members of the group began to demand action. This sentiment was brought to a head by the general chairman in a special meeting of the study group advisory committee and the committee chairmen.

It was decided that what the group needed was some definite, concrete action project in which everyone in the community could have a hand, which would require the active cooperation of all organizations in the area, and which—when completed—would become a symbol of community-wide effort. It had to be something tangible, something material that people could see and take real pride in doing. It had to be something which could be completed in a short period of time so that in the process of doing it people would feel an immediate sense of achievement. Above all, it had to be something which would have real meaning and significance throughout the community. And they wanted it to be work and fun all at the same time. These were the specifications they decided to use in choosing a project.

They sifted through the records of their discussions and recommendations from the previous meetings, and from their discussion of the questions in Section 3 they found just the project they were looking for: The community cemetery.

Ever since they could remember the cemetery had been a disgrace to the community. Covering six acres of ground, it was so badly grown over with brambles and weeds and thickets of trees that it looked as if no effort to take care of it had ever been made by anyone. Gravestones were knocked down, many were upset by roots of large trees, and many were completely hidden from sight. Bottles, tin cans, and other rubbish had been dumped on the cemetery grounds and much of this was entangled by vines. Roads were full of chuckholes and in places the tire ruts had eroded into small gullies.

Each spring one or two organizations would attempt to get up a work party to clean up the cemetery, but only a handful of people would turn out. After working all day they would have one or two small plots of ground nicely cleaned up but the over-all picture was unchanged.

The cemetery had become a symbol of community defeat.

If the study group could organize a community-wide effort to put the cemetery into first-class shape, here would be an action project that could pump vitality into the community and thereby generate a spirit of unity and progress that nothing could stop. This would be a spirit that would give them the momentum to start other projects and to launch the long-range community action program that participants in the study group had envisioned.

It was an enormous job, but they were determined that it could be done. In the study group there were members from virtually every organization in the community. The Beautification Committee submitted the proposal as a definite recommendation to the entire study group for immediate action.

The recommendation was approved unanimously and immediately the committee got busy drawing up a set of work specifications. The first step was to map the entire cemetery. They figured what heavy equipment would be needed. A landscape architect was invited in to help draw plans. Every organization in the area was asked to join in on the project, and tentative plans were worked out for permanent upkeep. The committee called for final completion of the project by Memorial Day, May 30.

The date for the big opening push was set for eight o'clock in the morning on Sunday, April 20, 1952, and a minister was asked to conduct community religious services. Arrangements were made for a community soup kitchen that would serve free coffee and hamburgers.

On Saturday, the day before the main effort was to start, advance crews moved in to get things ready, and that night they held pre-opening day get-togethers in homes around the community. Everyone kept a weather eye on the sky.

Next morning the sun rose high and bright and at seven o'clock the people began coming. By eight o'clock there were trucks of every size and description, tractors, bulldozers, mechanical loaders and farm haulers, graders, roto-tillers, blowtorches for the burning crews, and power saws for the loggers. There were rakes, hoes, mattocks, shovels, axes, and wheelbarrows. And there were people; it seemed they were everywhere. Across the road from the cemetery, automobiles covered a wide area. Five hundred people had turned out. Population of Winlock proper was 878, which, with the surrounding rural area, gave the entire community a total of around 2,000 men, women, and children.

A sound truck had been set up at the entrance to the cemetery and as people—whole families together—came in they were assigned to one of the fifteen sections into which the cemetery had been divided. By nine o'clock the air literally rang with activity.

With the minister standing in the back of a truck, the crowd gathered in a large semicircle and men, women, and children dressed in workclothes stood among the tombstones in prayer. There were Protestants, Catholics, and Jews, people of every denomination. Scattered about the crowd were the wheelbarrows, the trucks, the tools, and the heavy equipment that had been moved in for this community effort.

The minister began his text, "I will lift up mine eyes unto the hills . . ." This was hallowed ground. In it were buried the dead who had been friends, neighbors, and members of the families there assembled. And many of the older ones who had come there that day to work knew that one day not too far away they themselves would be laid to rest in this same six acres of ground.

It was dark before the last of the workers went home. Their first action project had been a success beyond the wildest dreams of even the most optimistic. But they had done more than clean up a cemetery. In one day they had achieved a spirit of unity and community cooperation that had not existed in the history of Winlock, and many other projects that had seemed impossible before now seemed easy.

Afterward they declared a local holiday and painted the entire town center. The momentum has never stopped, and inside their community there is a fire that people say will burn forever.

Winlock is a good example of what can be accomplished through community beautification if people do it themselves. Not only is the physical appearance changed, the community builds for itself a spirit, an inner pride of solidarity and determination.

In most communities there is room for sprucing up and in general improving the physical appearance. In most of them there is a project which if undertaken and carried out will accomplish the same kind of results in terms of unity and spirit that the cemetery project accomplished in Winlock. Community beautification offers perhaps the best opportunity for an immediate sense of achievement. From this kind of achievement, attained just as the study group is completing its study, can come the momentum for tangible action which will help in the launching of a long-range action program for the future development of the community.

This is a suggestion.

It is important to remember that all communities are different from one another. What applies in one may not apply in another. In other communities where outstanding success has resulted from the study, no concrete action was started until after the study was complete. Certainly it would be unwise for the study group itself to undertake any action project that might involve general controversy and thereby run the risk of damaging the over-all study program. The right answers to the questions of when and how plans for definite action should begin will depend upon the feelings of the study group concerned. People are never ready for concerted community action until they themselves really want it.

Questions for the Buzz Sessions

Question (1): Are there any needs for improvement in the physical appearance of our community?
A. If so, what specific improvements are most needed?
B. Should definite action be taken to make these improvements?
C. If so, what might such action mean to the general welfare of the community?
D. How might this action be started?
E. When should it be started?
F. If definite community action projects are recommended for purposes of beautifying the community, should any special order of priority be given them? If so, what project should be first, second, etc.? Should any of them be undertaken simultaneously?

Other questions for the buzz sessions should be prepared by the Beautification Committee in order to help center the discussion on the specific points and recommendations contained in the committee's report.

11

The Education of Our Community

THERE IS A COMMON TENDENCY TO THINK OF EDUCATION AND GO-ing to school as the same thing. But education and schooling are *not* the same, and going to school is only one aspect of education.

Every individual is born with certain natural capacities which are inherited from his parents. The extent to which he develops these capacities and the kind of use he makes of them are partly up to him, but to a major degree are determined by the community in which he lives.

When he goes to school his community provides him with an opportunity to acquire certain facts and information, to form certain attitudes of mind, and in this way helps him to develop and learn to make use of his native endowments. But not all of his education is obtained in school. Everything that happens to him from the moment he is born, everything that he experiences, whether in school or out of school, becomes a part of his education and in some way, either for better or for worse, influences his personal development.

In his early and formative years he is molded by his parents and by his relationships with other members of his family. He is influenced by his playmates and by every other person with whom he is in contact. He is influenced by the kind of quarters in which he is housed, by the type of neighborhood in which he is located, and by the human activities and events that take place around him.

His education comes from the experience of living. It is in the street, in the stores, in the places of entertainment. It is in the church and in the organizations he joins. It is in the mental attitudes, in the customs, and in the ways of acting and ways of doing things of his associates and of the people who live in his community. It is in every place that he goes and in all that he does. It is in everything that is a part of the community in which he lives. This is his environment, and it is this environment that will largely make him what he is.

Education, in short, is not limited to certain prescribed courses taught in the schoolroom or to the writings in certain textbooks. It is inherent in the whole process of living. The quality of an individual's education is therefore determined not merely by the courses offered in school, but to a great extent by the kind of life that develops in the community where he lives and works and makes his home.

Educationally, the community is a powerful force. And just as the community molds its people, so too does it mold its institutions. The school is no exception.

But the community is in turn molded by its people. It is molded by their personalities, by their attitudes of mind, by the extent to which they make use of their native talents, by their interests, their desires, their sense of personal responsibility, by their degree of citizen alertness. It is molded by the extent to which its families are in communication with one another, by its organizational life, by the kind of human relationships which develop among the various groups who live there. It is molded and shaped by its institutions. And, again, the school is no exception. Thus the influence which the community has upon its people is a two-way process. Each influences the other, and each helps to determine what the other will be. This means, as we have already emphasized, that by utilizing their resources—human and physical—to the greatest possible extent the people may make their community largely what they will. They may to a large extent actually create the kind of environment in which they live. And it is this environment which will largely make them what they are.

And so the community, not the school, is the ultimate training ground for American citizens. From it come our ideals, our aspirations, our qualities of human leadership. But the quality of that training ground can be largely determined by the extent to which the people make use of their resources—personal, institutional, and otherwise.

We are now in a position to look at the school as an institution in the life of our community, not as education *per se*, but as one of the important available educational resources. The question is: Are we as a community making the most of what we have in our school resource, are we getting the greatest possible return from our investment in the school as an institution? Or, is the school system, as an important educational resource in our community, being utilized to the best possible advantage?

As an institution which the community has created and which operates in the community the school may perform at least two important functions.

One of these functions is in the service it renders children and young people by teaching them certain facts and information and through the extracurricular activities it offers them. Probably the most effective school program from the point of view of service to children and young people will be one which has achieved some kind of balance between the academic and the practical. It will be one which helps to develop the creative powers that are latent in all human beings. This means that students will need a certain amount of book learning, but if they are to become effective citizens in a free society they must also learn to accept the responsibilities of that society.

The teachings of a good modern school will help its students to feel the full impact of their cultural and social past, and it will be geared to the concrete realities of today's changing world. For in time the effectiveness of the service which the school renders its students will be tested in terms of how well its teachings help them to meet the problems of life as it is, and to deal with the needs of their community.

How many young Americans have left school with honor grades but with no sense of community responsibility? How many students gain from their schooling an inspiration to help make their community a better place in which to live? How many of our graduates have a real interest in public issues or know how to analyze propaganda, investigate and weigh alternatives in order to become intelligent voters? What is there in our modern schools that tells our sons and daughters some of the requirements of parenthood and a wholesome home life? Do the schools have any influence on the sexual irregularities, the divorce rates, and the mishandling of children which are becoming an increasing threat to the stability of American society? These are some of the tests that might be applied to the effectiveness of the school program in terms of its service to the young people of our community, and that will help us to determine the extent to which we as a community are making use of the school as a community resource.

Another important aspect of the school's function in its service to youth may be in the extracurricular activities which it offers for personal and social growth. Here the school may function to provide opportunity for the entire student body, or it may serve only a select few. The test of this function is in terms of the extent to which it helps to develop the personalities of all the students, inspire and develop leadership, initiative, and self-confidence. All these things, the academic and the practical, the fundamentals and the art of living, the classroom study and the extracurricular, may be a part of the function the school performs in terms of service rendered the community's children and youth. Actually, it is a service of the community carried out through the utilization of the school resource which the community created.

The second important function which the school may perform is in the service it renders the people as a whole by helping the community to become a richer and more stimulating place in which to live. These two broad functions—service to the children through classroom teachings and extracurricular activities, and service to the community through helping it to become a more wholesome environment for people to live in—are necessarily interrelated and will in some degree overlap. But the extent to which the school carries out the second function will have a major influence on the kind of life that develops in the community, and will therefore have an important bearing on the effectiveness of the training it gives to individual students.

Inasmuch as the community and all that goes on within it constitutes the major part of an individual's education, the school has a job to do for the community if it is to provide the best possible education for the individual. Thus by performing both these functions —service to students, and service to the community—the school may

become a center of enlightenment and an instrument for the eleva-
tion of human living for the entire community, young and old alike.

The school is an important educational resource in every community, but its end value to the people who support it will depend
upon how much and for what purposes it is utilized.

If the school operates as a world unto itself with little or no relationship to most of the people except as a place where children are
sent for formal classroom instruction, then the community gets only
a partial return from its school investment, and the school makes
only a limited contribution toward improving the quality of the
community life in which its students are growing up.

Under these conditions school and community relationships are
usually weak. The majority of the people may take little interest in
school affairs and it is frequently necessary for a handful of school
patrons to put on special drives or campaigns to whip up even
enough public interest to provide adequate financial support. The
school under these conditions is left with little alternative but to
seek community support on the grounds that it is an institution to
which people owe a certain obligation, rather than an essential public servant whose functions are in fact so related to the total community life that taxpayers are involved in a direct way with the
school's operations. History has abundantly demonstrated that unless
the appeal for support of public schools is based on something more
than a drummed-up feeling of public obligation, the majority of
people are likely to take no more than a surface interest in school
affairs despite the fact that the school belongs to them.

Where the school is not related in a functional way to the rest of
the community, it tends to become more and more isolated from the
full stream of community processes, its program tends toward narrowness and sterility. The school is thereby cut off from much of
the richness of real life which might be used to improve its teachings
and make it a truly effective instrument of democratic living.

Utilization of the school as a community resource is obtained to
some extent from the service it renders in the teaching of academic
fundamentals. If it goes beyond these fundamentals and helps to
inspire the student, to stimulate his personality, his qualities of
leadership, his interests, his creative imagination, his sense of personal and social responsibility, if it helps him to become a more

effective citizen in his community, then the school has performed still another function and the community realizes a greater return on its school investment.

These are some of the ways in which the community may utilize the educational resources of its public school system. But this isn't all. There are still other ways in which the school resource may be utilized. This we have already touched upon.

With cooperation from the rest of the community the school may develop an extended program offering rich educational services to all the people of every age. Some of these offerings might carry academic credit, but most of them will have nothing to do with academic credit.

The primary purpose of such an extended school program is to help enlighten, enrich, and in numerous ways improve the general life of the community as a whole. This improvement might be brought about in terms of social growth and civic development; it might be in terms of cultural development through the release of creative energies and human self-expression, or in the fulfillment of artistic and recreational interests; it might have to do with assistance in providing objective information on matters of public concern, on social needs, and on family life; or it might be in terms of service for purposes of assisting the community in its economic development, in meeting the needs for health instruction, or in helping to develop an adequate program of year-round community recreation.

Full utilization of the school as a community resource may include educational activities in all these areas, but the over-all objective is to strengthen and improve the total life of the total community. Full utilization of the school resource means that an important influence will be exerted on the quality of the education that every individual, young and old, will get simply from the process of living in the community. Thus the school may help to create an even better community.

Certainly under these conditions the school is more than just a place where parents send their children for classroom instruction, but in which the majority of people show little interest. Here is no ivory tower. The school becomes to the fullest possible and practical extent involved in a direct way with the total community. Children and adults share personally in its functions, and in many instances may even participate together in the same educational project. This is the integration of school and community life; it is the full relating of an important institution to the rest of the community in which it operates. But it is not a one-way process. The school gains freshness from the community, as the community gains freshness from the school.

By the nature of things no part of the community can function apart from the rest of the community and long endure as an effective instrument of human welfare. This means that to remain as a worthwhile force in the affairs of man no one element of community life may be viewed as an end in itself, but only as a means for the building of a better community in which human beings may live a richer life.

As an institution of the community the school has no more claim to existence for its own right than does any other agency of the community. The school is not an end in itself but is only an instrument which the community has created for the improvement of human society. When the school ceases to serve community needs and social ends the very purpose for which it was created is forgotten and the community no longer derives an adequate return from its creation.

As people especially trained in school operations, the teachers and school administrators are delegated direct responsibility for technical supervision, for devising the methods of teaching, for the conduct of classes, and for the operation of other school activities. They, along with the elected members of the school board, are directly responsible for the school policy and for the construction of the school program. But all of them are accountable to the community.

And by the same token, since the school belongs to the community and is a part of the community, the problems of the school are not the school's problems. They are the community's problems. The school can go no further and can be no better than the community will permit. The community may utilize its school resource as little or as much as it wishes. The community may in the final analysis define its school policy and determine the kind of program it will have.

In evaluating the effectiveness of the public schools in our community we might consider to what extent and for what purposes we are actually utilizing this educational resource. We might also consider whether we have sufficiently developed the schools in our community through adequate support and understanding to make full utilization possible.

But the local public school is only the beginning of the community's educational resources. There are many others, formal and informal. They range from the Boy Scout troop to the government agency. Perhaps one of the most important of these educational resources, or at least potentially important, is the tax-supported university or college.

The same principles that have been set forth with regard to the community and its public schools apply equally to the community and its state institutions of learning. The state university, for example, is just as much a resource of the community and in many respects may become just as important to its enrichment and improvement as the public school. Indeed, the university and the college may offer many educational services which the public school would never be able to offer. But, just as with the public school, the value of the university or college as a community resource can be determined only by the extent to which the people wish to utilize it and make it available inside their own community.

The American public schools, universities, and colleges represent a potentially powerful force for human freedom and community development, but that force can be released only if the people in each community make full use of the resource. By thinking of our educational institutions as something only for the young many of us quit all effort at systematic learning by age twenty-five. As a result the most important resource of the community—the minds of the people who live there—is largely neglected.

The continuing development of the human mind after formal schooling ends is no less important to the strength of the community and hence to the strength of America than is the teaching we give our children. Indeed, it may well be that the extent to which the American adult keeps himself educated will in the long run determine whether the education we give our children is being canceled out. If American democracy is to survive, if the vast problems of modern society are to be solved, if world peace is to be achieved, and if our children are to grow up in the kind of community their parents hope they will, then the continuing development of adult minds and emotions is a major educational job that must be tackled with considerably more vigor than it has been in the past.

QUESTIONS FOR THE BUZZ SESSIONS

QUESTION (I): What do the members of this group feel should be the broad purposes of the schools in our community? Why?

A. Does this group agree with the report of the Education Committee in this respect? Why?

B. Are there any points of disagreement? Why?

QUESTION (II): In terms of attitude toward the local school system what percentage of the people in our community might be described as:

.... Very interested
.... Fairly interested
.... Slightly interested
.... Indifferent
.... Hardly know the schools exist

QUESTION (III): What reasons can the members of this group offer for the status of community interest in our local public schools as indicated by the answers given to the preceding question?

A. What is there about the schools to motivate citizen interest in our community?

B. What is there about the schools that might be cause for a lack of citizen interest?

C. Has there ever been a time in the history of our community when there was more citizen interest in the local schools than there is today? If so, why was there more interest?

D. What practical recommendations might this discussion point toward for substantially increasing the extent of community interest in our local schools?

QUESTION (IV): What are the objectives of the P.T.A. in our community?

A. To what extent are these objectives being accomplished at the present time?

B. To what extent, if any, are they not being accomplished? Why?

C. What is there about the P.T.A. in our community that makes people want to take an active part in its program and activities?

D. What is there about the P.T.A., if anything, that makes people not want to take an active part in its program and activities? Why?

QUESTION (V): How many people attend the meetings of the school board in our community?

A. Are there any particular reasons why people should attend meetings of the school board? If so, what are they?

B. Are there any particular reasons why people should not attend the school board meetings? If so, what are they?

QUESTION (VI): To what extent does our community permit the school to enter into total community life?

A. Are there any specific ways, or instances, in which the community has made it difficult or has actually prevented the school from entering into the adult life of the community? If so, what were the circumstances? Was any misunderstanding involved? If so, in what ways?

QUESTION (VII): Does our community make any specific effort to find employment within the community for its students and graduates?

QUESTION (VIII): Is the school in our community genuinely interested in tailoring its program to the needs of the community?

A. To what extent do the school board and administration welcome inquiry, suggestions, and advice from the community in matters pertaining to school programs and operations?

B. How can the school board and the administration keep the community well informed and up to date on school problems and school affairs?

QUESTION (IX): To what extent does the school in our community cooperate with local business, industry, and agriculture in an effort to help solve specific problems in these areas of community life?

A. Is the effort of the school in this respect about right, too much, or not enough?

QUESTION (X): To what extent does the school in our community seek out and make an effort to utilize in its programs people in the community with special knowledge or training?

A. In what ways is this sort of thing desirable? Why?

B. In what ways is it undesirable? Why?

QUESTION (XI): To what extent does our school help out and cooperate with other public agencies in our community?

A. Should there be more or less of this sort of thing? Why?

QUESTION (XII): Does the school program in our community place less emphasis than it should, too much emphasis, or about the right amount of emphasis on the academic fundamentals?

QUESTION (XIII): What courses in the school program help to equip students to deal with the practical problems of everyday life in our community?

A. Is the school's emphasis in this respect less than it should be, about right, or too much? In what specific ways?

QUESTION (XIV): What is there in our school program that helps to create in our students a sense of community responsibility?

A. To what extent do our young people take an active interest in helping to provide their own recreational activities and facilities? What significant factors about the school program might be indicated by this degree of interest?

B. To what extent do our young people exercise an active interest in community affairs? What might this indicate about the school program?

C. What effort is made by the school in our community to help students learn how to analyze propaganda, investigate and weigh alternatives in order to become intelligent voters? Is the purpose of this effort being adequately accomplished?

D. What effort is made by the school in our community to help students understand the democratic processes and the meaning of a free society? How effective is this effort?

E. What effort is being made by the school in our community to equip young people for marriage and parenthood?

F. To what extent are we making use of our schools to help stimulate the student's personality? Leadership ability? Creative imagination? Personal initiative and resourcefulness? Self-confidence?

G. What about the nonathletic extracurricular program in our schools? Does it adequately meet the needs of *all* the students?

H. What is the opinion of the group as to the school's athletic and physical education program? Does it adequately meet the needs of *all* the students?

I. Looking back over the points discussed under this question, are there any points on which our school program needs to be strengthened? If so, in what specific ways? How might these improvements be accomplished?

QUESTION (XV): What is the opinion of the group as to the recommendations of the Education Committee on the school program in our community in terms of the service it renders to children and young people? Are there any recommendations that this group would like to add to those of the committee?

QUESTION (XVI): Are there any programs in our school system that contribute toward better understanding of social and civic problems in our community? Should there be?

QUESTION (XVII): Are there any programs in the school that help to provide the community as a whole with objective information on matters of general public interest? On social needs? On family life? On health and health problems? On business and agriculture for purposes of economic development? Should there be such programs?

QUESTION (XVIII): Do we have any programs in our school system that help to develop expressive or creative activities in the community as a whole? Should there be?

QUESTION (XIX): Do we have any programs in our school system that help to develop cultural appreciation in the community as a whole? Should there be?

QUESTION (XX): Does our community utilize its schools to the fullest possible advantage for purposes of community recreation? Should we?

QUESTION (XXI): Does our community have an adequate program of education for adults? If not, should such a program be established?

QUESTION (XXII): If we were to establish an expanded program of education for adults in our community what things would be of interest to the members of this group?

QUESTION (XXIII): Does this group feel that our community would be willing to support the kind of programs that we have discussed under Questions XVI and XXII above?

QUESTION (XXIV): Are teacher salaries in our community high enough?

QUESTION (XXV): What measures are being taken to attract the best teachers to our community?

QUESTION (XXVI): Are the school buildings and equipment in our community adequate to meet present and future needs? Does this pose any problems? If so, what can be done about them? (See report of Education Committee.)

QUESTION (XXVII): Referring to the report of the Education Committee:

A. What is the financial status of our school system at the present time?
B. Does this financial picture present any problems? If so, what action might be taken to solve these problems?
C. Does this group feel that our community is getting full value from each dollar that we are putting into our school system?

QUESTION (XXVIII): In what ways might we utilize the tax-supported universities and colleges in our state in helping to develop our community education and improvement programs?

A. Are we making sufficient use of these institutions at the present time?

12

The Health of Our Community

"HEALTH," ACCORDING TO THE WORLD HEALTH ORGANIZATION, "IS A state of complete physical, mental, and social well-being and not merely the absence of disease or infirmity."

On the basis of this definition it is doubtful that most of us are as healthy as we ought to be. Certainly the modern concept of health is no longer limited to the physical, though a person's physical condition is still mighty important. Today science has learned that such intangible things as a person's state of mind, emotional make-up, economic status, relations with other people, and his adjustment to society in general play a vital role in determining his health and efficiency.

But because the health of the community is tied in with so many other factors that might at first glance seem to have no connection with health, the question of the community's health cannot be considered by itself any more than can any other aspect of community life.

It is influenced by the economy, the school system, the churches and organizations, by the whole basic social structure. A human being's environment—all or any part of it—may, in short, influence for better or for worse his personal health and mental stability. Good health is fundamental to the conservation of our most priceless resource—human beings. It is a major factor in determining the vitality of community life.

In a democracy the people have the responsibility of determining for themselves what their health needs are and for providing the means which they consider appropriate for meeting these needs. The research specialist, the physician, the dentist, the nurse, and all other health workers have a professional responsibility to help alert people to their health needs, but they alone cannot decide what kind or how much health service the community will have. This is for the community itself to determine.

Today America is faced by a serious shortage of trained personnel in every health field, and despite all countermoves made thus far the shortages seem to be growing. Numerous reasons have been advanced to explain this dilemma, but in effect they all boil down to the same conclusion. Our production of health personnel and facilities has not kept pace with the rising needs and demands.

Nearly fifty million Americans do not have the services of an organized local health department. Right now the nation needs thousands of new doctors, new dentists, new nurses, new clinical psychologists to do the job that needs doing. Laboratory technicians, sanitarians, medical social workers, medical record librarians, health educators—almost every kind of worker involved directly in health services is in short supply.

Hardest hit of all are the small communities and rural areas. Virtually all our people who do not have the services of a local health department live in small or rural communities. Everywhere authorities recognize this shortage of health services as America's number one health problem. Indeed, it is probably safe to say that if every small community in America could take effective action to meet its own health needs the over-all problem of supplying the nation with adequate health services would be substantially licked.

In general the small community is still a healthy place to live in, but perhaps not so good a place to be sick in. During World War II the highest per capita rate of draft rejections for physical reasons occurred in the rural countryside. Perhaps some of the reasons for this may be found in less medical care, less public health service, poorer provisions for sewage disposal, fewer school health programs, fewer immunizations.

There are many reasons why it is difficult to get doctors, dentists, nurses, and other members of the health professions to settle down and practice in the small community. One important reason is the feeling which many people have that the small town does not offer a sufficiently interesting life. This may not be a proper feeling, but the fact is that it prevails nonetheless. And in certain places there may be good cause for such an attitude.

Another important reason for the difficulty in getting enough health personnel for the small community is that the large city usually offers greater financial rewards. Higher salary schedules tend to pull the supply of nurses into the urban centers, thus keeping them away from the rural areas. For the young doctor the high cost of equipment and facilities may make a move to the small community impossible. In the city these facilities are available to him at no cost.

Many difficulties are posed in any effort to attract doctors, dentists, and nurses to our rural areas. But in the final analysis it is a problem that can be solved only through the self-initiative of the communities themselves. In Kansas a plan has been tried whereby small communities in need of doctors put up enough money to equip a medical office or small modern clinic if a young doctor will agree to come in and practice. The plan is worked out so that the doctor may eventually pay off the cost out of the proceeds of his practice and thus become the owner of his own office and equipment. Under this plan the community gains the benefits of a needed doctor, and the young doctor benefits by being able to establish his own practice without an initial financial outlay that he cannot afford.

Not every community can, or necessarily should, support a modern general hospital. Many of them could, however, establish well-equipped local clinics to work with hospitals in neighboring towns and thus gain the medical services they need at home.

In seeking a solution to its health problems the community has at its call the various professional health organizations, both private and governmental, for advice and information. By calling on such agencies as the state or county health department a community not only gains the benefits of professional help, it realizes a better return on its annual investment in taxes. These agencies are supported by the people whether they are used or not. Then there are the private professional organizations—the medical society, the nurses' association, the mental hygiene society, and many others—which have a great deal of information to offer for the asking. Some of them have expert consultants who are available on invitation to meet with community groups concerning local health problems. In some places there is a state or county health council consisting of representatives from most of the professional health groups. This council usually makes a study of specific health problems and recommends action. In some communities strictly local health councils consisting of both health personnel and citizens have been organized with profitable results. These councils are frequently the best means of helping the whole community to become aware of its health problems and of the steps necessary for the solution of these problems.

It would be well if the Health Committee would compile a list of the various health organizations and agencies that might be available as sources of information and help on the health problems of our community. It might be that some of these agencies would send representatives out to visit the study group and help suggest problems and types of information that the group would want to look into.

Health Personnel

In checking the health services and facilities that are available to our community it might be well to start by determining how many persons in each of the health professions are now living in the community and how many of them are in active practice.

We might ask first whether our community has all the doctors it needs to provide adequate medical service, and if it doesn't, how might more doctors be obtained. Obviously, it is impossible to provide adequate safeguards against poor health in a community that does not have enough doctors to keep up with the load. The doctor is the key figure in the health team.

In recent years it has become more and more difficult to get an appointment with the dentist. The shortage of dentists is even more severe than the shortage of doctors. Yet tooth decay is the most widespread disease known to man. Ninety-eight people out of a hundred have it in one stage or another, and the rate of decay is said to be increasing. Tooth decay is not a fatal disease, but medical and dental authorities know that, unless cared for, infected teeth will lead to many more serious consequences and ultimately lower the efficiency of the whole body. Science is now finding new hope that through preventive measures the tremendous economic and human loss caused by bad teeth can be largely eliminated. But these measures cannot be applied unless the community sees the need for them and makes them possible.

One of the essential members of the health team is the professional nurse. More and more duties that were once considered responsibilities that only a doctor could perform have been delegated to the professional nurse. This means that the doctor has been relieved of many exacting and time-consuming duties and is thereby free to distribute more and more of the services that only he is competent to perform to more and more people.

In the hospital it is the general duty or the private duty nurse who carries out the orders prescribed by the doctor. It is she who helps keep the patient progressing toward health, who must be able to detect and note changes in the patient's condition, and to know when to summon the doctor before complications become serious. No one knows how many of us are here today because of the prompt and skilled action of a professional nurse.

The public health nurse is a professional nurse with special training in public health. She is the connecting link between the health department and the home. She visits homes where her help is needed and upon request gives nursing care or offers advice and demonstrations to the family. She acts on the doctor's orders and gives nursing service and health education in the school. She also traces down cases of communicable disease in the community and attempts to get the infected person under proper treatment. She is available to conduct classes and give courses of instruction to community groups.

Nurses are the largest group of health workers, and although a tremendous effort is being made to get more young women to enter the profession, the supply is far behind the needs and demands for service. A partial solution which has been advanced for this problem has been in the training of practical nurses. This practice has helped, but there are limitations as to how far it can go. In the hospital more and more professional nurses are needed for supervision, and there are many nursing duties that the practical nurse is not qualified to perform.

Sanitation

Sanitation is one of the fundamental elements in community health. It concerns such matters as the supply of drinking water, the disposal of sewage, the proper handling of food in stores and public eating places, the regulation of milk supplies, the cleanliness of streets and alleys, and the elimination of breeding places for insects, rats, and vermin that may cause the spread of disease, or that may become a public nuisance. This is a job which the community usually checks on through its health department. But if there is no health department or no other community agency charged with the responsibility, then who is there to see that it is taken care of? Even where there is a health department, sanitation is a job that cannot be properly cared for without the help and cooperation of the entire community.

America has made great strides in the field of sanitation, but it is an area in which there are still many serious problems. Many communities still do not have the benefit of adequate public water supply systems, millions of Americans are not served by a sewer system, and only a small percentage have the facilities of a modern sewage treatment plant. Even in this day of modern health science it is not uncommon to find raw sewage running free and untreated, and because of the serious drainage problems faced by many communities this is becoming more and more a source of contamination.

In many places sewage wastes are being discharged untreated into fresh lakes, rivers, and coastal waters. Although disinfection of drinking water and the control of typhoid prevent great epidemics from breaking out, the danger is always present, and the pollution of rich natural waterways has become a problem of major importance.

The limiting factor in the solution of the problems of drainage, sewage disposal, and pollution, in most communities is one of inadequate finances. Yet even without public sewage disposal systems much can be done by cooperative community effort, and by individuals in their own homes.

However, as already indicated, sanitation embraces much more than a good water supply and adequate sewage disposal. Much has been learned about how to maintain cleanliness at home, on the farm, in the schools, in industry, and in other places where people gather. But a clean environment anywhere is possible only if the people feel a need to make it that way.

The modern sanitarian whose services are available from the state, county, or local health department, stands ready to advise and help all members of the community with any problem they might have in keeping the physical environment clean and healthful. We have come a long way toward making our communities cleaner places in which to live, but there is still a long way to go. A good look in any community will reveal many sources of potential contamination, a need for rat and other pest control programs. These are some of the jobs where a sanitarian can help. He can also help plan the home plumbing system and give advice on how to fix the septic tank with a proper drain field. Science has given us the knowledge to make our physical environment entirely sanitary. Only the people can put it to work. It will take more cooperation, more money, more time, more local effort.

Communicable Disease

The fight against communicable disease has been one of the outstanding health achievements of the American people. This success has been possible largely because Americans have learned to view their health problems with an open mind, the same sort of thing we are doing in this study group. Many of our younger doctors and nurses have never in their professional careers seen a case of smallpox. Tuberculosis, by far the leading cause of death in 1900, has been beaten back so far that it is predicted that within the next twenty-five years many of the nation's tuberculosis hospitals will be able to close their doors.

Owing to precautionary measures diphtheria today is practically unheard of. Deaths from children's diseases such as whooping cough and scarlet fever are getting fewer and farther between. Medical science with its powerful healing drugs has removed the fear from these and many other formerly dread diseases.

However, here again much progress has yet to be made. Poliomyelitis is yet to be conquered. The common cold still causes more economic loss than any other disease. These and other communicable diseases are still at large and cannot be licked until science finds an answer. But knowledge is of no use unless it is put to work, and this is largely the job of the community.

The quick cure of venereal diseases has already been discovered, but it is estimated that the vast majority of these cases never get into a doctor's office. Immunizations, mass chest X rays, and routine checking are free for the asking in many communities, yet many people are still reluctant to take advantage of them. Other communities are still waiting for the services and they are desperately needed. The fact that many of the communicable diseases have been checked is no reason to relax the efforts that have been made against them. A long period without fires is no cause to disband the city fire department. A period of few fires is only proof that the fire department is doing a good job. This applies equally to the health department. The question is not how many people in our community have died recently from a communicable disease, but how many have taken the proper precautions?

Child Health

The future of every community depends largely upon what happens to its children. It is in childhood that most of the diseases of adult life have their beginning, and it is during childhood that treatment and immunization have the most lasting effects. A big part of the job of caring for the health of the child is up to his parents, which is one of the important reasons why many parents are today willing to spend time in adult education classes devoted to the study of child health problems, including mental and emotional health.

However, much of the job of developing healthy children must be done by the schools. This applies particularly to the problem of preventing disease and ill-health. In school the children are thrown together in fairly large groups and if an infection gets loose this is where it is most likely to spread. It is therefore important that the school keep itself alert, and that the school health program is adequate to do the job.

A good school health program provides the teaching of proper health care and health habits which will be important to the child all through life. It offers health services which include immunization, periodic physical examination, attention to nutritional deficiencies, referrals to the public health nurse or to the doctor, conferences with the child's parents, and a complete set of health records which follow the child all through school. The school health program provides also for a good healthy school environment. This means that grounds, buildings, washrooms, lunchrooms, and all other school facilities are kept clean, sanitary, and adequately equipped at all times.

According to the U.S. Public Health Service one infant dies every nineteen minutes whose life could have been saved. Prematurity is one of the leading causes of infant deaths, and though medical science has provided us with the knowledge by which to prevent most of these deaths, many expectant mothers still make no effort to get modern instruction in prenatal care, and thousands of communities make no move to provide such instruction. This is most pronounced in our small communities and rural areas.

Here is an opportunity for concerted community effort.

All medical authorities advise that on the first sign of pregnancy the expectant mother should contact her doctor immediately. The U.S. Public Health Service, the state health departments, and many other agencies and organizations have published many practical and easy-to-read pamphlets on prenatal and mother and baby care. This material can be obtained cheaply, and much of it is free for the asking.

One of the causes of premature deaths is the lack of up-to-date facilities for caring for premature infants in many communities. Pediatricians have estimated that the installation of incubators within easy reach of every community would do a great deal to reduce the death rate due to prematurity. Doctors and other health personnel need to avail themselves of the latest techniques and information regarding the care of such cases, and mothers may do much to help by learning more about the danger signs to look out for.

Millions of our children are handicapped, and are in need of help. Mental illness has most of its beginnings in childhood. Accident rates among children are already high, and are getting higher. These are some of the areas in which the community may devote some intensive and profitable study, and it may be that after the Health Committee brings in its report the study group will want to pursue certain aspects of the findings in this connection in further detail.

Mental Health

Mental illness is not a disgrace. It is not necessarily inherited or incurable. It is a disease, just as heart trouble is a disease. But it is probably the greatest single destroyer of human beings in the modern world. It can, and may, afflict any of us.

According to the U.S. Public Health Service more than half of all patients in America's hospitals on any given day are mental patients. One out of every twenty people in the United States will require psychiatric care at some time during his life. Emotional disturbance accounts for up to half of all patients entering doctors' offices, is responsible for a major percentage of all accidents, and is the cause of more human misery than any other disease. Crime is on the increase, juvenile delinquency rates are increasing, chronic alcoholics are growing in numbers, and one out of every three to four marriages is ending in divorce. A large proportion of these problems is the result of mental ill-health, and for every case of mental illness on record it is estimated that many times that number have never been recorded.

Only a small fraction of the amount spent to fight all other diseases combined is spent on mental illness. We are still very much in the dark as to the nature of the disease and the best methods of treatment. Research is desperately needed.

Many states have no psychiatrists outside mental hospitals and in every state they are only a tiny fraction of the number needed. Only about 2 per cent of the practicing nurses in the United States are employed in mental hospitals, which means that this many nurses take care of about half of all hospitalized patients in the country. In every profession having to do with mental illness there is a seriously short supply of personnel, and more than half of all hospital beds occupied by the mentally ill are classified as below minimum standards.

But perhaps the greatest deficiency in the battle against mental illness is in society itself. Everywhere mental health workers are recognizing the vital importance of the social environment to the mental well-being of the human being. For, as we have said many times throughout this study, it is the environment in which we live that will largely make us what we are.

Even the healthiest person has certain tendencies toward emotional disturbances. Some are more able to withstand the stresses and strains of their environment than others, but if the environment becomes severe enough many of those who apparently are sound emotionally may break under the strain. From the standpoint of mental hygiene the social implication of our community life comes in for careful examination. Family tensions, juvenile difficulties, worry, economic stress, social injustices and maladjustment, inadequate opportunity for rewarding recreational and creative outlets— these and many other social factors that tend to cause unhappiness may lead to emotional disturbance and mental illness.

These are some of the gaps in the life of the community that may be filled by a healthier and more satisfying social structure and organizational pattern, by adult education activities, and by adequate programs of recreation. If more people can find opportunity for more self-expression through wholesome channels they will have less emotional need for self-expression in ways that make for poor mental hygiene and which thus help to contribute to the tragic loss of human resources resulting annually in America from mental ill-health. This applies especially to our children now in the process of developing habits and attitudes for a lifetime.

These problems are too big for any one individual. Neither can they be solved by professional or governmental leaders alone. They certainly cannot be solved at state and national levels. These are essentially problems which can be solved only in the local community. For it is here that the pressures of insecurity, discrimination, prejudice, and many other inequalities may be relieved in the personal lives of men and women. Here is where the individual through direct, personal, and whole relationships with other human beings may attain a sense of belonging, of being wanted, important, needed, and responsible, that will help to develop that inner strength which enables him to cope with his environment.

The positive approach to mental health is to prevent the illness, not only to cure the psychotic or the neurotic. From this point of view the successful founding of a needed new business which helps to provide more job opportunities and enriches the community's economy is a contribution to mental health. A new recreation center geared to the needs of the community, the improvement of a church, the creation of community music groups and other appreciative activities in which people participate just for the fun of doing—all may have important community functions. All of them may contribute to the community's mental health.

More local mental hygiene clinics, child guidance centers, parent education classes, and professional mental health workers are desperately needed in America. But all these may be to no avail unless there is created a better atmosphere for mental and emotional well-being through the development of better communities in which to live.

The Problems of Older People

America's population is growing older; the average age is rising. More than half of all our people are now past thirty as compared to a median age of only sixteen in 1800. By 1975 a third of all Americans will be 45 and over; in 1900 it was only 18 per cent. And in the smaller towns where most of the young people leave after high school graduation the average age is getting higher faster. Many of our communities are becoming communities of older people.

Meanwhile chronic diseases—heart trouble, cancer, arthritis, hardening of the arteries, mental and nervous disorders, and a host of others—are on the upswing. These are the leading causes of death and disability. They are most likely to attack after thirty and the frequency of infections rises steadily from that point on.

What implications does this, an aging population, have for our communities, and for our nation?

One thing is already evident. Millions more for relief and public assistance, higher taxes, more and more in need of care with proportionately fewer and fewer to take care of them. But this is only a material measurement of the problem. The hours of human suffering, untimely deaths, and family misery can scarcely be measured. Old age has gradually caught up with us.

As a youthful nation in which growth, expansion, and speed have been the keynotes of living, America has had little time to think about the problems of age. Ours has been a country of seemingly unlimited natural resources, and we have exploited them accordingly. In this environment there has been little place for people who were unable to produce at full capacity, and as a result many of our people have been thrown on the ash heap because they were considered too old to work. Even now it is not easy for many older people to find a job, and the age of retirement is still based on the calendar instead of being adjusted to the ability of the person concerned.

Perhaps it is time to back up a bit and take another look at our ideas toward age. Many employers are now finding that not all people are worked out as early as we once thought they were. Some men of eighty are still capable of keeping up with the best, and the personal qualities of wisdom and steadiness that come with maturity make many older people capable of doing superior work in jobs that are suited to them. Many older people are fully capable of part-time work and are well suited to jobs that require only light physical exertion. These are some of the means by which the productive power of our people may be conserved in order to maintain a rising standard of living. With the statistics as they are, the conservation of human resources has become one of the pressing needs of our time. Idleness is waste. It may also be a cause of chronic illness requiring expensive care, and dependency requiring that one earn the living formerly earned by two.

Although great strides have been made in the prevention and treatment of chronic disease, our efforts in the face of increasing age are lagging far behind. Much expensive research yet remains to be done before science will have the answers to the many questions concerning cause and cure. Much needs to be done in the way of education for professional health personnel in order to make full use of even the knowledge that we have. And, as in the case of nearly all other health problems, we need many times the number of health workers and health facilities now available.

But much of the problem is up to the older folks themselves. Patients may learn to cope with their own disabilities and may in many cases cure themselves. More people may learn to make their lives as productive as possible instead of "giving in" and becoming dependent on others before circumstances make it necessary. All of us might do well to give some thought to intelligent planning and preparation for old age. This sort of thing would go a long way toward making our people more independent and extending the activities of minds and bodies in proportion to age.

The belief that you can't teach an old dog new tricks is not necessarily so. People grow old mentally only when they no longer wish to keep busy and face life as it is. Physical old age does not have to mean that people can no longer change, acquire new interests, and become busy in new activities. Many older people are finding the first opportunity in their lives to study and do things that they have always been interested in but never had time for. The power to learn does not fall off with increasing age nearly so much as some would like to believe. Some of the best students are in the upper years.

Many of the greatest contributions to society have come from the so-called older people. A woman in her seventies supports herself and cares for a grandchild by teaching fifty children daily in her own private kindergarten. Her home has become a center in the community which people seek out for advice on children's problems. Many examples could be named of people who refuse to grow old because they have learned how to keep learning and keep doing.

There are many, however, who are physically or mentally infirm and are therefore unable to care for themselves. These must be cared for either in the home or in an institution. The U.S. Public Health Service has estimated that about 70 per cent of these persons can best be cared for at home if proper supervision and assistance are provided. Staying at home keeps the patient happier and more satisfied. And it is less expensive.

Where home care is not possible, then, of course, institutional care becomes necessary, and here the problem is often complicated by lack of adequate facilities. Many of our mental institutions are crowded with senile patients who are not mental cases at all but have no place else to go. Nursing and convalescent homes, usually most desired for patients with chronic illness, are in severe short supply, and many of those that we have do not meet minimum health standards. These are the problems of an aging population. They are primarily the problems of the community.

QUESTIONS FOR THE BUZZ SESSIONS

QUESTION (I): Does our community have all the doctors it needs? If not, why haven't more doctors settled here? What might we do to obtain more doctors? If more doctors moved here to what extent would they be patronized?

QUESTION (II): Do we have all the dentists that we need? If not, why haven't more dentists settled here? What might we do to obtain more dentists? If more dentists moved here to what extent would they be patronized?

QUESTION (III): Do we have all the nurses that we need? In public health? In hospital staff nursing? In private duty? If not, why haven't more nurses come here to practice? What might we do to obtain more nurses?

QUESTION (IV): What are the major nursing problems, if any, in the hospitals and public health agencies that serve our community? What might the community do to help solve these problems?

QUESTION (V): Does our community have a local health council? If so, is it active? What does it do? If not, is one needed? Why?

QUESTION (VI): Is the water supply in our community adequate, both from the standpoint of supply and from the standpoint of safety? If not, in what respects is it deficient? What might be done to correct these deficiencies?

QUESTION (VII): Is our community satisfactory from the standpoint of sewage disposal? If not, what defects are there? What can be done to correct these defects?

QUESTION (VIII): Do we have adequate drainage in our community? If not, what defects are there? What problems does this pose? What might be done about it?

QUESTION (IX): Is the collection and disposal of garbage satisfactory in our community? If not, what deficiencies are there? What might be done about this?

QUESTION (X): What are the most important sanitary defects, if any, in our community? What reasons exist for permitting them to remain? Are there any recommendations for action?

QUESTION (XI): What services are there in our community for immunization against communicable disease? Are these services adequate? If not, in what ways are they inadequate? What might be done about this?

QUESTION (XII): Is the school health program in our community adequate to meet the needs of all our children? If not, in what ways is it inadequate? What might be done about this?

QUESTION (XIII): What are the most important school health problems, if any, in our community? What steps would be necessary to solve these problems? Are there any recommendations for action?

QUESTION (XIV): Is there any organized effort in our community to provide instruction to young parents and expectant parents on mother and baby care?

A. If so, are these efforts being taken advantage of as much as they should?

B. If there are no such organized efforts, are such efforts needed? How might they be provided?

QUESTION (xv): What factors in our community life are most likely to make for poor mental hygiene? For good mental hygiene?

QUESTION (xvi): What might be some of the practical ways in which our community could eliminate the factors making for poor mental hygiene and at the same time increase and strengthen the factors making for good mental hygiene?

QUESTION (xvii): How might greater opportunity be provided for the children and adults in our community to better express themselves emotionally?

QUESTION (xviii): What might be done in our community, or state, to meet the need for more treatment of mentally ill patients?

QUESTION (xix): What are the major problems facing older people in our community?

QUESTION (xx): What are we doing in our community to help meet these problems?

QUESTION (xxi): Does our community have a sound program of education and recreation for its older people? If not, would the older people like to participate in building one?

QUESTION (xxii): Are there any ways in which older people in our community might turn hobbies and recreational activities, such as arts and crafts, into full or part time occupations?

QUESTION (xxiii): Do the employers in our community recognize the special assets of older people as employees?

A. Do we have any special unemployment problem as regards older people in our community?

B. Is there any effort in our community to adjust retirement policies to enable older people to contribute their full potential to the community's economy?

QUESTION (xxiv): What is happening to the older people in our community who have become disabled or infirm?

A. Is any special effort being made to help make it possible to give them good care at home?

B. What kind of institutional care is available for the older people who cannot be cared for at home? Is this care, and the facilities for it, adequate? If not, what are the deficiencies? What might the community do to correct these deficiencies?

13

The Recreation of Our Community*

ONE OF THE ESSENTIAL ELEMENTS IN A DEMOCRATIC SOCIETY IS THE self-expression of the people. This means expression of thoughts, of ideas, of emotions, of human spirits and personalities. And it means the free exchange of these expressions in a direct and dynamic way from person to person and from group to group within the community.

When people cease to express themselves in a wholesome and creative manner individuals will sicken, community life will wither, and the democratic processes will dry up. Likewise, if free exchange of human expression is blocked by social or economic barriers, by thwarted personal emotions, by community disunity, by indifference, misunderstanding, intolerance, or by any other barrier—tangible or intangible—then democracy cannot function.

Self-expression is also essential to the well-rounded development of human beings. It is essential to their mental and physical health. A person may be an intellectual genius, but completely out of step socially. Inside he may be gradually drying up or on the verge of blowing apart for want of an opportunity for emotional expression. Or he may be going to seed physically for want of exercise. If for any reason an individual is lacking in healthy emotional development, or if he lacks ability to get along with other people, then his whole personality is thrown out of balance and the community is that much poorer.

The lack of healthy self-expression has become commonplace in

* Acknowledgment is made to Jack E. Wright of the University of Washington for special assistance in the preparation of this section.

many of our modern communities partly because of the tendency to become passive and dependent on someone else. In no area of life is this dependence more marked than in the area of recreation. Instead of creating our own recreation we have gone overboard for commercial amusement. We hire someone else to do our entertaining for us while we sit by and watch. We worship the genius or the professional, and there is a tendency to think that unless certain standards of professional excellence can be attained a thing isn't worth doing. This tendency to judge literature, music, painting, drama, and all other art forms by the quality of the finished product rather than by the creative and emotional energy that is released in the process of doing is gradually killing self-expression and individual initiative in America. It is also hindering our cultural development, for it is dulling the appreciative side of our personalities and making us a nation of spectators. This is a trend which may destroy community life by making the community culturally barren and uninteresting as a place in which to live. As such, it is a direct and fundamental attack on democratic processes.

Recreation, or the opportunity to play, to get away from work and take an active part in interesting activities, to have fun by doing, to find wholesome outlets for creative and emotional energy, and to find healthy physical exercise for the body is as important to human happiness and the development of a rich community life as is the opportunity to work and earn a living.

"There's nothing to do in this town" is a remark which is not literally true, but it has become commonplace in communities throughout the nation. The mere fact that people are alive means that every minute they will be doing something. That something may be just sitting and worrying. But whatever it is—good, bad, or indifferent— everybody of every age does something every minute that he is alive. The feeling which so many people have that there is nothing to do recreationally probably means that there is nothing to do which interests them, or if there is, they haven't found it.

The fact that most communities have not planned and provided adequate facilities for the healthy outlet of human emotions and desires for stimulation is attested to each year by overcrowded mental institutions, increasing rates of crime, the inner fears and warped personalities, the continued breakdown of home life, and the premature wearing out of millions.

A well-planned program of recreation in which people of every age can find adequate and varied opportunities to enjoy themselves through active participation in activities that stimulate them and that provide wholesome outlets for pent up emotional and physical energy can go a long way toward the development of vital community life and the strengthening of democracy.

The personal and social barriers that tend to cause misunderstandings and keep people apart are likely to melt away on the softball field or the volleyball court. There is nothing like active play to relax tense nervous systems and overworked minds and bodies. The right kind of recreation can be a tonic for the idle, it can be a form of therapy for the emotionally distraught. For children and young people it is the positive substitute for the negative method of saying "don't." And when whole families can find opportunity to participate together with other whole families in mutually interesting recreation, then the full meaning of rich community living and democratic processes gets a personal application.

Disunity, group friction, and a lack of community spirit usually will not continue on any score when people begin to create for themselves and take part together in their own recreation. Active, creative recreation is perhaps the most effective single method that can be used to build a spirit of togetherness in which democratic vitality and a healthy community life can flourish.

The best program of community recreation will be an all-round program. It will serve all the people who wish to take part regardless of their age or their physical limitations. It will be a program for the old, the young, and the in-between. It will have something for all interests. It will stimulate and create new interests. And it will operate through different activities in all seasons of the year. It will become an established and integral part of the community life, contributing in an important way to the full development of the people —physically, intellectually, emotionally, and socially.

Recreation of this kind is within reach of every community. But to achieve it the people must first want a recreation program, they must be willing to plan and work to create it, and they must be willing to finance it. Much of the value of a community recreation program will come from the very process of the people creating it and providing it for themselves. When recreation is created for people by somebody else and handed to them, it is doubtful that it can even be called recreation in the true sense of the word. Certainly it will be lacking in interest and self-expression, and little will be accomplished toward the strengthening of democratic processes or toward building a sense of community pride, initiative, and achievement. If a recreation program is to take root and grow in the community it is important that the people themselves take the initiative in bringing it about and that it be supported from within. Outside agencies may help in an advisory capacity to get it started, but unless the program grows from within the community and is based on the needs and wants of most of the people, it is not likely to accomplish the purpose of community recreation, or to survive as a lasting function in the life of the community.

America is dotted with community recreation centers that are standing idle simply because they were created by a few well-meaning leaders for the rest of the people, but without proper consideration for the kind of recreation the community really wanted, and without giving enough people an opportunity to participate in the planning. It is almost commonplace to find youth recreation facilities and programs that are of no interest to the youth because the young people themselves were not included in the planning, or took no initiative in the starting.

Some years ago a group of young people decided that life in their town was dead, that there was nothing in it for them to do. With the guidance of a wise adult leader they took it upon themselves to form a committee to see what could be done. Ideas began to flow, and it wasn't long until they were talking about the possibility of building their own recreation program. In a few weeks they had a comprehensive plan worked out for a year-round program including the construction of a recreation center with complete facilities and equipment. Together they decided what actual work they could do for themselves to make the dream come true, and then they sent a special committee to call on every adult organization in the community. They didn't ask that it all be done for them or that the adults put up the money for a building. They merely asked for help and cooperation in matters that the young people couldn't handle alone. They needed help in the planning. They needed help in the financing. They needed a lot of things. But it was only help added to their own efforts. The teen agers were first doing everything they could up to the full limits of their ability, and beyond that they were seeking help. The adults were so amazed and gratified by this showing of initiative that no one could resist. Soon it became an enterprise of the entire community, and with people of all ages working together they renovated a building and equipped their own recreation center. Nobody worked any harder than the teen-agers themselves. Today the program is still growing, and the school board has hired a full-time recreational director. Here recreation has been established as a habit of the community. But the people did it themselves.

Said the high school principal, "Those kids learned more socially and did more toward the development of their own characters by building that recreation center than they ever could in a year of school."

A well-rounded community recreation program should be designed, as we have already indicated, to serve all ages in all seasons. It should offer enough variety to attract many different interests and to stimulate the well-rounded development of human beings.

Participative sports and games both indoor and outdoor will have a prominent place in the program. Hiking, camping, and other outdoor activities will have their place. But the program will not be limited to active sports and vigorous physical exercise. There will also be activities for those who are more quiet and for those whose physical condition does not permit vigorous exercise.

It is important that people have an opportunity to express themselves through creative activities. Here is a place for the full range of arts and crafts, for things that people can do with their hands. The finished product need not meet professional standards, though obviously the more proficient people become at anything they do the more they enjoy doing it. But it is the process of doing for personal relaxation, for pure enjoyment, and for creative expression that is of prime importance. Most of us cannot be master artists, but that should in no way subtract from the joy of doing. These things that people do with their hands make a particular contribution to the building of community life when done by people in groups. And often it is the opportunity to show off the results in community exhibits that brings the final sense of inner expression and satisfaction.

In one community each merchant converted certain windows into a kind of community art gallery where arts and crafts made by groups of residents were put on display. These displays were changed from time to time and the merchants would vie with one another to make the most attractive arrangement of the things being shown. One week it would be the work of amateur photographers, another it would be ceramics, or things made of wood. Another time it might be floral arrangements contributed by the people who made a special hobby of growing flowers. One time it might be displays contributed by the Boy Scouts and another time by the 4-H Club. It might be collections of Indian craft, or whatever became available from the various activities in the community. From this sort of thing the interest of the whole community was stimulated in creative activities and more and more people began to take part. Incidentally, extra crowds of people were attracted into town to see the displays and retail trade got an additional shot in the arm. And in the process of getting these results the community spirit was strengthened and moved upward.

Creative writing groups offer another important outlet for self-expression and community recreation. Here, again, the writing need not meet any particular standards of literary excellence. Anyone who likes to write should be urged to try. It might be fiction or nonfiction, and it is of particular value from the standpoint of community life if it concerns regional or local subjects. Writing is an art that anyone can learn and enjoy, and with competent guidance it may achieve a high quality of expression.

An idea that might be of interest to local writing groups would be to publish a community magazine which might be printed only four times a year. If printing was not possible it could be mimeographed. In it could be any type of writing by anybody in the community, and preferably on subjects with a local setting. The writings might concern interesting incidents or people in the community's past, or it could concern contemporary happenings. The publication could include factual articles or sheer fiction, and it could be sold for just enough to break even on the production costs. But the important thing is that the community group would act as their own editorial board and an opportunity would be provided for anyone in the community to realize the inner satisfaction that comes to all writers from seeing their work published. Undoubtedly the community could obtain help for activities of this kind from their state university and other educational institutions.

Community music groups, both choral and instrumental, are always of interest and provide valuable outlets for self-expression and creativity. This might include quartets or glee clubs that reach a high point of perfection. Or it might be simply in informal groups who get together for an evening of singing. The idea that one shouldn't sing because one knows nothing about music or because one's voice is flat is nonsense. Some of the most enjoyable moments in recreation come from a group of people who can't sing for sour apples standing around a piano in the church basement or in somebody's home.

The collection of folk music native to the region in which the community is located is another activity which holds interest for almost everybody who has a love of music. But the point is that, although Beethoven provides a great lift for the spirit, there are other forms of music in which people can participate without any special training. These might vary from the latest popular swing to the native folk songs, but the important thing is participation and active self-expression with a community group who are enjoying themselves in a wholesome hour of fun.

Square dancing and folk dancing have been coming back and are making a real contribution as worthwhile community recreation. The only danger in these activities from the standpoint of democratic community life is the possibility that they will cause special cliques which exclude others in the community from the opportunity to participate. This kind of thing is always a danger to watch out for in any community recreational activity, but can usually be avoided with a bit of precaution against setting the same standards for everyone.

Community drama is an activity which has yielded outstanding results in terms of heightened interest in community life and has made a major contribution toward creating a spirit of unity and solidarity among all groups and families in the community.

Drama may take many forms, but the kind of drama referred to here is a form of pageantry in which the community writes and produces its own story. Here is an opportunity to combine all the art forms, music, writing, painting, dancing, and crafts, in one great production wherein the people portray their own past and present, and project themselves into the future. Here they can dramatize the problems of their community, social and economic, and act out on the stage their proposed solutions. The community drama is done entirely by the people themselves without bringing in trained actors and professionals from the outside. It is simply a method by which the community can express itself to itself, and to anyone else who might like to come and watch.

In the Mount Adams area around Bingen and White Salmon in southern Washington a drama of this kind was done with a cast of five hundred and in one way or another virtually every family in the entire community actively participated in making the production possible. It was a difficult common community enterprise which required the cooperation of all, and in its production the people achieved a monument of community effort.

Jack E. Wright, of the University of Washington, who acted as adviser in the production of *The Mount Adams Story*, which attracted people from the entire Northwest, said, "The history of each American community is rich in the drama of human struggle, human love, yes, and in human blood. Each community's history is its own story. It makes the community individual. This story is as irretrievably a part of the community as the community is of the nation. What's more, America is young in history. Much of the country's history is still to be heard from the very lips of the pioneers who made it. Here is an opportunity to record, in dynamic form, the very roots of our culture."

All community drama does not, of course, need to be done on such a large scale. Each community has its own limitations, the same as individuals have theirs, and an attempt to do something beyond the capacity of the community to handle may end up by doing more harm than good. One-, two-, or three-act plays and simple skits are all valuable forms of community expression and offer fertile opportunities for recreation and enjoyment through the release of creative energies.

In Lonepine, Montana, the people took historical incidents from their community and wrote them into a series of plays which they produced to the delight of an audience that was larger than the community's population. Older people in the community played the parts of their own parents, and members of the younger generation played the parts of their parents. This kind of thing can be done with outstanding success without any attempt to promote an audience from outside the community. It can be done in the form of brief skits at community picnics or on a winter evening at community gatherings in the high school. This sort of activity also makes highly enjoyable program material for local groups of all kinds and offers an opportunity for wholesome fun and self-expression.

The report of the History Committee of this community study group should be an excellent source of material for community drama and writings of all kinds.

One of the newer developments in recreation and education is creative dramatics. Creative dramatics for children, to paraphrase Winifred Ward, is not for the development of the exceptional child but rather for the development of the exceptional in each child.

Wright says: "Creative dramatics is one of the most effective methods devised in recent years for developing proper emotional outlets. Under competent guidance it is one of the best ways of training children in democratic living that has yet been developed. Each child participates actively in group dramatics, improvising around a story, an experience, or a lesson in history. It is great fun for it has all the elements of make-believe that stimulate the imagination of all of us. It has a more important aspect too, for it allows the greatest amount of individual expression that is compatible with the freedom of expression of the rest of the group. No one is allowed to take over, and, by the processes of this small society itself, the shy youngster gradually is drawn out into a responsible active role. Here we see, as in the community, that independent, individual action with respect for the rights of others is vital to group accomplishment."

Baker Brownell, one of the leading philosophers of the present age, has suggested this: "It might be worthwhile to work out a tentative program for one year's community cultural events adapted to our particular interests. For example: January, New Year's celebration and winter sports day; February, Lincoln dinner and home orchestra concert; March, community drama day; April, singing night; May, garden day; June, graduation day and chorus; July, community picnic; August, ice cream night; September, school and teachers' night; October, hunter's day and game dinner; November, harvest festival and Thanksgiving dinner; and December, Christmas chorus and community tree."

And so some of the important tests of a well-rounded community recreation program are that it grows from the wants and desires of the people, that it is democratic in origin, and that it serves the needs and interests of all people of all ages in the community in all seasons of the year.

In virtually all communities some start has been made toward recreation, but in most of them much yet remains to be done. The school's physical education program is one form of recreation. Also there is the school athletic schedule for the few students who are able to play. But these usually fall far short of meeting the needs of a community's children and young people, and from the standpoint of the community as a whole they hardly scratch the surface.

In checking the community for the facilities necessary for a good all-round recreation program, perhaps the best place to begin is to examine the facilities that are already available. Everywhere there is space, idle most of the time. School buildings and grounds may be used only five days of the week, nine months of the year, and this chiefly in the daytime. Church buildings, lodge halls, and private clubhouses may get even less use than that. Also there may be vacant or abandoned buildings which could be renovated and put to use for recreation. These are community resources. They have cost the people a great deal of money. The question, as in other phases of community development, is simply a matter of determining how local resources may be utilized to full capacity. The same principle applies to vacant lots, streams, and other outdoor areas.

Leadership of the right kind is probably the first essential. And here again the best place to begin is with the people who live in the community, or with the community's own human resources. It would be ideal, of course, if the community could hire a full-time recreation director who is trained to guide this kind of program. Such a director would work largely as a coordinator of volunteer leadership. But even without a full-time paid director, a good community recreation program is still possible.

Probably there are a good many natural leaders who are ready and willing to come forth when there is a showing of genuine community enthusiasm. Also there are probably a good many potential leaders who have gone unnoticed in the community because they have never had the right opportunity to develop and express their leadership ability. And in almost every community there are certain people whose hobby or profession has made them well enough acquainted with some particular activity which could be incorporated into a recreation program, and which they might be willing to teach to others. Another method of developing the necessary leadership is to form a corps of local volunteer leaders who will meet at certain intervals with professional recreational people from the state university or from some other tax-supported agency or institution who could be brought into the community to give special instruction sessions. Sometimes graduate students from the state university will welcome the opportunity to gain experience by working in a community to help get the recreation program started. By drawing on the university and other tax-supported institutions for assistance the community simply utilizes more fully the resources which it helps to pay for whether it uses them or not.

Another question which must be considered in establishing a good community recreation program is the matter of finance. The cost will, of course, vary with the size of the program and the kind of activities it includes. But almost every recreation program, if it embraces the interests and wants of the entire community, will involve a certain amount of cost.

There are numerous methods of financing a community recreation program. The one which has worked best and which has proved the most desirable in communities that truly wanted a recreation program has been to raise the funds through a small tax millage within the community. The main idea is to spread the load so that it isn't a burden on anybody and so that everyone has an opportunity to share in carrying it. Certainly this is the democratic way, and even for an elaborate program the cost per person may be less than most people spend for their Sunday newspapers. If the program includes dramatic and other events that people come to watch, it may largely pay for itself.

But in the long run the success or failure of a good program of community recreation will be determined by how well it meets the needs and desires of all the people, the extent to which all groups and organizations in the community are involved, and the degree to which each group is willing to subordinate its own special interests to the larger interest of the community as a whole.

QUESTIONS FOR THE BUZZ SESSIONS

QUESTION (i): Is there adequate opportunity in our community for all the people to express themselves through recreation?
A. Preschool children?
B. Grade school children?
C. High school age?
D. Young adults?
E. Adults?
F. Older people?

QUESTION (ii): Do the opportunities for recreation in our community include all that they should in terms of:
A. Active physical exercise? Indoor? Outdoor?
B. Activities such as chess, billiards, etc., which do not require strenuous physical exercise?
C. Creative activities such as arts and crafts, writing, etc.?
D. Appreciative activities such as concerts, etc.?
E. Community affairs such as barbecues, picnics, etc.?

QUESTION (iii): Are there sufficient opportunities for whole families to participate in recreational activities with other whole families?

QUESTION (iv): Is there a good balance in our community between commercial entertainment and opportunities for participative recreation?

QUESTION (v): Would our community be interested in community drama? If so, what kind? How might it be brought about?

QUESTION (vi): Does our community have an organized year-round recreation program for all ages?
A. If so, is it adequate?
B. If not, should one be established?
C. Who would do it, and how might it be financed?

QUESTION (vii): What facilities does our community have that could be used for purposes of recreation?
A. Are we making the best use of these facilities at the present time?

B. If not, how might better use be made of them?

QUESTION (VIII): Does our community need any additional facilities for recreation?

A. If so, what facilities are needed?

B. How might they be obtained?

QUESTION (IX): Does the present school athletic and physical education program adequately serve the needs of all our school age young people? If not, what improvements are needed?

QUESTION (X): Do the nonathletic extracurricular activities in our school system adequately serve the needs of all our school age young people? If not, what improvements are needed?

QUESTION (XI): What is the consensus as to the recommendations of the Recreation Committee?

A. Should any of these recommendations be dropped?

B. Should any new ones be added?

14

The History of Our Community

BACKGROUND FOR DISCUSSION

THE COLOR, THE HUMAN INTEREST, THE TRADITIONS, AND THE INCI-dents that give the community its own peculiar characteristics are a heritage from the sum total of all that has taken place in the years that have gone before. And the thoughts and events of today will shape the community of tomorrow. If people always remembered how certain problems came about, it might be a good deal easier to deal with today's community needs.

In a certain western community an early-day feud between two pioneer families split the area into two sharply divided sections which historically prevented the residents of the two sections from working together for their common interests. The early families are now gone, and the majority of people are no longer aware of what caused the split. But the split continues and the people seem unable to get together. As a result, progress in both sections is seriously retarded and many over-all problems go unsolved.

Many times a certain situation in the community exists through the years because at one time circumstances made it necessary. As years pass, the situation remains unchanged despite the fact that the circumstances which once made it necessary have changed completely. This may give rise to serious problems, even to sharp accusations and misunderstandings which all would recognize as unnecessary by a simple examination of the historical incidents that brought the situation about.

By examining the community's history people are able to find a good many clues to the solution of present-day needs. The history of a community likewise offers lessons for the future, and may help people to avoid making the same mistakes that have been made before.

Then there are the incidents and events that have gone into the making of a community's history. A knowledge of these incidents by the people of today will usually make life in the community more interesting and worthwhile. There are the legends, the folklore and folk songs that are native to every community, or that were brought in by the early settlers. There are the yarns of the old-timers, and the stories that have been passed down from one generation to the next. These are all a part of the community's cultural heritage. And it is this that has made the real Americana. By an understanding and appreciation of this heritage people may find a reason for wanting to maintain our democratic processes which goes deep into the basic culture of the nation.

It might be well to consider why our community was founded and what factors operated to make it grow. Through the years since it was founded various periods have come and gone. For each of these periods there were certain definite causes, and there were equally definite causes for their decline and the rise of new periods. By an understanding of the reasons why each of these periods came and went it may be possible to understand better the direction our community is taking today or to understand what we might do to alter this direction as we would like.

History may be the best teacher we have. No community can ex-

pect to get far if the people can look only at the past. But a study of
the past with a view toward better understanding the present and
future can be highly profitable.

QUESTIONS FOR THE BUZZ SESSIONS

QUESTION (I): Why was our community founded, and what factors
caused it to grow?
A. What influence has this had on life in our community today?

QUESTION (II): What definite periods can be identified in the history
of our community from the time it was founded up to the present time?
A. What factors brought each of these periods into being?
B. What factors caused each of them to decline or change into a new
period?
C. Does this offer any lessons for the present? If so, what lessons? How
might the community today profit from what has happened in the
past?

QUESTION (III): What are some of the highlights in the history of the
economic life of our community? The educational life and public schools?
The churches? The organizations?
A. What specific influence have these historical highlights had on the
life of our community?
B. What object lessons might they offer in terms of present-day planning
and action?

QUESTION (IV): What are some of the interesting incidents and events
in the history of our community?
A. How might these incidents and events be used to help make life in
the community today richer and more interesting?
B. Do they offer any possibilities for purposes of community drama?
For purposes of writing and other forms of self-expression?

QUESTION (v): What are some of the interesting legends and folklore
in the life of our community?
A. What influence have they had on the community during the course of
its development?

QUESTION (vi): Would the members of this group be interested in the
writing and dramatization of colorful incidents from the history of our
community for purposes of future recreational activities? If so, is there
any action that might be suggested for bringing such activities about?

15

The Future of Our Community

SUMMATION

WE HAVE NOW DEVOTED OUR ATTENTION TO AN ANALYSIS OF LIFE IN
our community with an eye toward finding out how it might be improved. Our community is the place where nearly all of our life activities occur, and that is why we should be interested in making this the best place in the world to live.

Our community is where we earn our living, it is the place where we raise our children, where we have our friends and neighbors, our personal and family interests—material and spiritual. It is the place where we *live*. And so it is up to us to determine what kind of place it is going to be. Many of our problems are difficult. Many of them will require a mighty effort by all of us if they are going to be solved.

From what we have discussed in these weeks of study we might make a list of some of the factors that play an important part in making a really good community where life is rich, satisfying, and dynamic. If all these factors are developed to the fullest possible extent in communities throughout our nation, the full power of democracy will be felt everywhere.

Let us look now at some of these factors. As we run through the list let us stop long enough to give each point careful consideration, and to check where our community stands. For these are some of the principal factors upon which the future of every community will rise or fall:

1. *A stable and ever-expanding economic base.* This is why we have had our Economic Development Committee—to take an inventory of just what opportunities we have for making a living, to find out how these opportunities can best be used, and to study ways and means of actually creating new opportunities. In America we think we are the kind of people who can make many of our own opportunities. And so we have tried

to find out how this might be done in our community. If this is to be a really thriving place in which to live we can never let up in these efforts which we have started to build a strong economy. For it is the economy which supports our families, our churches, our schools, our institutions, and most of the other worthwhile activities that go into a well-rounded community life.

2. *A strong sense of community unity and solidarity.* This means an ability and healthy willingness to cooperate and work together to overcome handicaps and get things done. It means an attitude of "it can be done" instead of the defeatist attitude of "it can't be done." Without this kind of group spirit, it is doubtful that any community can ever realize its full capacity for the best kind of community life. With this spirit, almost nothing is impossible.

3. *Open recognition of community needs, and a willingness to face community problems constructively and realistically.* This is closely related to the second factor listed above and means, first of all, the ability and willingness to be honest, to face conditions as they actually exist regardless of how bad they might be. No community can be really thriving and vigorous in the fullest sense if it is always satisfied with just what it already has and is unwilling to discuss or publicize anything but its best points. This does not imply that the people should be chronic complainers. On the contrary, it does mean that in a really progressive community the people who live there have the "gumption" and the moral courage to dig out and face up to their community weaknesses in order that these weaknesses may be remedied or eliminated.

4. *An attitude of tolerance and understanding of the other fellow.* Class distinction, attitudes of class superiority, factional strife, and intolerance of other people's ways of doing things can have no place in a truly democratic community. If the great traditions of America are to survive, all groups in America must make every effort to understand each other, and the problems of all groups must find solution. There must be a spirit of friendliness, neighborliness, and an honest soul-searching attempt to be objective and fair in the judgment of others and their points of view.

5. *A well-developed force for moral and ethical behavior.* This is the quality which the church has traditionally brought to the American community. Today other institutions help to reinforce this quality. But no community can develop fully in terms of human values unless it has in it a well-recognized force for truth and moral conduct.

6. *A good program of community education.* This means sound, vigorous, and well-supported public schools. It means an educational pro-

gram that fits the community's needs. It means a well-rounded program of education that offers an opportunity to everybody who lives in the community, young and old alike. Some of this program will be established in the formal sense, some of it will be informal. But the future of every community depends largely on an alert, reasoning citizenry, capable of independent thinking, of objective, factual analysis, and of arriving at intelligently considered conclusions. This has been the special problem of our Education Committee.

7. *Healthy citizens and a healthy environment.* This means the best possible physical health for everybody in the community. But it means more than that. It means a healthy society. It means well-adjusted people. It means good mental hygiene, it means community cleanliness and sanitation, and it means the best possible facilities and enough trained personnel to maintain the community in "a state of complete physical, mental, and social well-being." It means, in short, the conservation of the most valuable resource a community has—the people who live in it. This is why we have had our Health Committee.

8. *A physical environment that is neat and pleasing to the eye.* This, in certain respects, is related to the preceding point. But specifically it refers more to the aesthetic values. It means a community of well-kept buildings, grounds, and streets. It means landscaping, flowers, shrubs, and gardens. It means a sense of pride in the appearance and over-all beauty of the community. It is one of the factors that reflects the difference between a lazy community and a progressive community. This is why we have had our Beautification Committee.

9. *A good community recreation program, including ample opportunity for the people to express themselves creatively.* The full development of this quality of community life has been the purpose of our Recreation Committee. This means an all-season, all-year program in which all the people can learn to play together as well as work together. It means creative, participative recreation as well as the spectator type of amusement.

Unless a community can provide all its people, young and old, sufficient opportunities to enjoy life, the people will either seek these opportunities elsewhere or their personalities will tend to stagnate and the community will grow more and more dull and uninteresting as a place in which to live. A sufficient outlet for recreation and creative expression on a community-wide basis is one of the urgent needs of modern America. Without these outlets the spectator-type citizen is becoming more and more numerous and the democratic way of life is becoming less and less a reality.

10. *An effective means of spreading news and of publicizing and promoting worthwhile community events.* One of the best means of keeping a community awake is a good community-minded press. Indeed, a good local press or an adequate substitute such as a town bulletin board that is attractive and kept up to date is one of the greatest assets that any community can have.

11. *Leaders, citizens, and organizations that are interested in the community as a whole.* The first emphasis of our study has been on the whole community and, second, on each of the various parts that go into the making of a good whole. We have considered each part only in its relation to the whole, for we have said that life is not a part, life is a whole. One of the great disintegrative forces in every American community is the breakdown of life into parts; the separation of people into narrow, specialized interests, into compartments, each walled off from the others, and each working for its own special ends without consideration for the whole community.

The multiplicity of organizations, of duplicating and overlapping purposes, of, as someone has said, "too many irons in the fire and not enough fire," have not only become major handicaps to community progress, they have brought the defeat of human values. The age of specialism has brought us many things of value, but it has been overdone to the point where the greater values of the whole human being and the whole community have been forgotten. No one specialist, no one special interest, no one institution, and no one organization can make a good whole community. No community can ever realize its best potential as long as only a small percentage of the people participate in community affairs while the majority stand by idle and lost in the hopeless maze of parts.

And so in the place where community life is fully developed each part is only an instrument in the general scheme of things. The interest of each is in some measure the interest of all. Life is knit together, it is integrated. The efforts of all organizations are coordinated, all the people and all the groups work together as a team.

Probably there are a good many more things that we have yet to accomplish, than have been accomplished to date, but certainly we should have become better acquainted with each other. We should have developed more skill in discussing our mutual problems, in formulating conclusions, and in evolving logical solutions to the problems we have found. We should know more about our community now than we knew before we started this study, we should better understand the points of view of each other. We should be more adept at facing our community problems honestly, objectively, and without emotion and prejudice. And we should have had a good time doing something constructive.

FINAL REPORTS OF THE COMMITTEES

At this point each of the standing committees, and any other committees that are recommending action, should present to the entire study group a summary of their findings, conclusions, and recommendations. These recommendations should include those made by the committees themselves at the time of their original reports as they were accepted by the study group, plus any additional recommendations that may have developed from the buzz sessions.

After each committee makes its presentation and time is allowed for any discussion that may be called for, a vote may then be taken from the entire group for acceptance or amendment of the recommendations. The recommendations that are accepted from all the committees then become the final recommendations for action by the study group.

WHERE DO WE GO FROM HERE?

We have emphasized that one of the most effective and intelligent approaches to community action is through group study and discussion. In the course of these weeks of study we have uncovered many problems and their causes. We have discussed many possibilities and opportunities by which we might make our community a better, more secure, and more satisfying place in which to live and raise our children. Our committees have worked hard and brought in long reports which we have discussed. Together we have made many recommendations for action. We know that most of this action cannot be accomplished without a lot of hard work and pulling together. But the future of our community is in our own hands. By concerted effort in which all groups and organizations are united we can make the future of our community largely what we wish.

The question now is by what machinery are these recommendations to be carried out? Or, where do we go from here?

This is a question for which there can be no stock reply. We have said that every community has its own peculiarities, its own limitations, its own capacities, and its own ways of doing things. The right way of bringing about the action we desire is by whatever means the group feels is right for our community. Perhaps our community already has the machinery necessary for carrying out the action we desire. But one thing is certain: Community action is never possible unless some group wants it badly enough to go after it. And there is one thing that should be remembered above all else: It is community spirit, unity, and solidarity that is of ultimate importance in the life of a community, not any one specific action project.

Following is a plan for translating community study into community action which, with variations, has been used with high success in other communities. The main idea in this plan is to bring about community unity and action.

The suggested plan is this:

Shortly before the regular study group meetings are to be concluded the general chairman appoints a special committee on permanent organization. This committee is asked to draw up a tentative plan for a kind of community assembly through which all citizens and established organizations in the community can mobilize themselves or pool their combined energies for one concerted community-wide effort; this assembly to be permanent and continuous in nature. Through this assembly people from the entire community can get together to discuss community development projects of all kinds and to initiate the action necessary to carry them out. In general these will be projects that are too large for any one group or organization to handle alone, though other projects may be initiated as well.

The plan calls for each organization in the community to elect or appoint one representative to the community assembly, this assembly to meet once each month or at whatever intervals might be decided upon. These representatives, or delegates, are key persons in the group, for they are responsible for making regular reports to their respective organizations on all matters discussed and voted on at the meetings of the assembly, and for presenting to the assembly any projects, proposals, or programs in which their organizations are particularly interested. By this means it will be possible for each organization in the community to obtain, wherever desirable, community-wide support and cooperation for special projects or programs which that organization might sponsor. Also it will be possible to mobilize all organizations in the community behind projects initiated in the assembly, or to initiate other community improvement projects which may not require the efforts of the entire community but which badly need doing for the betterment of the community. From the recommendations of the study group there will be a long list of action projects to get the assembly started.

Meetings of the assembly function in the nature of a typical American town meeting which all citizens of the community are welcome to attend and speak their piece, and in which everybody has a vote by virtue of his being a resident of the community. It is, in short, thoroughly democratic, there is no special privileged group, and it is open to everyone. This is merely an instrument through which all citizens in the community can exercise a direct voice in the shaping of their own community destiny, and through which the community can utilize all its potential power for citizen action and progress. This also gives all who have devoted their time and energy to the community study an opportunity for the realization of their hopes and aspirations for a better community life.

The assembly elects from the community at large a president or general chairman, a vice-president, and a secretary-treasurer. It may, of course, provide for any other officers which the people desire.

The plan calls also for a number of standing committees to be set up as a part of the assembly. These committees include: Economic Development, Community Beautification, Education, Health and Welfare, Recreation, Legislation, Finance, Publicity, and any others which the group desires. The chairmen of these committees, together with the president, vice-president, and secretary-treasurer of the assembly, might form a kind of executive council or advisory committee for purposes of detailed discussions which would be difficult to accomplish in a large meeting. Plans may be drawn up by this smaller group in the form of proposals for presentation and general discussion in the regular meetings of the community assembly.

The community assembly is not in any sense just another organization that will overlap and duplicate other groups or organizations in the community, but is actually a kind of organization of all organizations and people in the community through which all groups and people may coordinate their efforts in matters of common interest to bring about general improvements and over-all community development by united effort.

The community assembly does not in any way dictate to any of the organizations or tell them what to do, but is instead a means through which the wishes of the various affiliated organizations for community-wide action may be more effectively accomplished. The assembly should result in strengthening the community's various individual organizations and at the same time help to unite them and the citizenry at large for common community objectives. It should be emphasized that the community assembly does not infringe upon the functions of individual organizations. These organizations carry on their own programs just as they always have, but if they want help on a certain project of general interest, they have in the assembly a means of getting that help and of mobilizing if necessary the entire community.

As indicated above, there may be certain instances where only one or two of the affiliated organizations will be needed to carry out action projects set up in the assembly. In such cases individual organizations may volunteer through their assembly representative to assume responsibility for this action. For other projects the combined effort of all organizations will be needed. Action projects may be originated either by the assembly or by any of the affiliated organizations.

The committees of the assembly function in a research capacity, and act as spearheads for planning and organizing various action projects that are assigned to them by the president, by the executive or advisory committee, or by the entire assembly. For example: a certain proposed action project may call for a set of facts and figures which are not currently on hand or for further study in order to determine the need and feasibility of the project. This research would be the job of the proper standing committee. The committee then makes its report of findings and recommendations, and a decision is reached as to what definite action should be taken, if any, when it is to be started, and how it is to be accomplished.

On the basis of what has happened in other communities it has been found that it is wise to retain the same committee personnel who have served in the study group for at least the first six months of the community assembly. This provides continuity and gets the assembly well established before entirely new personnel are expected to take over all committee functions. The important thing at this early stage is not to lose the enthusiasm and community spirit which has been built up through the community study.

The committee which is appointed by the general chairman of the study group to draw up the tentative plan for the permanent action organization should present its report to a special meeting of the study group's advisory committee which is called for this purpose prior to the completion of the study. After the proposed plan has been discussed by the advisory committee and accepted or modified, it is then presented for discussion and approval or modification to the entire study group. After this has been done and the plan is in a shape which is agreeable to the whole group, it is then ready for presentation to each individual organization in the community.

Letters describing the proposed plan, together with an invitation to affiliate, may be prepared for delivery to each established organization in the community. The less delay there is in the organizations discussing the plan and appointing their representatives the better.

It is a good idea to have such letters delivered to the various organizations by a member of the study group in person, and the purpose and objectives of the proposed action machinery properly explained. Delivery can be made either to a regular meeting of each organization or, if this is impossible, to the organization's head. It is important that a definite statement be obtained from each organization as to its intentions of affiliating or not affiliating with the community assembly.

It is highly desirable that all this be accomplished before the study group completes its regular series of meetings, but just at the end of the series. This will make it possible to get a response from each organization in the community in time to launch the community assembly immediately following the completion of the study.

It is suggested that consideration be given at the last meeting of the study group, or before, to the possibility of holding a large citizens' mass meeting, at which time the study group may report to the entire community its findings, conclusions, and recommendations. A date may be set for this meeting to come immediately at the close of the study group's series of regular weekly meetings.

This large mass meeting might be scheduled for a night on which there will be no other meetings in the community, and all citizens should be urged to attend. This could well be one of the most important meetings in the history of the community.

On this night the general chairman of the study group outlines the purpose of the meeting, describes what has gone on in the course of the study group meetings, and calls on each committee chairman to give a summary of his final report and recommendations for community action. The last committee to report is the committee on permanent organization. After this report has been made, the general chairman calls the roll of community organizations and the entire membership of each organization rises. A spokesman for each group signifies the willingness of that organization to affiliate with the proposed community assembly and to support the community action program. After the organization roll call has been taken the general chairman announces a date for the first meeting of the community assembly for purposes of actual organization. The citizens' mass meeting thus becomes a celebration of the end of the community study and the beginning of a long-range community action program. This meeting may be held in such a way as to make it an outstanding community event. In some communities it has included the band, group singing, and the governor of the state.

At the first meeting of the community assembly the final reports and recommendations of the community study are gone over for purposes of actual planning and action. The talking stage is over. The study group has finished, and the community action program is under way.

As already indicated, the above plan of procedure has been used with modifications and variations in other communities where this community study program has been conducted, and has brought outstanding success. It is given here merely as a suggestion. The actual method of initiating community action on the recommendations of the study after the study group has completed its series of meetings must be determined by the people involved. Each community is a special case, and whatever decisions are made must be made by the people who live there. But the importance of these decisions cannot be overemphasized. The future of America depends upon them, for America can be no stronger than the local communities of which she is made up.

Part IV

Special Outlines

1

For the General Chairman

THE GENERAL CHAIRMAN IS THE KEY FIGURE IN THE COMMUNITY STUDY program. His job is essentially that of an over-all executive. He should not be expected to serve on any one committee or be directly responsible for any of the committee work.

He should first make himself as familiar as possible with the entire contents of the study guide. He should review each section to be covered in each meeting of the group in advance of the meeting, and be prepared to answer questions or make decisions on all matters of procedure. After having read and thoroughly digested the contents of the study guide it is suggested that he draw up an outline of his own of the things that he feels should be done in the order in which they should be handled. It is the general chairman who will guide the group through its beginning stages, prepare the ground for each step that follows, and lead the final translation of community study into community action.

It is important that at no point the study program be allowed to become entangled in partisan political conflict or get involved in factional strife. Always it should be geared to include all factions and elements in the life of the community for the over-all interests of the community as a whole. Remember, one of the major aims of this program is to help solve the problems of all phases and aspects of community life in an effort to help build a stronger democratic society in the local community, and thereby to help undergird the American traditions. This should be a program in which all groups and all special interests in the community may unite in the single cause of cooperative effort for a richer and more vigorous kind of community life.

To accomplish these ends it is of utmost importance that the general chairman have the full cooperation of all participants in the program, and that scrupulous attention be given to the many fine details of organization and procedure. Every detail that is allowed to slide will weaken the potential of the study group. Therefore, a rather comprehensive schedule of suggested procedure is set forth below for the guidance of the general chairman. This procedure is not, however, intended to be an inflexible or set pattern, but is offered only as a tool. It may be altered by the general chairman wherever in his judgment, or in the judgment of the group as a whole, it can be made to fit more precisely the local situation.

Following is a list of points which the general chairman should bear in mind.

1. If more meetings are needed than are indicated in the schedule outlined below to complete the discussion on any particular section in the study guide, the discussion on that section should be allowed to continue into the next meeting.

The question of just how many extra meetings to allow for the discussion of any given section is a matter to be determined by the general chairman, or by him in consultation with other participants in the group. While it is important that the discussions not move so fast as to leave people with a feeling that they do not have time to come to grips with basic issues, it is equally important that they not be allowed to drag. In general it has been found wise to adhere as nearly as possible to the schedule outlined in the guide, although a few extra meetings will not be out of line. The thing to remember is that it is impossible for the community study group to cover every single subject in full and complete detail. In general the committees will make a considerably more detailed study of their respective subject matter than will the entire study group. But the discussions in the buzz sessions should enable all participants to gain a broadened knowledge of the community life as a whole, to improve their understanding of community problems, and to educate themselves as to what needs to be done to solve these problems and bring about the desired improvements. The committee reports in combination with the group discussions will also help to develop a recognition by the community of the need for further and more detailed study into certain specific areas of the community life. These are some of the factors to be taken into consideration in attempting to determine how rapidly the study should move.

In some instances it may be found that certain questions raised in the study guide are of little or no consequence in this particular community. In these instances the questions may be skipped over lightly, thus allowing more time for the questions that are of greater importance to this particular community.

2. Call for progress reports at least once every two weeks from all committees whose sections are yet to come up for discussion.

3. Keep in touch with each committee to make certain that its report will be in the hands of the secretary at least one full week in advance of the date it is due for discussion by the study group.

4. Check with the secretary to make certain that each committee report is received on time.

5. Whenever possible visit meetings of the various committees.

6. Check with discussion leaders and recorders in advance of each meeting to make certain they will be present, and that they have the material needed to make advance preparations for the discussions.

7. Make it an established routine to meet with discussion leaders and recorders a half hour early before each weekly meeting for a final review of the questions and material to be taken up and the procedure to be followed that evening.

8. Make a personal check of meeting rooms before each weekly meeting to make certain that all equipment, chairs, tables, blackboards, chalk, erasers, heat, etc., necessary for the meeting are in readiness.

9. Immediately before the opening of each meeting of the study group copies of the secretary's report, and copies of whatever committee report is due that evening should be distributed by placing them at each participant's seat. This will save from five to ten minutes which would be lost at each meeting by passing out the reports after the meeting has begun.

10. At the close of each meeting remind all participants in the study group to read and study the section in the study guide to be covered next week and to bring the guides and study group reports with them to the meeting. The more advance thought given the questions for discussion the more fruitful will be the discussions. If people wish to make advance notes and jot down extra questions they want to bring up, so much the better.

Each participant in the study group should have a special folder in which to keep a file of all study group reports so that these materials will be in order and handy to bring to the meeting. It is suggested that if possible a supply of these folders be made available at the first meeting of the study group on Section 2, Part III, for this purpose.

11. The Advisory Committee meets only on call by the general chairman. It should be called whenever the situation warrants.

12. The general chairman should not feel limited to the suggested procedure set forth in this outline, or in the rest of the guide, but should feel free to make use of his own imagination and improvisation to meet whatever problem arises and to create an atmosphere that will contribute to the success of the study group.

SCHEDULE OF MEETINGS

The plan of operation for each weekly meeting of the study group is outlined in detail in Part II of the study guide. Below is a check list of special reminders to bear in mind for each meeting.

SECTION 1, PART III (ONE MEETING)

Follow the schedule outlined in this section.

Remind all members of the group to read Parts I and II, and Section 2, Part III of the study guide before the next meeting.

FIRST MEETING OF THE ADVISORY COMMITTEE

Completion of study group organization and committee appointments. Notify each committee chairman of appointment.

SECTION 2, PART III (TWO MEETINGS)

First Meeting

Review purpose and objectives of the community study group.

Read secretary's report on the organizational meeting and the first meeting of the Advisory Committee. It will not be necessary at all future meetings to read the secretary's report aloud, but merely to distribute a copy of it to each member of the group.

Read aloud the *Background for Discussion on the Report from the Boundary Committee.*

Chairman of Boundary Committee presents report and discussion follows. A definite decision should be reached at this time on the boundaries to be accepted for purposes of the study.

Go into buzz sessions and make Community Characteristics Survey as set forth in this section.

A written report on the returns from this survey should be prepared and mimeographed for distribution to all participants in the study group for discussion at the next weekly meeting. In the report list each question, and under it give a consolidated résumé of all the answers to that question. Names and other personal references that might prove embarrassing to a particular individual in the community should be deleted. Many, if not all, of the answers may be quoted directly either in whole or in part. The main objective in writing this report is to convey as clearly and fully as possible all shades of opinion of the group as a whole, but without identifying any specific individual, so that at the next meeting the discussion in the buzz sessions may be centered on what the participants as a group actually said about their own community.

Copies of the report on the Community Characteristics Survey should be placed in the hands of each discussion leader and recorder at least one full day before the next study group meeting.

Reassemble from the buzz sessions. Alert all committees to hold their first meeting this week and to be ready with a brief progress report at the next meeting of the study group.

Adjourn.

Second Meeting

Roll call of committees and progress reports.

Discussion of report on Community Characteristics Survey in buzz sessions.

Section 3, Part III (one meeting)

Report of Population Committee.

Section 4, Part III (one meeting)

Roll call of committees and progress reports.
There is no committee report to be discussed at this meeting.

Section 5, Part III (one meeting)

Report of Community Organizations Committee.

SECTION 6, PART III (ONE MEETING)

Roll call of committees and progress reports.
Report of Church Committee.

SECTION 7, PART III (ONE MEETING)

Report of Government Committee.

SECTION 8, PART III (ONE MEETING)

Roll call of committees and progress reports.
Report of Social Agencies Committee.

SECTION 9, PART III (THREE MEETINGS)

First Meeting

No report is due for this meeting. Go into buzz sessions and discuss material outlined in this section for first meeting on the general factors concerning the community and its economy.

Second Meeting

Roll call of committees and progress reports.

Report of Subcommittee on Agriculture and Industry, of the Economic Development Committee.

These reports are given in the form of a panel discussion by the entire membership of these subcommittees. If it is believed that there will be time for only one of these subcommittees to report, then an extra meeting should be added for this section of the guide, and each subcommittee will have a separate meeting for its panel discussion. It is likely that this panel discussion will take up the entire study group meeting. If this is the case, no buzz sessions will be necessary at this meeting, but time should be allowed for a discussion from the floor of the study group general assembly, and all members given an opportunity to participate.

Third Meeting

Report of Subcommittee on Trades and Services, of the Economic Development Committee. Follow the same procedure as indicated above for the second meeting on this section.

SECTION 10, PART III (ONE MEETING)

Roll call of committees and progress reports.
Report of Beautification Committee.

SECTION 11, PART III (THREE MEETINGS)

First Meeting

Report of Education Committee. If the committee wishes, this report may be given in two parts, the first part at this meeting and the second part at the next meeting.

Second Meeting

Roll call of committees and progress reports.
Continue in buzz sessions with the discussion on education.

Third Meeting

Report of Library Committee.
In buzz sessions complete discussion on education as outlined in this section and discuss questions presented by the Library Committee in its report.

In the final summary at close of meeting give résumé of conclusions and recommendations for action for all meetings on education in the community, and summarize conclusions and recommendations for action in report of Library Committee.

SECTION 12, PART III (TWO MEETINGS)

First Meeting

Roll call of committees and progress reports.
Report of Health Committee.

Second Meeting

Complete discussion on health.
At this meeting the general chairman should begin preparations for the last scheduled meeting of the community study group by appointing a special Committee on Permanent Organization. The job of this committee is to draw up a tentative plan for whatever permanent citizens action machinery is deemed necessary to carry out the community action projects to be finally recommended by the study group. These projects together may constitute a community action program which is both immediate and short range in nature, and which will be ever expanding as time goes on and new needs and problems arise. It may be that the necessary action machinery for this purpose already exists in the community, but needs only to be expanded or elaborated to include all

organizations and all citizens who wish to join hands in concerted community-wide effort. This committee should first work out a tentative proposal, and then discuss the proposal with other participants in the study group and leaders in the various established organizations in the community. Before beginning its actual planning, all members of the committee should read carefully Section 15, Part III, of the study guide.

The general chairman should call a special meeting of the study group Advisory Committee and committee chairmen, at which time the Committee on Permanent Organization may report its proposal for discussion and approval and/or alteration. The proposal as accepted at this special meeting should then be presented for final approval and/or alteration to the entire study group at the meeting on Section 15, Part III.

SECTION 13, PART III (ONE MEETING)

Report of Recreation Committee.

MEETING OF THE ADVISORY COMMITTEE

During the week before the regular study group meeting on Section 14, Part III, the general chairman should call a meeting of the Advisory Committee and committee chairmen, plus anyone else who would like to attend. This important meeting is for the purpose of making necessary preparations for winding up the weekly meetings of the community study group and the beginning of an over-all action program through which the community may accomplish the recommendations for improvement that have grown out of the study.

The main items for consideration at this meeting are:

1. The suggested plan for community-wide action machinery which has been worked out by the special Committee on Permanent Organization, and a definite plan for discussing it with the various established organizations in the community.

2. A date, and definite plans, for a community-wide citizens' mass meeting to be held immediately following the last regular meeting of the community study group. At that time the study group reports its findings, conclusions, and recommendations for action to the entire community. This meeting may be held as a kind of celebration to mark the transition from a community study program to a community action program, and on that night whatever action machinery that has been adopted may be officially launched.

3. The adoption of one specific community-wide action project which can be carried out immediately following the community-wide citizens' mass meeting.

4. The presentation of the final summary of conclusions and recommendations for action from each committee of the study group at the regular meeting on Section 15, Part III.

Each person attending this special meeting of the Advisory Committee should be specifically asked to read in advance of the meeting Section 15, Part III of the study guide.

SECTION 14, PART III (ONE MEETING)

Give an account of the meeting of the Advisory Committee, the conclusions and proposals of which are to be discussed by the entire study group at its last meeting on Section 15, Part III.

Report of History Committee.

Alert the entire study group to be prepared for the last scheduled meeting next week on Section 15, Part III, at which time the final recommendations for action are to be presented, and a decision is to be made on the question "Where do we go from here?"

Alert the entire study group to the date set for the community-wide citizens' mass meeting scheduled to follow the last meeting of the study group next week.

SECTION 15, PART III (ONE MEETING)

This is the last scheduled meeting of the community study group and is perhaps the most important in the entire series. We have come now not to the end but to the beginning. This is the beginning of the translation of democratic study into democratic action. If this translation can be made effectively the democratic way of life will always survive and the community's future should grow richer and stronger with each passing year.

Read aloud the *Summation* given in the study guide.

Presentation of final reports and recommendations as called for under *Final Reports of the Committees* in the study guide. Allow time for discussion and/or amendment by the entire study group. These recommendations as approved then become the recommendations for action from the entire study group to the community.

Report from the special Committee on Permanent Organization as discussed and recommended to the study group in the last special meeting of the Advisory Committee. Allow time for general discussion and/or amendment by the entire study group. The plan of action as approved then becomes the recommendation from the entire study group to the community.

Report from the Advisory Committee on all other matters discussed and recommended at its last special meeting.

Complete final plans for the community mass meeting at which time the study group reports to the entire community.

2

For the Secretary

THE COMMUNITY STUDY IS ESSENTIALLY A PROCESS OF LEARNING TO understand the local community and of creating from within a stronger and more dynamic community life. An important element in this process is the keeping of a complete record of the proceedings of the group, which will serve not merely as an account of the various items brought up at meetings, as do the minutes of the ordinary club secretary, but which will serve as a written review of the thinking, the discussions, the problems, and the recommended action that each meeting brings out.

This is a responsibility of the study group secretary.

The secretary's report should be written in the form of a detailed narrative which conveys as nearly as possible the full meaning and sense of what is actually said and discussed in each meeting. Do not be concerned about making the report too long. Completeness, not brevity, is the thing to be sought. The more comprehensive the better. Actual quotes, anecdotes and interesting situations, points of view and agreements or disagreements of opinion, problems and recommended solutions should all be included in the secretary's report. If there are points of humor they should be included. The report should be written also from the standpoint of reader appeal so that in so far as possible it will make interesting reading such as a nonfiction magazine story or a narration that brings out the human content of a historical event.

At the end of the report there should be a brief summary which lists in one-two-three fashion the problems posed, the suggested solutions, and the recommendations for action from the buzz session discussions. Thus the secretary's report on each study group meeting should be written in somewhat the following order.

1. A narrative account of proceedings and discussions before the buzz sessions.

2. A narrative account of proceedings and discussions in each buzz session, as taken from the recorders' notes.

3. A narrative account of proceedings and discussions after the buzz sessions reassemble for the final summary.

4. Summary and conclusions giving a listing of the problems posed and the action recommended.

At the end of each study group meeting the secretary collects the notes from each recorder for inclusion in the report.

Each week the secretary's report is mimeographed so that copies can be distributed at the opening of the next weekly meeting to all participants in the group.

At the end of the study the entire proceedings of the group, including all reports of the secretary and the reports of all of the committees may be re-run and bound into a single volume for permanent use in the community. Enough copies of this volume may be made for all persons who might be interested. Copies of this volume will be of especial value to whatever community action body or program is formed to carry out the action follow-up of the study. In this volume will be a report of all discussions, findings, conclusions, and recommendations for action reaching into nearly every phase and aspect of community life. Copies of this complete volume may be sold for a sum modest enough to make the price a negligible item, but which is enough to pay off the actual cost of production.

In order to simplify the production of this final volume, the secretary's report and all other records of the group, including the reports from the committees, should be typed each week according to a standard size page with standard size margins. Each stencil should be cleaned and filed away for safekeeping. Then when the study group reaches the end of its scheduled course, or just prior to that time, the stencils may simply be re-run to make the pages for the final volume of proceedings. Thus, a big job of retyping will be avoided.

Part II of the study guide calls for the appointment of a Secretarial Committee. The secretary serves as chairman of this committee, which has the job of doing the actual typing and mimeographing of the secretary's report and the reports of the committees.

Typing and mimeographing of each issue of the secretary's report and of the reports of the various committees should be finished early enough each week so that copies can be given to the general chairman and to each discussion leader and recorder at least two days in advance of the weekly meeting for which it is due. The secretary is responsible for seeing that this timetable is maintained and that the advance copies of reports are actually distributed. This will enable the general chairman, discussion leaders, and recorders to make adequate preparations for each meeting of the study group.

SUMMARY

Responsibilities of the secretary are, in summary, as follows:

1. To make a complete record of all meetings of the study group, and of all meetings of the Advisory Committee.

2. To collect the recorders' notes at the end of each study group meeting.

3. To receive all committee reports as they are due for typing.

4. To act as chairman of the Secretarial Committee and see that all reports are mimeographed for distribution to all participants in the study group.

5. To see that advance copies of these reports are distributed to the general chairman, discussion leaders, and recorders at least two days in advance of the meeting for which they are due.

6. To supervise the production of the final volume containing all reports of proceedings of the group.

The secretary should read and become familiar with the entire study guide, and make a special review of the outline for the general chairman in Part IV.

3

For the Discussion Leaders

Responsibilities of the discussion leaders are:

1. To lead the discussions in the buzz sessions.
2. To read immediately and become thoroughly familiar with the entire study guide, and to make a special review of Part II, the outline in Part IV for the general chairman, and of all other references in the guide which pertain to the duties of discussion leaders.
3. To obtain at least two days in advance of each meeting a copy of the secretary's report, and a copy of whatever committee report is due for discussion.
4. To study all material from the study guide and the reports to be taken up next in order to make adequate preparations in advance of each meeting for leading the discussion.
5. To meet with the general chairman and recorders a half hour before each weekly meeting of the study group to iron out any last-minute procedural problems and get ready for the discussions that evening.
6. To notify the general chairman far enough in advance to get a substitute in case circumstances are going to prevent a leader from attending a study group meeting.

At the opening of the buzz session the discussion leader reads or summarizes the background for discussion as given in the study guide while each participant follows from his own book. All participants should be encouraged to interrupt the reading at any point they wish to raise questions or make comments. Whenever such an interruption leads naturally into a group discussion pertinent to the subject of the evening the leader may encourage the development of the discussion until a definite conclusion has been reached.

After reading aloud or orally summarizing the background for discussion and reviewing briefly the committee report that is up for discussion, the leader then reads the first question and opens the buzz session to discussion.

Every member of the group should be encouraged to take part and speak his piece in this discussion. For this purpose the leader should make it a point to call on everyone by name for his opinion until the discussion is under way and all members of the group feel the opportunity to enter in.

It is the responsibility of the leader to help keep the discussion from running too far off the subject and to guide it toward definite conclusions and recommendations. The leader may do little talking himself, but by elaborating on the questions with other questions of his own and by summarizing points that have been made and asking more questions, he may stimulate a full and lively discussion from the group as a whole. The general objective is to attempt to bring out all points that may be pertinent, to help get ideas and thoughts exchanged freely, to blend and alter individual prejudices into group understanding, and to attempt to reach as nearly as possible a group consensus.

Try to avoid merely listing and observing facts, but attempt to develop in the discussion an interpretation of the meaning and significance of facts.

If any member of the group disagrees on any point that has been made, the leader should attempt through asking more questions to develop the reasons for the disagreement and to work again toward bringing out all shades of thought in the group until some kind of conclusion has been reached.

It is the leader's responsibility to keep the discussion from bogging down on unimportant details and to keep it moving so that the group will come to grips with major issues and then work toward group understanding and recognition of the facts or principles involved. If the group gets stuck on every small detail it will never be able to get onto the major points and the discussions will become dull and uninteresting.

The last few minutes of each discussion should be devoted to a summing up of what has been said, the major points that have been made, and a definite listing of the problems posed and the recommendations for action.

Every effort should be made to prevent any one person from dominating the discussion or freezing out other members of the group by talking too much. This can usually be accomplished by announcing in a good-natured manner at the beginning of the discussion that everybody's opinions are wanted, but that the more long-winded members should not feel hurt if the leader has to cut them off by asking what someone else in the group thinks about this or that particular point. Everything possible should be done to create an atmosphere of friendly give-and-take and to help motivate people to say what is actually on their minds without fear of being censured or of hurting other people's feelings. It is only when the mental barriers, either real or imaginary, which prevent people from saying what they feel like saying are broken down that the true processes of democracy can function. And this is the basic aim of the community study group.

Remind each member of the group to read and study the material in the study guide which is scheduled for discussion next week.

4

For the Recorders

RESPONSIBILITIES OF THE RECORDERS ARE:

1. To keep a complete record on the questions raised, the points made, the conclusions reached, and the recommendations for action in the buzz sessions.

2. To read immediately and become thoroughly familiar with the entire study guide, and to make a special review of Part II, the outlines in Part IV for the general chairman, the secretary, and the discussion leaders, and all other references in the guide which pertain to the recorders. It is especially important that the recorders' notes are written in such a way as to make it possible for the secretary to prepare the kind of report called for in the outline for the secretary given in Part IV.

3. To obtain at least two days in advance of each meeting a copy of

the secretary's report, and a copy of whatever committee report is due for discussion.

4. To study all material from the study guide and the reports to be taken up next in order to make adequate preparations in advance of each meeting for working with the discussion leaders. This preparation will help to provide the recorder with a good background knowledge of the subject being discussed and will thus make it easier to do a good job of recording.

5. To meet with the general chairman and discussion leaders a half hour before each weekly meeting of the study group to iron out any last-minute procedural problems and get ready for the discussions that evening.

6. To report in a panel on the discussion of their respective buzz sessions before the entire study group after the group reassembles at the close of each weekly meeting.

7. To notify the general chairman far enough in advance to get a substitute in case circumstances are going to prevent a recorder from attending a study group meeting.

The recorder should not hesitate to stop the discussion in order to get a clear record of a point when the discussion is going too fast for the recorder to keep up.

Devote the last few minutes of each buzz session to summarizing orally the notes that have been taken to make certain they are correct, and to make an actual listing of the problems posed and the recommendations for action.

In reporting on the discussion after the buzz sessions have gone back into the study group general assembly, keep the report brief and to the point. Emphasize conclusions, and specific problems and recommendations. If a point is already covered, simply indicate that it has been covered by the other group and that this group had nothing to add. Each recorder should exercise as much care as possible to report the group's actual conclusions and to give a complete picture wherever there has been a difference of opinion.

At the end of each meeting the recorders should make a specific point to see that notes on the discussion are handed to the secretary.

5

For the Boundary Committee

THE BOUNDARY COMMITTEE IS RESPONSIBLE FOR MAKING A SURVEY TO
help the study group determine what area constitutes our community. It is important that the committee's report and recommendations be completed immediately after the organization of the
study group so that the group may make this decision without delay.
The area decided upon will be the area to be covered by the community study.

A copy of the Boundary Committee's report should be available
for distribution to all participants in the study group at the opening
of the meeting on Section 2 in Part III of the study guide.

As soon as the study group has made a definite decision on the
area that constitutes our community, the Boundary Committee is
responsible for seeing that each committee of the group gets a copy
of a map.

It has been found from experience in other communities that it is
unwise to extend the boundary lines out into what is normally considered by local residents as another community. Areas or centers
outside the natural community boundaries may be thought of as
neighboring communities, and in the course of making the study a
great deal of attention may be given to intercommunity relationships
that influence the future of several communities. But remember, this
is essentially a study of *our own local community*. Care should also
be taken, of course, not to leave out any area that is normally considered by local residents as actually being a part of this community.

To make the boundary survey it is suggested that the committee
travel out each road leading away from the town proper, or the
community center, call on a few families along the outer reaches of
the community, and ask a few questions such as the following:

197

1. What do you consider your home town? Or what community do you generally feel that you belong to?

2. In what shopping center do you do most of your trading?

3. Where do you go chiefly for meetings of the various organizations to which you belong?

4. In what center do you, or most of the people around here, go to church?

5. In what center do you visit most frequently for informal social contacts?

6. Where do your children attend school? Is the school located in the same community you live in?

7. What is the last house down this road that you consider as being located in this community?

Make a notation of the approximate point on each road leading away from the town or community center where people cease to feel that they belong to the community being studied. After plotting this point on each road, connect up the points on a map and draw in the boundaries. The lines connecting these points are the approximate natural boundaries of the community.

The committee should then write up a report for presentation to the study group. This report should show what the committee did in making its survey, the results of the survey, the conclusions reached, and a description of the boundaries which the committee recommends for adoption by the study group.

SUMMARY

Suggested steps for getting the work of the Boundary Committee completed are as follows:

1. Set a date for the first meeting of the committee as soon as possible after the study group is organized.

2. Each member of the committee prepare himself in advance of this meeting by reading carefully (a) the *Background for Discussion on the Report from the Boundary Committee,* which is set forth in Section 2, Part III, of the study guide, and (b) this special outline.

3. At the first committee meeting adopt a plan of operations and assign jobs with deadlines for completion to each member of the committee.

4. Make the actual boundary survey. Suggestions for this purpose are given above.

5. Agree on the description of the community's boundaries which the committee may recommend to the study group.

6. Write up the committee's report and mimeograph enough copies for each participant in the study group.

7. After the study group has made a definite decision on what boundaries to accept, draw a large-scale map and make enough copies for use by each committee in the group.

8. Distribute the copies of this map to all committees.

The area thus defined will constitute our community for purposes of this study.

6

For the Population Committee

THE POPULATION COMMITTEE HAS THE RESPONSIBILITY OF MAKING A house-to-house census of the entire community. This is by far the largest survey called for in the community study program, but from it will be obtained many of the basic facts needed by other committees and of particular value for purposes of future planning for specific community action.

An outline is set forth below showing the kinds of facts and information that should be included in the committee's report, and a suggested questionnaire is provided for the purpose of collecting most of this information.

The committee should make its survey as detailed and inclusive as may be desired and for this reason may wish to add a good deal of research and investigation not called for in this outline.

It should not be expected that the full report will be covered in every detail by the discussions in the study group buzz sessions. To attempt this would mean several weeks of discussion on this one aspect of the study alone, and that is not necessary. All that is needed in the buzz sessions is to discuss and interpret the main points of the report enough so that all participants in the study group will acquire a general insight into some of the basic needs and problems of the community. Also much of the information in this report will come up again in discussing the material in other sections of the study guide.

Thus the report from the Population Committee will become a valuable and useful reference in the community for many different purposes. All participants in the study group, as well as other persons or agencies who might have a definite interest, should receive a copy in order that they may have an opportunity to read and study it as thoroughly as they wish.

The first step in getting started is for the committee chairman to set a date for the first meeting. Because there is not too much time for the completion of the population report before it is due for the discussion outlined in Section 3, Part III, of the guide, the committee should make every effort to get started without delay.

In some communities it might be a good idea to get the population survey completed entirely even before the community study group is actually organized. Various organizations in the community may be willing to help do this as a special project, and undoubtedly the school will be interested in assisting. A survey of this kind should be of considerable educational value to students. On this point, however, a word of caution is in order. It has been found in other communities that it is unwise to send out immature interviewers who are unable to explain properly the purpose of the survey or to make a diplomatic approach to persons being interviewed. It is strongly recommended that any idea of obtaining the needed data by sending questionnaires home with school children be immediately discarded.

In any event, the population survey should make a good project for the steering committee that is working to get the community study started if it is desired to complete this particular survey before the community study is actually organized. Also it might provide a good opportunity to inform people throughout the community and secure their interest in the study program.

Each member of the Population Committee should prepare himself in advance of the first meeting of the committee by *reading carefully* Section 3, Part III, which contains material for discussion in the study group buzz sessions. At that meeting of the study group every member of the Population Committee should be an expert on all questions that might be raised for discussion, and should be prepared to interpret the meaning and significance of all facts contained in the report.

The main job at the committee's first meeting is to design a procedure for making the community census and for collecting all other information called for from the committee but which cannot be obtained by house-to-house interviewing.

At its first meeting the committee should review all items asked for in this outline under *Basic Facts for the Report of the Population Committee,* which appears below, and check these items against the suggested *Questionnaire for Community Census.*

As already indicated, it will be noted that not all the information asked for in the committee's report is included in the suggested census questionnaire. This is not an oversight. It has been learned from experience in working with other groups of this kind that it is unwise to include in the census questionnaire such personal questions as those pertaining to income, rent, frequency of voting, etc. Also it is important that each question in the census questionnaire be worded in as statistical and impersonal a manner as possible. If certain people being interviewed are offended by even one question they may refuse to answer any of them. Even worse, a false rumor might be unnecessarily started about the whole community study program. Moreover, much of the information asked for from the Population Committee is not of the type that can be obtained by making a house-to-house census.

However, the information that is asked for from the committee but which cannot be obtained from house-to-house interviewing is nonetheless important. Facts pertaining to the community income and effective buying power, for example, will be highly important for purposes of future planning for economic development.

Therefore, in addition to the information which will be obtained by filling out the community census questionnaires, it will be necessary for the committee to decide how it is to obtain the other information called for. This might be done by simply making a list of the various places where this information can be found, and then assigning different members of the committee the job of actually going to these places to collect the facts that are needed.

Remember, the Population Committee has a lot of work to do, but if it is divided up among all members of the committee, and each member does his or her share, the total job should be relatively simple. And it should be a highly interesting and enlightening experience.

After it has been determined what facts are to be obtained by the house-to-house interviewing and what information is to be obtained by other means, the committee is then ready to begin organizing itself for the actual collection of data.

The first step in preparing for the census is to make sure that the questionnaire to be used contains all the questions that the committee wants it to include.

Next, have enough copies of the questionnaire mimeographed to cover every household in the entire community, plus a few extras.

Next, block out the community into districts, using as the community boundaries the area determined from the report of the Boundary Committee. If the census is done as a special project before the community study group is organized, it will be necessary first to determine as nearly as possible what boundaries are going to be used for the community study. For this purpose refer to the special outline for the Boundary Committee and to other references to community boundaries in the study guide.

In making that portion of the census which pertains to a classification of the population by age groups it is recommended that special attention be given to the boundaries of the local school district so that specific data will be provided which can be used in planning for the future needs of the school. This suggestion is made here so that in case the natural boundary lines of the community and the legal boundaries of the school district do not coincide, a special report on age groups can be made for school purposes.

After the community has been blocked out into districts, the committee should organize enough interviewing crews to cover the entire area. Each crew should have a crew leader. One crew should be assigned to each district that has been blocked out. It has been found in other communities that wherever possible it is a good idea to assign interviewers to districts of the community where most of the people are well known to them personally.

On the day the census taking is to begin all the interviewing crews should meet together to pick up their supply of questionnaires and receive final instructions, and should then all start out at the same time. At the end of the day they should all meet again to compare notes and reorganize or adjust their plans for covering the places that have been missed and completing the census.

The committee chairman and crew leaders should establish a checkoff system and all interviewers should keep tab of each house as it is covered so that there will be a definite method of avoiding duplication and of making certain that the entire community is covered.

The major responsibility for the success of the census falls necessarily on the interviewers. If their approach to the various homes is made in a diplomatic manner there should be little difficulty in getting the census complete. For this reason the interviewers should make certain that each person contacted understands the general purpose of the census and that the answers to all questions are impersonal and confidential, and for statistical use only.

On approaching a person to be interviewed it is a good idea first to make a pleasant personal greeting, give just enough explanation to place the person at ease and get him in a cooperative frame of mind, then proceed with the interview. Complete the interview as quickly as possible, check to make certain that every question has been answered, and then get on to the next house. In general *it is not advisable* to leave the questionnaire form to be filled out and picked up later. This will result only in needless delays, many of the forms will not be filled out at all, and many of those that are filled out will be answered so incompletely or will be so badly confused that they will be almost worthless when it comes to tabulating the information.

In all cases the interviewer should be sure to check off each house as soon as the interview is completed so that an accurate count may be kept of which places have been covered and which places have not.

Before the census is actually started, the fact that it is going to be taken should be well publicized and every possible effort made to alert the entire community so that everybody will be expecting to be called on. Radio broadcasts, newspaper publicity, announcements in the meetings of community organizations and in church, word-of-mouth street conversation, and every other possible publicity medium should be utilized in order to inform the community in advance of the day the interviewers actually start out. Public announcements by the mayor or other public officials and by organizational heads calling for full community cooperation, dramatizations and panel discussions over the radio, and all other worth while means of publicizing the census will be helpful. Then, to follow up this publicity, similar efforts should be made to keep the entire community informed of the progress of the census as it goes along, and of the final results after it is completed.

After the actual taking of the census has been completed the next job is to tabulate the results and to write up a report which will present these results with an interpretation of their meaning and significance in as clear and understandable a manner as possible. At the end of the report there should be a summary which pin-points the problems, the basic needs of the community, and the opportunities of the community revealed by the report. The report should be set up in such a way that it can be used as an easy reference by the study group buzz sessions in discussing the questions set forth in Section 3, Part III, in the study guide. If any graphs or drawings will be helpful for this purpose, the committee should endeavor to make use of them.

The final report is due in the hands of the study group secretary in plenty of time to have it mimeographed for general distribution at the study group meeting on Section 3, Part III, and each discussion leader and recorder should have a copy at least two days in advance of this meeting.

SUMMARY

Suggested steps for getting the work of the Population Committee completed are in summary as follows:

1. Set a date for the first meeting of the committee.
2. Each member prepare himself in advance of this meeting by reading carefully (a) Section 3, Part III, of the study guide, (b) this special

outline for the committee, and (c) all other references to the Population Committee as noted in the index of the study guide.

3. Decide which of the facts called for from the committee can be obtained by the house-to-house census, and which of these facts must be obtained by some other means.

4. Make a list of places or sources where you can obtain the information that cannot be obtained through the census. Then assign members of the committee to go to these places and collect the needed data.

5. Check the suggested census questionnaire form given below to make certain that it includes enough questions to get all the information the committee wants it to get.

6. Mimeograph enough copies of the questionnaire to cover the entire community, plus some extras.

7. Block out the community into districts, using the area to be covered by the rest of the community study program, but with special attention to the school district so that a special count of age groups can be made for school purposes. Be sure to count *all age groups* for both the natural community area and the local school district.

8. Organize enough interviewing crews with crew leaders to cover the entire community, and assign one crew to each district. Wherever possible have the interviewers work in neighborhoods where they are well acquainted. The more interviewers the committee has the more opportunity there will be for people to participate, and the easier it will be to make the census. *But be sure to have interviewers who can do a good job.*

9. Establish a checkoff system for the committee chairman and crew leaders, and a tally system for interviewers as a method of avoiding duplication and of making certain that the census is complete for the entire community.

10. Have all interviewers, crew leaders, and the committee chairman meet together on the day the census is to be taken to get their supplies of questionnaire forms and to review final instructions. Then all start out at the same time.

11. All meet again at the end of the day or that evening to compare notes and make any adjustments in plans that may be necessary to complete the census. The census should be completed in as little time as possible, and if most of it can be done in one day so much the better.

12. Make all interviews in a diplomatic manner and wherever possible fill in the answers to a question without actually asking the question. Make no calls that are not necessary, and use the telephone only where people are well known to the interviewer calling. Remember, however, it is important that the community census be as accurate and complete as

206 DEMOCRACY IS YOU

possible. This is basic information for a good deal of the rest of the community study, and for purposes of actual planning and action.

13. Give the census plenty of publicity throughout the entire community—before, during, and after.

14. Tabulate the results of the census. Add the data collected by other means and write up the report. Arrange the report in a manner which will make it an easy reference by the study group buzz sessions in discussing the questions outlined in Section 3, Part III, of the study guide. Use graphs and drawings wherever possible. At the end of the report give a summary which interprets the meaning and significance of the facts, and which sets forth in pin-point fashion whatever community needs, problems, and opportunities have been revealed by the population survey.

15. The report should be ready for distribution at the opening of the study group meeting on Section 3, Part III, and copies should be in the hands of discussion leaders and recorders at least two days in advance of this meeting.

16. Each member of the Population Committee should make himself or herself an expert on all questions that might be raised by the study group in the discussion scheduled in Section 3, Part III.

17. One or more members of the Population Committee should sit in on the discussion in each buzz session of the study group and help to keep the discussion going in a lively and constructive manner.

BASIC FACTS FOR THE REPORT OF THE POPULATION COMMITTEE

Population

1. Total population of the community, and the total number of families in the community.
   A. Trends in the population and number of families over the past ten years, showing rate of increase or decrease, or fluctuations including both increases and decreases.
   B. Number of people and number of families who live inside the town or city proper, and the number who live out of town. Give percentage of the total population and families that live in town and that live out of town.

2. Sections of the community that are undergoing the greatest growth in population, and sections undergoing the least growth in population at the present time, and reasons why.

3. Annual birth rates and annual death rates in the community, showing trends over the past ten years.

4. Length of residence of adults in the community.

A. Those here:
   less than 1 year
   1 to 5 years
   6 to 10 years
   11 to 15 years
   16 to 20 years
   20 years or longer
B. The number of persons who intend to stay in the community indefinitely, and the number of persons who intend to leave the community either immediately or later on.
   (1) What percentage of the total number of persons in the community have intentions of leaving?
   (2) Give principal reasons for intentions to leave.
C. An estimate of the approximate number of persons who have left the community for good during the past ten years and the principal reasons for leaving.
D. Number and percentage of persons in each high school graduating class during the past ten years who have left the community to stay. (This could be at any time since graduating. Give principal reasons for leaving.)
E. Number and percentage of people now juniors and seniors in high school who intend to leave the community to stay after graduation. Give reasons for intentions to leave.

5. Classification of population by age.
   A. The number of people in this community who are:
      under 1 year old
      1 year old
      2 years old
      3 years old
      4 years old
      5 years old
      6 to 12 years old
      13 to 17 years old
      18 to 20 years old
      21 to 29 years old
      30 to 39 years old
      40 to 49 years old
      50 to 59 years old
      60 to 64 years old
      65 years old and over
   B. What percentage of the total population does each of these age

groups represent? Give any information that might be available to show the trends in each group.

6. Classification of population by sex.
   A. Total number of males.
   B. Total number of females.
   C. Ratio of males to females.
   D. Total number of adult males.
   E. Total number of adult females.
7. Classification of population by marital status.
   A. Total number of married persons in the community. What percentage are these of the total adult population?
   B. Total number of single adult males.
   C. Total number of single adult females.
   D. Ratio of single adult males to single adult females.
   E. Number of marriages during the past ten years.
   F. Number of divorces during the past ten years.
   G. Ratio of divorces to marriages during the past ten years.
   H. Trend of divorce rate in the community, whether increasing or decreasing.

Labor Force

1. Total number of employable persons in the community. (The word "employable" is used here to mean persons who are employed by themselves or by someone else, or who would be employed if they could find a job.)
   A. Percentage of total population employable.
   B. Number and percentage of employable persons male.
   C. Number and percentage of employable persons female.
   D. Number and percentage of employable persons in business for self.
   E. Number and percentage of employable persons employed by someone else.
   F. Number and percentage of persons actually employed at present who are employed full time, part time, seasonally.
      (1) How many of those persons employed part time or seasonally would accept full-time year-round employment if it were made available?
   G. Number and percentage of employed persons who work in *this community,* and the number and percentage who work in *some other community.*
2. Total number of unemployed persons in the community at the

present time. (All persons who are employable, but who are out of a job.)

    A. Percentage of the total labor force. ("Labor force" is used here to mean all persons in the community who are employable.)

    B. Principal reasons for the unemployment.

    C. Seasonal variation, describe and give details.

3. Classification of employed persons by type of economic activity.

    A. Percentage engaged in agriculture.

    B. Percentage engaged in industry.

    ("Industry" is used here to mean manufacturing or processing, logging, mining, fishing, and other such activities which may be distinguished from agriculture and trades and services.)

    C. Percentage engaged in retail and wholesale trades and commercial services.

    D. Percentage engaged in professional services. (Medicine, law, nursing, teaching, etc.)

4. List all occupations represented in this community.

    A. Number and percentage of employed persons in each occupation.

    B. Number and percentage of unemployed persons in each occupation. Which occupations lead the list of unemployment?

    C. Occupations or skills in this community that are not now being used. Number of *employable* persons in each. (A person may be employed in one occupation, but skilled in another.)

5. Number and percentage of persons in the local labor force who are union organized.

    A. Unions represented.

6. Total annual income of the population in this community.

    A. Per capita income.

    B. Total and per capita bank deposits.

    C. Percentage of population filing federal income tax returns.

    D. Average wage scales.

    E. Compare figures on per capita income, per capita bank deposits, percentage of population filing federal income tax returns, and average wage scales with similar figures for the county, state, and nation.

    F. Effective buying power of the local population. (Total income less taxes.)

Birth, Nationality, and Racial Groups

1. List all nationality and racial groups in this community, and estimate the percentage of the total population in each.

2. Are there any nationality or racial groups in this community who live in segregated areas, or are they all mixed in together throughout the whole community?

3. Percentage of the local population born in this community.

4. Percentage of the local population born in America.

5. Percentage of the local population born in this state.

6. List states of the United States that are represented in this community in order of numerical importance.

Formal Educational Attainment

1. Number of persons in this community twenty-one years of age or over who:

> never went to school
> completed 1 to 4 years of school
> completed 5 to 8 years of school
> attended high school but did not finish
> completed high school
> attended college but did not finish
> completed 4 years of college
> completed more than 4 years of college.

2. Number of adult persons in this community who cannot read or write.

3. Compare figures on formal educational attainment with similar figures for the state and nation.

Political Characteristics

1. Number of eligible voters in this community. (Count all persons 21 years of age or older.)

> A. Percentage of these persons now registered to vote. How does this compare with ten years ago?
> B. Percentage of eligible voters who *actually voted* in the last election. How does this compare with other elections for the past ten years?

2. Percent distribution of local voters by political party during the past ten years. (Check from election returns. *Do not ask anyone what political party he or she belongs to.*)

Housing

1. Total number of dwelling units in this community.

> A. Number in town.
> B. Number out of town.

C. Number of these dwelling units that are:
detached houses
apartments or duplexes
auto court units intended for regular living quarters
rooms not elsewhere mentioned that are intended for regular
living quarters
trailers intended for regular living quarters
D. Number of these dwelling units that are:
occupant owned
rented
vacant
2. Condition of dwelling units in this community.
A. The number in good living condition.
B. The number in poor living condition.
3. Number of dwelling units now under construction in this community.
4. Range of rental prices in this community for a dwelling unit.
5. The number of dwelling units in this community that have:
indoor plumbing
outdoor plumbing
private bathroom
shared bathroom
electricity
no electricity
running water
no running water
hot water heater
no hot water heater
6. The number of families in this community who have a telephone,
and the number who do not.
7. The number of families in this community who own an automobile,
and the number who do not.

Following is a suggested form for use in making the population
survey, or census. It should be stressed that this form is for purposes of gathering the basic facts needed to complete the committee's report, and as such the information obtained in this form
should be treated confidentially and used for statistical purposes
only. In taking the census the interviewers should explain this to the
persons being interviewed, and also explain briefly the nature of the
community study as a whole. Some of the questions in the form

given below can be answered by the interviewers themselves without actually asking the questions. It is highly important that no one be given any misunderstanding as to this census, otherwise it will be difficult to obtain the necessary information, and the community study may be injured through the starting of false rumors.

FORM FOR COMMUNITY CENSUS *

Interviewer...Date................Questionnaire No..........
Address ....Enumeration District ....
INTRODUCTION: This is a survey for the .... Community Study. All information is confidential and for statistical purposes only. Your name does not appear anywhere on the questionnaire.

a. Check location of *dwelling unit:*
   1.............Inside City Limits   2.............Outside City Limits
b. Check type of living quarters:
   1.............House   2.............Duplex or flat   3.............Apartment
   4.............Other (Write in.........................) such as trailer, boat, tent, quarters in a structure devoted primarily to business or other non-residential use, etc.
   5.............SPECIAL DWELLING PLACE such as a large rooming house (10 or more lodgers), institution, hotel, tourist court, military installation, etc.
   (*Note to interviewer:* If this is a SPECIAL DWELLING PLACE, do *not* ask remaining questions. A special committee will enumerate these. Write in name and address of structure and turn in your questionnaire to your crew leader.)

1. What things do you *like most* about living in this community? ....
   ....

2. What things do you *dislike most* about living in this community? ....
   ....

3. Do you rent this house?
   1.............Occupied by renter   2.............Occupied by owner
          3.............Vacant
   If vacant, check if—
   4.............Vacant, for sale
   5.............Vacant, sold, not yet occupied

* Acknowledgment is made to Edith Dyer Rainboth of the Washington Public Opinion Laboratory, University of Washington, for special assistance in the preparation of this form.

6............Vacant, for rent

7............Vacant, rented, not yet occupied

8............Vacant, not for sale or rent

9............Vacant, seasonal

4. How many rooms in this dwelling unit, not including bathrooms?
............rooms

5. How many bedrooms in this unit?............bedrooms

6. Does this unit have a telephone? 1............Yes   2............No

7. Does this unit have electric lighting? 1............Yes   2............No

8. Does this unit have central heating? 1............Yes   2............No

9. Does this unit have a water heater? 1............Yes   2............No
If "yes," check whether............electric,............gas, or............other
(specify)............

10. How many radio sets in this unit?............

11. How many television sets in this unit?............

12. How many automobiles are owned by members of this household?
....
(Exclude automobiles used solely for business.)

13. Piped water supply:

1............Hot and cold piped running water inside this structure

2............Only cold piped running water in this structure

3............Piped running water outside this structure

4............No piped running water (Hand pump, well, etc.)

14. Installed bathtub or shower:

1............For this unit's exclusive use

2............Shared with another unit

3............No bathtub or shower for this unit

15. Type of toilet:

1............Flush toilet inside this structure

2............Flush toilet outside this structure

3............Privy, outhouse, or chemical toilet

4............No toilet for this unit

16. Toilet—exclusive use:

1............For this unit's exclusive use

2............Shared with another unit

3............No toilet for this unit

17. Kitchen sink:

1............For this unit's exclusive use

2............Shared with another unit

3............No kitchen sink for this unit

18. Heating equipment:

1............Piped steam or hot water

    2............Warm air furnace

    3............Other means with flue

    4............Other means without flue

    5............Not heated

19. Heating fuel most used:

    1............Coal or coke

    2............Wood

    3............Utility gas

    4............Bottled gas

    5............Liquid fuel

    6............Electricity

    7............Other fuel (write in............)

    8............Not heated

20. Cooking fuel most often used:

    1............Coal or coke

    2............Wood

    3............Utility gas

    4............Bottled gas

    5............Liquid fuel

    6............Electricity

    7............Other fuel (write in............)

    8............No cooking

21. How many members of this household were born in this community?............

22. How many persons are members of this household?............

    (Note to Interviewer: Count as members of the household, all persons who are living in this dwelling unit.)

23. Please fill the columns on p. 215 for each member of this household.

24. Please fill in the columns on p. 216 for each member of the household 14 years of age and over. Enter the numerical designation for each person 14 years of age and over that was used in question 23. To facilitate asking these employment questions, copy from question 23, the relationship to head, sex and age of each of these persons.

25. How many persons from this dwelling unit are in military service?
....

26. Are there any physically handicapped individuals in this household who are available for employment? If "Yes" list type of employment capable of doing. (Copy same numerical identification of person used in question 23.)

(Note: Persons being counted are identified by a number as indicated across the top of columns.)	Person 1	Person 2	Person 3	Person 4	Person 5	Person 6
a. RELATIONSHIP: Enter relationship of person to head of household, as HEAD, WIFE, DAUGHTER, SON, GRANDSON, MOTHER-IN-LAW, LODGER, LODGER'S WIFE, MAID, HIRED HAND, ETC.	HEAD					
b. SEX: Enter code M-Male, F-Female						
c. RACE: Enter code W—White, N—Negro, IND—American Indian, JAP—Japanese, CHI—Chinese, FIL—Filipino, other —spell out.						
d. How many years has .... lived in this community?						
e. How old was .... on his last birthday? (If under one year of age, enter month of birth as May, Dec., etc.)						
f. Is .... now married, widowed, divorced, separated, or never married? Enter code: Mar, Wd, D, Sep, Nev.						
g. What State (or foreign country) was .... born in?						
h. If foreign born, is .... naturalized? Enter Yes, No, or AP if born abroad of American parents.						
i. What is the highest grade of school .... has attended?						
j. Did .... finish this grade?						
k. Did .... attend business college or other type of vocational school?						
l. Does .... intend to stay in this community indefinitely? Enter yes or no.						
m. If .... intends to move away from this community, enter briefly the reason why.						

	Person	Person	Person	Person
a. RELATIONSHIP (Copy from question 23a)	HEAD			
b. SEX (Copy from question 23b)				
c. AGE (Copy from question 23e)				
d. What was .... doing *most* of last week? Enter codes as follows: WK—Working for pay or profit or without pay on family farm or business H—Keeping house S—Going to school U—Unable to work OT—Other (write in)				
e. Was .... looking for work last week?				
f. If "Yes," was .... looking for (enter code)— F—Full-time work P—Part-time work S—Seasonal work				
g. What is reason for unemployment?				
h. How many hours did .... work last week? (Working for pay or profit or without pay on family farm or business)				
i. How many weeks did .... work during the last 12 months?				
j. If now working part-time or seasonally, would .... accept full-time-year-round work if offered?				
k. (Fill items k, l, and m for present job if now employed. If unemployed, enter for last full-time civilian job or business.) What kind of work was .... doing? (Example: Heel nailer, file clerk, sales clerk, farmer, farm helper, never worked)				
l. What kind of business or industry was .... working in? (Example: Shoe factory, State Tax Commission, retail grocery store, farm)				
m. Was .... working for: P—Private employer G—Government O—In own business NP—Without pay on family farm or business				
n. Other work or skills for which suited				
o. Is place of work located in this community?				
p. Is place of work located in some other community?				

*Special Instructions to Interviewers Using
the Community Census Form*

1. Count living quarters as dwelling units *if* they fit the following definition: In general, a dwelling unit is a group of rooms or a single room, occupied or intended for occupancy as *separate living quarters,* by a family or other group of persons living together, or by a person living alone. Where there is doubt apply the following tests:
   (A). Does it have *separate cooking facilities,* or:
   (B). Does it have *two or more rooms and a separate entrance?*
2. Special Dwelling Places (listed in the census form) should be enumerated by a special crew appointed for this purpose by the chairman of the Population Committee. In counting the persons who live in these places many of the questions in the census form will not apply. Therefore, the special crew will use only those questions that do apply.
3. *Do not* count persons who are in the community as temporary visitors or as travelers, or tourists, or just passing through—*unless* they have *no usual residence elsewhere.*
4. In the census form, Question 23, parts d through m, a blank (...............) is used in place of the words "he" or "she" to refer to each person of the household about whom the questions are being asked, i.e., Person 1, Person 2, etc.
5. Wherever the answer to a question asked in the form is obvious (such as race), the interviewer should simply fill in the answer without asking it.
6. For purposes of race the interviewer should simply assume that all members of the same household are the same.

7

For the Community
Organizations Committee

THE COMMUNITY ORGANIZATIONS COMMITTEE HAS THE RESPONSIBILITY of making an analysis of the organizational life of the community. Its report should contain all facts and information needed by the buzz sessions to discuss intelligently the questions set forth in Section 5, Part III, of the study guide. These questions should be used by the committee as its outline of research, and the report written up in such a manner as to make it an easy reference for purposes of discussing these questions in the buzz sessions.

A suggested questionnaire is provided in this outline which the committee may use for purposes of collecting the basic information from which to write its report. One of these questionnaires should be filled out for each organization in the community except churches. The churches will be covered by the Church Committee.

In the report no mention should be made of any organization by name, other than to make a list of those that exist in the community and to give a calendar of organizational meetings. It is highly important that the head of each organization in the community understand the nature of this survey so that no false ideas will be created, and so that the committee will be able to get the kind of cooperation needed to make the survey.

In order to fill out the questionnaires a member of the committee should call on the head or the secretary of each organization *in person* and explain the purpose of the survey. Each organizational head or secretary, or both, should be informed that the information requested in the questionnaire is for statistical purposes only and is simply one phase of the effort to make a realistic study of the overall life of the community. The community organizations constitute an important part of that life and have a great deal to do with the vitality and progress of the entire community. It should be explained that the committee is not concerned with any particular organization by name, but that in order to make a factual report on the over-all picture of the community's organizational life, it is necessary to collect the data requested in the questionnaire on each organization individually. The information from all the questionnaires will then be consolidated for the final report and no organization will be identified by name in connection with any of the information obtained.

It will be noted that in Section 5, Part III, of the study guide several questions are asked in regard to the total number of organizational memberships in the community as compared with the total number of actual persons who hold these memberships, the total number who are active as compared to the number who are inactive, etc. Also there are questions pertaining to the total number of organizational offices and committee chairmanships as compared to the total number of persons actually holding these posts, the total number who are active as compared to the total number who are inactive, etc. These questions also ask what percentage of the total population of the community is active in organizations and what percentage is inactive.

In order to answer these questions it is necessary to obtain a list, first, of the officers and committee chairmen of each organization, and to note which of these are active and which ones are inactive. Second, it is necessary to obtain a list of the entire membership of each organization in the community.

From the first list a count can be made of the total number of organizational offices and committee chairmanships in the community. A count can also be made of exactly how many persons hold these offices and chairmanships. And by placing an "A" for active or an "X" for inactive in front of each name, a count can be made of how many of the organizational officers and committee chairmen in the community are active and how many are inactive. Once these statistics are obtained, the list of names can be destroyed.

From the organizational membership lists the committee can make up one consolidated list of names, and by placing a mark after each name for each time it appears on an organization's roster, and by placing an "A" for active or an "X" for inactive in front of each name, the statistics called for in the report can be obtained by simply making a series of actual counts. Again, the list of names can then be destroyed.

But unless the purpose of this information is properly explained at the time the questionnaires are filled in, the committee may find that some of the organizations will not be willing to cooperate. If these matters are explained so that each organizational head understands why the information is being requested and that it is for statistical purposes only, there should be no difficulty in getting the necessary cooperation and information requested.

In no case should the questionnaires be mailed or simply handed to someone in the organization to fill out and then return. It has been found from experience in working with groups of this kind in other communities that once a questionnaire gets out of the hands of the committee the possibility of misunderstanding and incomplete returns is greatly increased.

In addition to collecting the basic facts needed to answer the questions set forth in Section 5, Part III, the Community Organizations Committee is also responsible for drawing certain conclusions as to the meaning and significance of these facts, for pointing up any community problems that may be reflected, and for recomending action that might help to bring about a solution of these problems.

Beyond the information called for in the study guide, there may be certain organizational problems in this particular community. If this is the case, the committee should point out these problems and call for a discussion of them in the study group. If the committee wishes to change any of the questions asked in Section 5, Part III, or add to them in order to make certain that the discussion covers all problems and recommendations that pertain to this particular community, it should do so.

Part of the information for this committee's report will be obtained from the report of the Population Committee.

Following is a suggested outline for the committee's report:

1. Purpose of the report.
2. How the information was collected.
3. Findings of the committee.
4. Summary of conclusions.
5. Summary of community needs and problems posed.
6. Recommendations for action.

The committee may also wish to add another heading to cover further questions which it feels should be brought up for discussion in the study group with regard to specific problems not covered by the questions given in Section 5, Part III.

SUMMARY

Suggested steps for getting the work of the Community Organizations Committee completed are in summary as follows:

1. Set a date for the first meeting of the committee.
2. Each member prepare himself in advance of this meeting by read-

ing carefully (a) Section 5, Part III, (b) this special outline, and (c) all other references to the Community Organizations Committee as noted in the index of the study guide.

3. Make a list of all organizations in the community.

4. Review Section 5, Part III, and check the organizational questionnaire given below in this outline to make certain that it includes all the questions the committee wants it to include.

5. Have enough questionnaires mimeographed to cover all the organizations, plus a few extra.

6. Divide up the list of organizations among the members of the committee and give each member the proper supply of questionnaires. Set a deadline for their return.

7. Call in person on the head or the secretary of each organization, explain the purpose of the survey, and by personal interview fill out the questionnaire. Stress the fact that the information being asked for is confidential and urge that the answers be given as *bluntly and honestly as possible. Remember, the purpose of this survey is to seek FACTS which will reflect the true picture of organizational life in this community as it actually is, not a glowing version of what somebody wishes it were.*

8. Tabulate the data as collected in the questionnaires.

9. Write up these data for the report, presenting the facts and the committee's interpretations as to their meaning and significance in as clear and understandable a manner as possible. Add to the report any additional information obtained through means other than the questionnaire. If graphs or drawings will help to make the report clearer they should be used. Summarize and pin-point any community problems posed, and the committee's recommendations for action.

10. The committee's report is due in the hands of the study group secretary at least one full week in advance of the meeting of the study group on Section 5, Part III.

11. One or more members of the committee should be present in each buzz session of the study group and should be prepared to help keep the discussion moving toward constructive ends.

FORM FOR USE IN SURVEY OF
COMMUNITY ORGANIZATIONS

Fill out one of these forms for each organization in the community. This will give the committee most of the basic data needed for preparation of its final report. Information obtained in this form is confidential and for statistical purposes only. Names of individual organizations are not to be used in the committee's report. The committee is not interested in any one organization specifically, but is interested only in an over-all picture of the organizational life of the community as a whole.

Name of organization: ....

Purpose for which organized: ....

Principal activities: ....

Has the original purpose of this organization changed at any time? Yes .... No .... If answer is "yes," what changes have been made? ....

....

How many members are there in this organization? ....

What is the approximate attendance at meetings? ....

Type of membership:

    A. Sex .... B. Age group ....

    C. Occupational groups represented ....

    D. Major interests represented ....

What are the qualifications for memberships?

Restrictions as to membership, if any:

What are the annual dues? .... Assessments? ....

Are there any groups in the community who are not included in the membership of this organization, but which the organization would like to have included? Yes .... No .... If "yes" what are these groups? ....

When are the meetings of this organization held? Date ....

Time .... Place ....

Does this organization have any active cooperative relationships or joint programs with other organizations? Yes .... No .... Is this an established practice, or does it happen only once in a while? ....

If this organization does have active cooperative relationships or joint programs with other organizations, please give names of other organizations:

Name of Organization	Nature of Relationships or Joint Programs
....	....
....	....
....	....
....	....
....	....

Are there any organizations in the community whose policies or aims are in opposition to this one? Yes .... No .... If "yes," give names of other organizations and nature of differences:

Name of Organization   Nature of Differences

....
....
....
....

Are there any organizations in this community whose organizational functions and activities (other than regular meetings) conflict in scheduling with this one? Yes .... No ....
If "yes," give names of other organizations, and activities that conflict:

Name of Organization   Activities that Conflict

....
....
....
....
....

What have been the most outstanding accomplishments of this organization for community improvement within the past year?

....
....
....
....

If none, state "none."
How would you rate this organization (being absolutely honest) on a scale of ten, assuming that zero is very inactive, and ten is very active?
    0–1–2–3–4–5–6–7–8–9–10
Very   Very
inactive   active   Rating:
Do the committees of this organization function as well as they should?
Yes...............No...............If answer is "no," please give some of the reasons why:

....
....
....
....

Is this organization one in which strangers quickly feel at home?

Yes .... No .... Sometimes .... If answer is "no," or "sometimes," please give reasons why:

....

....

What are the outstanding problems, if any, of this organization at the present time?

....

....

....

Is there active participation in this organization by all or most of the members, or do a few usually do most of the work? ....

In order to make possible a count of the total number of memberships, the number of different persons holding more than one membership, the number who don't hold any, and other such statistical data, please give the information asked for below. This information is for statistical purposes only.

List all existing offices and committee chairmanships in this organization, give names of persons holding same, and indicate by a check mark which of these officers and committee chairmen are active and which are inactive:

Name of Office or Committee Chairmanship	Name of person holding same	Active	Inactive
1.			
2.			
3.			
4.			
5.			
6.			
7.			
8.			
9.			
10.			

On a separate sheet of paper please list the entire membership of this organization. In front of each name please indicate by an "A" those who are regarded as active workers in the organization, and indicate by an "X" those who could be regarded as inactive. The word "active" in this case means more than the mere payment of dues. This information will make it possible to count not only the total number of organizational memberships in the community, but the actual number of members, how many hold more than one membership, and other such statistical data. Give in the space below any other comments concerning this organization that might be useful to the committee for purposes of analyzing the organizational life of the community. ....

....

....

....

....

8

For the Church Committee

THE CHURCH COMMITTEE IS RESPONSIBLE FOR MAKING A REPORT THAT will present all facts which the study group should have in order to discuss intelligently the questions set forth for the buzz sessions in Section 6, Part III. These questions should be used by the committee as its outline of research.

The Church Committee may initiate any research that it deems necessary to present a well-rounded picture of the role of the church in the life of the community, but should avoid issues that would tend to create a controversy over religious beliefs. The main job of the committee is to show in a factual way the activities and functions of the church in the life of the community at the present time, and to make recommendations for action which will help to strengthen the church as a force for the further development of a wholesome community life.

Included in this outline is a suggested questionnaire which may be filled out for each church in the community. The information obtained from these questionnaires, together with any other information the committee wishes to present, may then be assembled for purposes of writing the final report. This report should be designed to cover the following points:

1. A statement on the purpose of the committee.
2. Methods used in collecting the information.
3. Findings of the committee.
4. A summary of problems and needs.
5. Recommendations for action to be discussed by the study group.
6. Any special questions in addition to those given in Section 6, Part III, of the guide which pertain to specific local conditions, and which the committee feels should be brought up for discussion in the study group.

The committee should organize its report in such a manner that it will be an easy reference for the various buzz sessions in discussing the questions outlined in Section 6, Part III, and any other questions which the committee may wish to pose for discussion.

Before starting its research, personal contact should be made with each minister in the community in order to make certain that he understands the committee's purposes and is willing to cooperate with the program.

SUMMARY

Suggested steps for completing the work of the Church Committee are in summary as follows:

1. Set a date for the first meeting of the committee.
2. All committee members prepare themselves in advance of this meeting by reading carefully (a) Section 6, Part III, (b) this special outline, and (c) all other references to the Church Committee that are indexed in the guide.
3. Check the questionnaire given below and make certain that it covers all the information the committee wants it to cover.
4. Assign jobs to each committee member and set deadlines for completion of the work.
5. Make enough copies of the questionnaire for each church in the community and get them filled out by members of the committee through personal consultation with the minister or other proper persons in each church.
6. Decide what additional information the committee should have, if any, and make necessary arrangements for getting it.
7. Assemble all information collected.
8. The report is due in the hands of the study group secretary at least one full week in advance of the meeting of the group on Section 6, Part III.
9. At least one member of the committee should sit in on each buzz

session at this meeting and be prepared to help keep the discussion moving toward constructive ends.

Church Survey Questionnaire
(To be filled out for each church in the community)

Name of church ....

Location of church ....

Name of pastor ....

Size of membership .... Average attendance at regular church worship services .... Number of members active .... Number of members inactive .... How does this compare with the situation ten years ago? ....

Twenty years ago? ....

Pastor's opinion on the extent to which people in this community participate in church activities. Is participation sufficient: Yes .... No .... If participation is not sufficient, why isn't it? ....

....

....

What practical suggestions can be made for increasing attendance and participation in this church? ....

....

....

....

List all programs and activities offered by this church for people to participate in: ....

....

....

....

Which of these programs are designed especially for young people? ....

....

What age levels are served by the youth programs? ....

To what extent do the young people actually participate in planning these programs? ....

....

How many young people are active in these programs? ....

Is this regarded as enough? Yes .... No .... If "no" give reasons why more young people do not participate: ....

....

Which of the programs or activities in this church contribute directly and specifically toward furthering worthwhile community projects? ....
....
....
....

Explain how or in what way: ....
....
....
....

To what extent does the community ask assistance from this church in specific projects for community improvement? ....
....

Does this church have any established cooperative relationships or joint projects with other churches in the community? Yes .... No ....
If it does, what are the projects? ....
....

Is this church building adequately suited to serve the needs of this community? Yes .... No .... If the answer is "no" what changes should be made? ....

Is there an active council of churches or ministerial association in this community? Yes .... No .... If not, should one be organized?
....

Does the physical appearance of this church add to the beauty of the community? Yes .... No .... If not, what changes are needed?
....

Are repairs needed? Yes .... No .... If the answer to this question is "yes" please list below the repairs needed:

Interior	*Exterior*
....	....
....	....
....	....
....	....

Is landscaping needed? Yes............... No .... Is exterior clean-up and paint up needed? Yes .... No .... What general improvements, if any, are needed to improve the exterior appearance of this church?......
....

Is this church adequately identified by an attractive sign? Yes ....
No ....

In summary, the most important needs of this church for improving its service to the community are: ....
....
....

Statement of the pastor as to the value of the church to community life:
....
....

Recommendations for action which might help the community to gain greater values from its churches: ....
....
....
....

9

For the Government Committee

THE GOVERNMENT COMMITTEE IS RESPONSIBLE FOR DRAWING UP A RE-port which will help all participants in the study group to gain a better understanding of their municipal and county governments. If the committee wishes to go further and assemble information on state or federal government it should do so.

The committee should make certain that its report covers all facts and information necessary for an intelligent discussion in the study group buzz sessions of the questions set forth in Section 7, Part III, and that the report is arranged in such a way as to make it an easy reference for this purpose. The report should be written in narrative form with whatever charts or drawings may be necessary to help make it clear and readily understood.

In addition to the questions for discussion in the buzz sessions as set forth in Section 7, Part III, the committee may wish to add other questions for discussion which pertain more specifically to particular local conditions or situations. Or it may wish to substitute other questions for some of those asked in the guide. The committee should not hesitate to do this if it is deemed necessary in order to bring out in the discussion questions of specific local importance.

Following is a suggested outline for the committee's report:

1. Purpose of the report.
2. How the information was collected.
3. Findings of the committee.
4. Summary of community needs and problems posed.
5. Recommendations for action that might help to meet these needs and problems. These recommendations should be given in as specific and direct a manner as possible. They may have to do with actual changes or improvements in governmental services, or they may have to do with educational activities which will help to develop a better informed citizenry.

The committee may also wish to add another heading to cover further questions which it feels should be brought up for discussion in the study group.

In order to present the basic facts that will be needed for the discussion in the study group buzz sessions, the report should cover at least the following points:

1. An organizational chart showing the structure of municipal government in this community. This chart should show all departments and offices and their relationship to each other. It should be accompanied by a written explanation which tells clearly what the chart means and how the municipal government operates.

2. A detailed written description of the functions of each office and department shown in the organizational chart. This description should (a) describe duties and responsibilities, (b) tell how much each office and department costs the taxpayers, (c) state how the holder of each office is chosen, (d) give the term of office, and (e) describe the kind of background and qualifications, or the kind of knowledge and experience that a candidate should have to do a good job in each office.

3. Needs and problems, if any, in the services, functions, or operations of each of the municipal offices and departments. See Questions II and III in Section 7, Part III.

4. An organizational chart showing the structure of county government for this community. This chart should show all departments and

offices and their relationship to each other. It should be accompanied by a written explanation which tells clearly what the chart means and how the county government operates.

5. A detailed written description of the functions of each office and department shown in the organizational chart. This description should (a) describe duties and responsibilities, (b) tell how much each office and department costs the taxpayers in this community, (c) state how the holder of each office is chosen, (d) give the term of office, and (e) describe the kind of background and qualifications or the kind of knowledge and experience a candidate should have to do a good job in each office.

6. Needs and problems, if any, in the services, functions, and operations of each of the county offices and departments. See Questions V and VI in Section 7, Part III.

7. A description of the relationships between the local municipal government and the local county government. This might also be extended to include state and federal governments.

8. If the committee wishes to go beyond municipal and county governments in its report, information similar to that asked for on municipal and county governments under Points 1 through 6 above may be given on state or federal government. This might be given in less detail.

9. The percentage of eligible voters in this community who are registered and the percentage who vote. See Question VII in Section 7, Part III. This information may be obtained from the report of the Population Committee. The Government Committee's report should also include a statement in this connection from the study group secretary's report on the discussion which the buzz sessions had on Question XV in Section 3, Part III, and a recommendation for action by means of which the percentage of eligible voters who vote might be increased.

10. A description of the principal techniques of propaganda that are commonly used in political campaigns and that are used by organizations and individuals for purposes of molding public opinion one way or the other on political issues. The reason for including information on this point in the report is to help stimulate people in the community to want to learn how to sift out and weigh facts in order to become more intelligent voters. It may be possible to develop considerable interest in a special course of study for this purpose. Such a course could well become a part of a community program of education for adults.

11. The report should include whatever factual information the Government Committee can make available on Questions VIII through XI in Section 7, Part III.

12. In addition to the questions for the buzz sessions given in Section

7, Part III, the committee should set forth in its report specific information on each of the following points:

A. How candidates for public office in the local municipal, county, and state elections are placed in nomination.
B. A calendar of election dates and pertinent information for becoming a registered voter.
C. The organizational structure and operation of American political parties.
D. The legal controls over expenditures and operations of political parties.
E. The method of choosing election officials and the duties of these officials.

SUMMARY

Steps for getting the work of the Government Committee completed are in summary as follows:

1. Set a date for the first meeting of the committee.
2. Each member of the committee get prepared in advance of this meeting by reading carefully (a) Section 7, Part III, (b) this special outline, and (c) all other references to the Government Committee which are indexed in the guide.
3. Work out a plan of procedure for collecting the information called for in this outline.
4. Assign jobs to each member of the committee and set deadlines for the completion of assignments.
5. Assemble the information and write the report.
6. The report is due in the hands of the study group secretary at least one full week in advance of the study group meeting on Section 7, Part III.
7. At least one member of the committee should sit in on each buzz session at the meeting on Section 7, Part III, and be prepared to help keep the discussion moving toward constructive ends.

10

For the Social Agencies Committee

THE SOCIAL AGENCIES COMMITTEE IS RESPONSIBLE FOR DRAWING UP A report which will help all participants in the study group to gain a better understanding of the objectives and functions of the social agencies that operate in this community. The committee should make certain that its report covers all facts and information necessary for an intelligent discussion in the study group buzz sessions of the questions set forth in Section 8, Part III, and that the report is arranged in such a way as to make it an easy reference for this purpose. The report should be written in narrative form with whatever charts or drawings may be necessary to help make it clear and readily understood.

In addition to the questions for discussion in the buzz sessions as set forth in Section 8, Part III, the committee may wish to add other questions for discussion which pertain more specifically to particular local conditions or situations. Or it may wish to substitute other questions for some of those asked in the guide. The committee should not hesitate to do this if it is deemed necessary in order to bring out in the discussion questions which are of specific local importance.

Following is a suggested outline for the committee's report:

1. Purpose of the report.
2. How the information was collected.
3. Findings of the committee.
4. Summary of community needs and problems posed.
5. Recommendations for action that might help to meet these needs and problems.

The committee may also wish to add another heading to cover

further questions which it feels should be brought up for discussion in the study group.

The committee's report should cover facts and information concerning at least the following points:

1. A list of all social agencies whose services are available in this community at the present time with a description of each agency covering information on the following points:

    A. What services does this agency perform? Describe in detail. To help clarify the functions of the agency two or three case histories out of the agency's files may be written up briefly from a human interest point of view for inclusion in the report. These histories should, of course, be written in such a manner as to not reveal personal identities.

    B. Are there any good motion-picture films that would illustrate the functions and services of this agency? If so, where might these films be shown?

    C. What groups of people does this agency deal with?

    D. How and under what conditions may an individual obtain the services of this agency? Whom must he contact? What is this agency's address?

    E. Does this agency see any needs in this community for social services that are not being met at the present time? If so, describe the needs that exist, give reasons why they exist, and reasons why they are not being met. What definite action might be taken by the community that would help make it possible to meet these needs?

    F. Could the operations of this agency be improved or performed more efficiently? If so, what changes should be recommended?

    G. Where does this agency's financial support come from? Is it privately supported or tax supported? How is the money obtained? Does it have any financial problems? If so, explain each problem.

2. What institutions or organizations other than the specialized social agencies render social services to the people in this community?

    A. What services is each of these institutions or organizations equipped to render?

    B. Are these institutions or organizations able to meet the need for such services as they see it? If not, why aren't they? Explain.

    C. Do these institutions or organizations see any needs in this community for social services in addition to those listed under "B" immediately above, that are not now being met? If so, describe each of these needs, explain the cause for each one, and state reasons why these needs are not now being met. What definite action might be taken by the people of the community that would help make it possible to meet these needs?

3. Problems which the committee sees, if any, in addition to those brought out in the information covered above, that are not now being adequately dealt with.

A. What about family guidance services?

B. Home nursing instruction?

C. Instruction in mother and child care?

D. Instruction in prenatal care?

E. Children's counseling and guidance services, particularly with regard to personality and emotional problems?

F. Services to help the aged help themselves to make their lives happier and more productive?

G. What about rehabilitation of maladjusted and handicapped persons?

4. Information covering Question V in Section 8, Part III.

5. Draw up a chart, accompanied by adequate explanation, showing the welfare load in this community at the present time. Show the trend of this load, whether it is rising or falling, and the variation by season of the year.

To obtain this information, contact in person the administrator of the local welfare office. It is important to see the administrator first and get his or her cooperation. Do not start with an office clerk or receptionist.

The committee's report should show the total number of persons receiving public assistance and the total cost of this assistance on a monthly and annual basis. In some places this often amounts to one of the largest payrolls in the community.

Break down the total public assistance load into the various categories listed by the Welfare Department and make a list of the various causes for people being dependent in each category.

The report should also contain a statement explaining the current public assistance laws in the state and the policies of administration in current practice.

Although unemployment compensation is not the same as direct public assistance, the committee's report should contain the same kind of information in this category as is called for on the public assistance load.

What constructive action could be taken by the people of this community to help remove the causes for public assistance and unemployment compensation in each of the various categories listed above? Or what could be done from within the community to help reduce the need for public assistance and unemployment compensation in this community? The committee should draw up recommendations on these questions for presentation to the study group.

SUMMARY

Steps for getting the work of the Social Agencies Committee completed are in summary as follows:

1. Set a date for the first meeting of the committee.

2. Each member of the committee should prepare himself in advance of this meeting by reading carefully (a) Section 8, Part III, (b) this special outline, and (c) all other references to the Social Agencies Committee which are indexed in the guide.

3. Work out a plan of procedure for collecting the information called for in this outline. This will mean personal contact with each social agency and other institution rendering social services in this community.

4. Assign jobs to each member of the committee and set deadlines for the completion of assignments.

5. Assemble the information and write the report. Make certain that it is presented in such a way as to stimulate a lively discussion.

6. The report is due in the hands of the study group secretary at least one full week in advance of the study group meeting on Section 8, Part III.

7. At least one member of the committee should sit in on each buzz session at the meeting on Section 8, Part III, and be prepared to help keep the discussion moving toward constructive ends.

11

For the Library Committee

THE LIBRARY COMMITTEE HAS THE RESPONSIBILITY OF MAKING AN analysis of the community's needs and resources for public library services and facilities, and of writing a report which will present all the facts necessary for the study group to conduct an intelligent discussion of this aspect of community life.

The report of this committee is scheduled for discussion during the last meeting of the study group on Section 11, Part III. The study guide does not include a list of prepared questions for discussion in the buzz sessions on the library and its services in the life of the community. Therefore, one of the responsibilities of the Library Committee is to prepare for inclusion at the end of its report a list of questions for discussion in the buzz sessions on the facts and needs which the report brings out.

In preparing these questions every effort should be made to stimulate a lively and constructive discussion which will come to grips with the actual needs and problems set forth in the report, and which will help to provide an opportunity for all participants in the study group to gain a better understanding of the services the library is rendering at the present time, and of the services it could render if certain needs were met. If there is no library in the community, the committee should investigate the extent of the need for establishing a library, outline the meaning it would have in terms of helping to develop a richer community life, the problems that would have to be met in obtaining library services, and present a suggested plan for achieving this objective.

SUMMARY

Suggested steps for getting the work of the Library Committee organized are in summary as follows:

1. Set a date for the first meeting of the committee.

2. Each member get prepared for this meeting by reading carefully (a) Section 11, Part III, and (b) this committee outline.

3. At the first meeting of the committee review the material in Section 11, Part III, and discuss how it applies to the services of a library, and the various ways that a good library might contribute to the educational life of the community.

4. At this meeting adopt a plan of operations, and decide how the information needed for the committee's report is to be obtained.

5. Assign jobs to each member of the committee and set deadlines for completion of assignments.

6. Conduct the research, tabulate and assemble data, and write the report. Write questions for discussion in the buzz sessions, and include at the end of the report. The report is due in the hands of the study group secretary at least one full week in advance of the night the study group holds its last meeting on Section 11, Part III.

7. At least one member of the Library Committee should sit in with each buzz session and be prepared to help keep the discussion moving in a lively manner toward constructive ends.

Following is a suggested outline for the committee's report:

1. Purpose of the report.

2. A statement on the role and significance of a library in the life of the community.

3. How the information was collected.

4. Findings of the committee.

5. Summary of conclusions as to community needs and problems posed.

6. Recommendations for action, including a proposed plan for meeting whatever needs were disclosed by the committee's investigation.

RESEARCH OUTLINE FOR THE LIBRARY COMMITTEE

1. List and describe all library services and programs that are in operation in the community at the present time.

2. Describe the extent to which the present library program provides adequate services in each of the following areas.

    A. Reference and technical books.

    B. Nonfiction books of general and specific interest.

    C. Fiction—quality and quantity.

    D. Magazines and newspapers.

E. Book reviews which keep the local public informed as to new books worth knowing about.

F. Adult education activities, including such things as discussion groups and forums, film service, efforts to help local citizens keep themselves informed on matters of community and public interest.

3. Describe the present library and current needs from the standpoint of physical facilities.

A. The building itself.

(1) Appearance inside and outside. Is it an attractive place, and if not, in what ways is it unattractive? What needs to be done to improve it, if anything?

(2) Available space for books, for reading, for meetings and various educational activities. If there are needs for improvement, what are they, and how might they be obtained?

(3) Maintenance, lighting, heat, etc.

B. Equipment and supplies.

(1) What does the present library have? What is needed, if anything, and how might it be obtained?

4. Personnel, and personnel needs, if any.

5. Budget. Describe the present cost of operation and show where the money comes from. If there are needs for increasing the budget, what are they, and how might this be accomplished?

6. Extent to which the present library is actually being used. Does the committee feel that it should be used more? If so, why isn't it? What changes would have to be made to bring about greater use?

7. If the community has no library service, is such a service needed? If so, what should such a service include? How might it be obtained?

8. Make a list of all agencies and persons who might be in a position to furnish special advice for purposes of assessing the community's needs for improved library services, and the best methods for meeting these needs. The committee or one of its members should make personal contact with each of these agencies and obtain from them whatever information they may have to offer for inclusion in the report.

12

For the Economic Development Committee

THE ECONOMIC DEVELOPMENT COMMITTEE IS RESPONSIBLE FOR MAKING an inventory of all resources and possible opportunities for the diversification and development of the community's economy.

In order to accomplish this job in an effective manner the Economic Development Committee is divided into three subcommittees. These are Trades and Services, Industry, and Agriculture. There should be a chairman for the entire committee to coordinate the work of the three subcommittees, and a subchairman for each subcommittee.

This committee is also responsible for the collection of all facts and information which will be needed by the study group for an intelligent discussion of the material given in Section 9, Part III. It should not expect that the study group buzz sessions will be able to cover the committee's entire report in complete detail, nor would such a complete discussion by the study group as a whole be necessary. However, the committee should endeavor to make its report as complete as possible in order that the study group may have available a factual document which may be used for purposes of actual planning and action. In it should be material from which special reports for interested persons may be written on specific investment opportunities. The report as a whole should constitute a reference source on all opportunities which offer the possibility of developing new jobs and payrolls throughout the community.

A research outline is set forth below showing the kinds of facts and information that should be included in the committee's report. Part of the information for this committee will be available from the report of the Population Committee.

It will be noted that Section 9, Part III, is divided into subject material which may be used for three meetings of the study group.

The first of these study group meetings is intended as a general discussion of the over-all picture of the economic life and potential of the community, and a set of questions is provided for this purpose. These questions are not intended to develop the kind of detailed information needed in actual planning and direct action. However, it is of utmost importance that a good background of group thinking, general knowledge, and points of view be focused on some of the broad factors that in general condition the local economy so that the study group as a whole may have an opportunity to understand some of the reasons why the present economy is what it is, and to decide for themselves what type of new development, if any, they would like to see brought about.

This is the essential purpose of the questions for discussion for the first meeting on Section 9, Part III. The discussion on these questions should also help to create a better understanding of some of the factors that are likely to shape the community's economic future, and it should help to generate many ideas as to what the people themselves may do to mold the future of their economy as they would like it to be. This discussion should help to point up ideas on what changes, if any, the community would like to see made in the present treatment of economic resources, and it should help to stimulate a fuller appreciation of what must be done from within the community itself if the full potential for economic development is to be realized.

Therefore, inasmuch as the questions for discussion in the first meeting on Section 9, Part III, are for purposes of discussion only, no report from the Economic Development Committee should be distributed at this first meeting. However, it is nonetheless essential that all members of the committee come to this meeting well prepared to help ensure a lively and thought-provoking discussion which will end with a set of definite conclusions and recommendations.

In order to make this kind of preparation the committee should hold a thorough discussion of its own on each question posed for discussion in the first meeting of the study group on Section 9, Part III, some time in advance of that meeting. Complete notes on the committee's discussion on these questions should be written up in full and a copy given to the study group secretary for distribution to each discussion leader and recorder several days in advance of the study group meeting. This will enable the discussion leaders and recorders to have the benefit of the committee's thinking and thus to help prepare themselves for leading the discussion. Also, one or more members of the Economic Development Committee should sit in on each of the buzz sessions at this study group meeting and be prepared to help keep the discussion moving in an interesting and constructive manner.

The second meeting on Section 9, Part III, is devoted to the committee's report on agriculture and industry. Copies of this portion of the report should be distributed to the study group at this time, and the Subcommittees on Agriculture and Industry should present an oral summary in the form of a panel discussion. It is quite likely that this panel discussion will take up most of the meeting, and for this reason there may not be time for the usual study group buzz sessions. If there is not time for the buzz sessions, the study group's procedure for this meeting may be one of questions and discussion back and forth from the floor to the panel. Questions for discussion at this meeting should be designed to help focus the attention and thinking of the study group on whatever specific points and recommendations are brought out in the committee's report. Many of these questions will be asked extemporaneously by participants in the study group at the time of the panel discussion. However, the Subcommittees on Agriculture and Industry should prepare in advance a list of questions which it is felt deserve particular discussion in the study group. These prepared questions should be mimeographed along with that portion of the report covering agriculture and industry, and copies distributed with the report at the beginning of the meeting. These questions can then be posed for discussion immediately following the oral presentation of the panel. The report on agriculture and industry, and the prepared questions, are due in the hands of the study group secretary at least one full week in advance of the second study group meeting on Section 9, Part III.

The third meeting of the study group on Section 9, Part III, is devoted to the committee's report on trades and services and follows the same procedure as that set forth above for the second meeting. Questions for discussion at this meeting should be designed to focus the attention and thinking of the study group on whatever specific points and recommendations are brought out in this part of the committee's report, and should also be prepared by the committee.

The report on trades and services, and the prepared questions for discussion, are due in the hands of the study group secretary at least one full week in advance of the third study group meeting on Section 9, Part III.

As indicated above, the report of the Economic Development Committee will be written in three parts, one part on agriculture, one part on industry, and the third part on trades and services. Each of these parts should be written by the appropriate subcommittee in consultation with the over-all committee chairman. The suggested outline for each part is as follows:

1. Purpose of the report.
2. Description of the local economy as it is at the present time (as it concerns the subject of the appropriate subcommittee).
3. How the information was collected.
4. Findings of the subcommittee.
5. Summary of community needs and problems posed.
6. Summary of opportunities for future development and recommendations for action necessary to bring this development about. These recommendations may be divided into immediate action, intermediate action, and long-range action.

When all three parts of the report are completed the chairman of the Economic Development Committee and the three subchairmen should get together and draw up an over-all summary which coordinates the information from all three parts, plus any additional ideas and information that came from the study group discussions. This summary should set forth in concrete form the final recommendations for action, and should be ready for presentation to the study group at the meeting on Section 15, Part III.

SUMMARY

Steps for the Economic Development Committee are in summary as follows:

1. Set a date for the first meeting of the entire committee at which

time there should be a discussion of the questions asked in the guide for the first study group meeting on Section 9, Part III. Each member of the committee should prepare himself for this meeting by reading Section 9, Part III, particularly that portion of the material which is to be covered in the first study group meeting on this section. Notes should be kept on this discussion and written up in full for the study group secretary.

2. Set a date for the first meeting of each subcommittee.

3. Each member should get prepared in advance of his respective subcommittee meeting by reading carefully (a) Section 9, Part III, (b) this special outline, and (c) all other references to the Economic Development Committee in the study guide.

4. Work out a plan of procedure in each subcommittee for collecting the information called for in the research outline set forth below, plus any other information that the subcommittees feel they should have.

5. Assign portions of this outline to each member of the respective subcommittee and set deadlines for the completion of assignments.

6. The Subcommittee on Trades and Services should make special plans for the survey of consumer buying habits outlined below.

7. Assemble the information in each subcommittee and write the report. Each subcommittee does its own part.

8. These reports are due in the hands of the study group secretary at least one full week in advance of the night they are to be presented.

9. Each subcommittee should make plans with the over-all committee chairman for its panel discussion at the second and third meetings of the study group on Section 9, Part III. The Subcommittees on Agriculture and Industry should form two panels, each with an allotted time limit, and plan to give their reports on the same evening. If there is not time for buzz sessions at this meeting, the questions for discussion should be discussed in the study group general assembly.

10. Write one final summary covering all three subcommittee reports. This summary is due in the hands of the study group secretary at least one full week in advance of the meeting on Section 15, Part III.

Research Outline for Survey of Economic Resources

Subcommittee on Agriculture

1. Climate—a description of each of the following factors in this community:
   A. Temperature.
   B. Precipitation.
   C. Sunshine.
   D. Growing season.

2. Water—a description of each of the following factors in this community:

    A. Rivers, streams, lakes, springs, and other sources of water. The volume of water available from each, and a list of uses to which they could be put.

    B. Current irrigation available. Irrigation needed, and possibility of expansion. What expanded irrigation would mean in terms of increased production, the cost, and how it could be accomplished.

    C. Drainage needs. What it would mean in terms of increased production, the cost, and how it could be accomplished.

    D. Temperature of water, the level of water table, the feasibility of wells and uses to which they could be put.

3. Soils.

    A. Give a description of soil types and classes in this area, soil depth, and present condition of soils.

    B. Describe present land management practices, and state whether these practices should be changed or improved. If present practices should be changed in any way, give reasons why, and explain what results could be expected.

    C. Give the total land area suitable for cultivation, and the percentage of this area now being farmed. State what would have to be done to bring the rest of it under cultivation, the advisability of same, and what would be gained for the community and for the individual farmer by doing it.

    D. List all crops and farm products for which this community is best suited and give reasons why. Write a brief description on each of these products showing requirements for growing, methods and practices recommended, sources of detailed information, market outlets, investment required, etc.

    E. List all crops and farm products that are actually being produced in this community at the present time. List in order of importance from a volume standpoint and estimate the percentage of the community's total farm production that each product represents.

    F. Compare the list of farm products for which the community is best suited with the list actually being produced at the present time. State whether any changes should be made in the present agricultural production pattern. State whether any new products could be introduced that would make for an expansion in current farm incomes, and what these new crops or products would be. State whether any new farm products could be introduced that would make possible more local processing industries, such as canneries, distilleries, cheese plants, etc., which would add more payrolls to the community.

G. State what could be done, if anything, to increase the production of present farm products in this community, and the advisability of doing same.

H. Describe the current use of fertilizers, green manure crops, etc. State whether or not these practices could be improved, if so how, and what results could be expected.

I. Describe current practices with regard to crop rotations, and indicate any needed improvements.

J. State whether any diversification in agricultural production is needed, and if so, give changes that should be made.

K. List the agricultural products now being grown in this community that are processed within the community. Could this processing be increased? If it could, what steps would have to be taken to bring increased processing about?

L. Make a list of the farm products that are grown in this community at the present time, but which are *not* processed here. Could any of these be processed here, and if so, explain what would have to be done to accomplish same.

M. State whether present storage facilities for farm products are adequate.

N. Is there a need in this community for a community demonstration or experimental farm? If there is, explain what might be accomplished in the long run in terms of increased agricultural production and better land management by establishing such a farm. Describe how the people of this community could go about establishing such a farm. Make a list of all agricultural agencies and outside experts that could be expected to help get such a project set up. Describe how the school might fit into a project of this kind.

4. Farms.
A. State the total number of farms in this community, and classify them by size. How many of them are locally owned and operated, how many are operated by absentee owners, how many are rented, how many provide the total income of the families living on them, and how many are operated for supplemental income only?

B. State how many people in this community are currently engaged in agriculture, and indicate what this means in terms of available jobs and payrolls during each season of the year.

C. Give the total farm valuation in this community, and indicate how the value of farm properties might be increased.

D. Give the approximate annual value of farm products in this community, the estimated total farm income, the approximate per capita farm income, and estimate the approximate amount these figures could be increased by making the various changes or improvements in farm practices that can be recommended by the committee.

E. State the approximate percentage of the total farm income that is spent within the community, and state what would be necessary from the farmers' point of view to increase this percentage.

F. State whether there are any opportunities for more full-time farmers in this community, and if so, describe these opportunities. Give the same information for part-time farming.

G. Make a list of all sources of agricultural information that are available to farmers in this community which might be used to increase farm productivity, and indicate the extent to which these sources are actually being used at the present time. State whether greater use could be made of these sources, and if it could, describe the possible results that could be gained. What should be done to encourage greater usage?

5. Range lands.

A. Give total area and location within the community.

B. Give information on ownership, the size of ownerships, the amount that is private, and the amount that is public.

C. Describe present condition of range and current range management practices.

D. Give information on current utilization, and possibilities for additional utilization.

E. Describe all needed improvements, if any.

6. Wild plants other than trees and range vegetation suitable for foods and other uses.

A. Give area, volume, and location of species.

B. Describe current use.

C. Describe all possible additional uses for economic purposes.

D. Give information on the need for restocking and other improvements, if any.

7. Farm markets.

A. Describe what farm markets are now available to the community.

B. State to what extent these markets are local, regional, national, or foreign.

C. Give information on how secure these markets are.
D. State what prospects there are for expansion of markets, and what definite plans have been made for such expansion. If no definite plans have been made for market expansion, then explain what plans should be made, if any.
E. Give information on what needs to be done to assist in market expansion. Make a list of all outside agencies, private, state, or federal, that might be able to help. How might the community help?

8. Transportation. (This item will be covered by the Subcommittee on Industry.)

Subcommittee on Industry

1. Analysis of present industries in the community.
   A. Make a list of each industry now operating in this community, and for each one give the following information, plus any other information that might be considered pertinent:
      (1) A listing of the various products that are manufactured, and a listing of other products that could be manufactured. How much room there is for expansion with present facilities and equipment.
      (2) A listing of all waste products that are not now being used. For each such product list potential uses and state what would have to be done in order to take advantage of these uses.
      (3) A listing of raw materials, parts, and supplies that are used, together with the following information:
         (a) The annual cost of these materials, parts, and supplies.
         (b) The percentage of these items obtained from within the community, and the percentage obtained from outside the community.
         (c) Of those items now being purchased outside this community, about how many of them could be made available or produced from within the community? Would this firm buy them from within the community provided they could be obtained here under the right conditions?
      (4) Location of market; percentage local, regional, national, and foreign.
      (5) Extent to which present market could be called secure, and whether it is sufficiently diversified.

(6) Prospects for market expansion, and what is needed to help in this respect.

(7) The number of persons employed, and size of payroll.

    (a) Seasonal variation.

    (b) Number of employees male, and number female.

    (c) Wage scales.

    (d) Extent of labor turnover and absenteeism.

    (e) Kind of labor-management relations.

    (f) Employment policies, whether training facilities are available in plant or in community, and whether local people get first consideration for jobs.

    (g) Could anything be done to make it possible to increase the number of employees in this firm, and if so, what?

B. State the total amount spent by all local industries annually for raw materials, parts, and supplies. Give the percentage of this amount that is spent within the community, and the percentage that is spent outside the community.

C. Give the estimated total amount that could be profitably spent within the community for raw materials, parts, and supplies that are now being purchased elsewhere. State what would have to be done locally to make this possible, and what this would represent in terms of added local payrolls.

D. Total industrial employment now provided in this community by season, and by sex. Total annual payrolls by season.

E. Indicate the extent to which present employment in local firms might be expanded, and state what steps would have to be taken to make this expansion possible. Would it involve new equipment, or could present equipment be used to expand production of present products or to make additional products?

F. Describe any unused capacity for industrial production with present facilities now available in the community.

G. Describe wholesale facilities available at the present time for local industry and agriculture, whether or not expansion is needed, and if so, how this expansion might be accomplished.

2. Natural resources.

A. Check the report of the Subcommittee on Agriculture for a list of all crops and other agricultural products in this community.

B. Water. (See report of Subcommittee on Agriculture.)

C. Forests and wood lots by species and types.

    (1) Volume and location.

    (2) Quality or grade of material.

(3) Ownership and availability.

(4) Economic accessibility.

(5) Current utilization, type of land management, where materials are now being processed, and status of future supply.

(6) Uses for which suited. List all possible uses, including fuel, power, and all products that could be made from local materials whether chemical or otherwise.

(7) Waste products and by-products, volume and present utilization.

(8) Extent to which local processing or utilization could be economically increased.

(9) Give a specific write-up on each raw material available for local processing and/or utilization which is thus far undeveloped. Include in this write-up all uses and possible products that could be made from each material either locally or elsewhere, and the conditions that would have to be met to make the projected utilization possible.

D. Fish and wildlife.

(1) Volume at present time.

(2) Current utilization.

(3) Need for restocking and other improvements.

(4) Possible additional use for economic purposes.

E. Seafood and other marine products.

(1) Present supply and use.

(2) Possibilities for expansion for economic purposes.

F. Mineral deposits.

(1) Examine each deposit in terms of points suggested under "C" above.

3. Analysis of possible new industries or possible production of new products by industries already established.

A. Make a list of all natural resources and raw materials available in this community that are now being only partially utilized, or not utilized at all.

B. Make a list of all waste materials from agricultural and industrial operations in this community, either past or present, that are now being only partially utilized or not utilized at all.

C. Describe and list each opportunity for possible industrial expansion that is offered to this community by these unused or only partially used natural resources, raw materials, and waste products.

D. For each possible opportunity listed, describe what conditions would have to be met in order to take advantage of the opportunity.

In describing these conditions think of such factors as available plant facilities and plant sites, kind of equipment, amount of needed power, water supplies, transportation, markets, labor, investment, housing, etc. List all conditions necessary for the development of each opportunity. State which of these conditions exist at the present time, and what must be done to provide those that do not exist.

E. Describe what new industrial or agricultural enterprises are most needed to balance out the economy in this community.

    (1) To promote more job opportunities.

    (2) To provide greater opportunities for young people.

    (3) To take up the slack during seasonal slumps.

    (4) To achieve better utilization of local resources.

    (5) To build a stronger and more stable community life.

4. Utilities.

A. Give information on the local drinking water supply system, including present capacity, annual volume of use, amount of surplus, chemical content, needed improvements, possibility of future expansion and the estimated cost of such expansion.

B. Sewage and waste disposal system. Capacity, need for expansion, estimated costs, etc.

C. Electric power.

    (1) Capacity available at present time.

    (2) Present surplus.

    (3) Amount of expansion needed, amount possible, and how soon it would be available.

    (4) Residential and commercial rates, and comparison with other localities.

    (5) Industrial rates and comparison with other localities.

    (6) Conditions under which power is available to new industries.

    (7) Stability of supply.

D. Gas.

    (1) Availability.

    (2) Cost and comparison with other localities.

    (3) Address of company from which available.

    (4) Feasibility of new gas wells.

E. Other fuels.

    (1) List kinds and availability.

    (2) Quantity and quality.

       (3) Costs.

       (4) Companies from which available.

5. Markets.
   - A. For consumers' goods.
     - (1) Within the community.
     - (2) Within the region.
       - (a) Size of market.
       - (b) Distance.
   - B. For capital or producers' goods.
     - (1) Within the community.
     - (2) Within the region.
       - (a) Size of market.
       - (b) Distance.

6. Transportation.
   - A. Railroads.
     - (1) Lines running into the community. State whether branch or main lines.
     - (2) If there is no railroad into this community, state nearest rail connection, give distance, and how it is reached. Is there any possibility of building a spur into the community?
     - (3) Rates to and from major cities.
       - (a) Freight.
       - (b) Passenger.
     - (4) Schedules.
   - B. Motor and truck routes.
     - (1) Lines running into the community.
     - (2) Capacity for freight.
     - (3) Rates.
       - (a) Freight.
       - (b) Passenger.
     - (4) Schedules.
   - C. Air.
     - (1) Distance to nearest airport facilities.
     - (2) Commercial airlines.
     - (3) Availability of chartered services.
     - (4) Rates.
       - (a) Freight.
       - (b) Passenger.
   - D. Water.
     - (1) Port and shipping facilities.

  (2) Distance by water to market centers, and time involved by
      boat.
  (3) Rates.
E. Highways.
  (1) Distance to major cities.
  (2) Condition of highways.
  (3) Adequacy and condition of road network through local and
      immediate surrounding area for purposes of local transpor-
      tation, particularly of local raw materials and agricultural
      products.
7. Plant facilities and plant sites.
  A. Existing buildings available for occupancy of industrial or
     wholesale firms.
    (1) Location with reference to transportation, power, water,
        and sewage disposal.
    (2) Floor space.
    (3) Ownership.
    (4) Terms available.
    (5) Condition and age of buildings.
    (6) Repairs needed.
    (7) Previous use.
    (8) Current taxes.
    (9) Other data required for specific industrial purposes.
  B. Plant sites suited to development.
    (1) Full description of real estate.
    (2) Ownership.
    (3) Terms available.
    (4) Location with reference to transportation, power, water,
        and sewage disposal.
    (5) Current taxes.
  C. Local sources of building capital.
  D. Local contractors available for construction of plant. Give names
     and addresses.
8. Fire insurance rates.
  A. Industrial and commercial.
  B. Residential.
  C. History of fire losses.
  D. Kind and availability of fire protection facilities.
9. Governmental finance.
  A. Taxable valuation of real property in the community.
  B. Current tax rates, local, county, and state.

C. Current bonded indebtedness of local municipality and school district.

D. Legal bond and millage limits.

E. Present debt service charges.

F. Total annual tax income of local municipality and school district.

10. Attitude of the community toward potential industrial development.

11. History of present industries with respect to community attitudes and public relations.

12. History of labor-management relations in this community.

13. Capital.

    A. Give the names of all banks located in the community.

        (1) Give the total assets of each.

        (2) Give a statement on the trend of bank deposits over the past five years in this community.

    B. Give information on available financial services for commercial and agricultural developments.

        (1) Commercial bank credit.

        (2) Mortgage credit.

        (3) Building and loan service.

        (4) Savings and loan service.

        (5) Veteran's loan service.

        (6) Farm credit.

    C. List any other sources of credit that are available in this locality. Are there enough sources of risk capital for the development of local business and industrial expansion? To what extent might the people of this community be expected to subscribe to a stock issue for the development of sound local industry?

14. Labor.

    A. Give the total number of employable persons in this community by sex and by occupation.

    B. The total number of persons actually employed at the present time.

        (1) The number of these people in business for themselves.

        (2) The number who are employed by someone else.

        (3) The number dependent on the production of military goods for their jobs.

    C. Total number of persons unemployed at the present time by sex and by occupation.

    D. Describe the seasonal pattern of employment in this community.

E. Make a list of skills and occupations in this community that are not now being used.

F. Total number of high school or college graduates in this community who annually enter the labor market.

G. Total number of students in this community who annually seek seasonal or part time employment.

H. Give information as to whether there is any concerted effort by employers in this community to find employment for local students and graduates. Have any specific cooperative relations been established for this purpose between the schools and local employer groups?

I. Give information as to whether the schools in this community provide training for students which helps to fit them for local employment. Can the present school curriculum adequately meet the needs of a local industrial development program? If not, what could or should be done about it, if anything?

J. Describe the pattern of migrant workers in this community.

K. State how many unfilled job opportunities exist in this community at the present time.

L. State whether or not this community has a labor surplus at the present time. What predictions can be made in this connection for possible future developments?

M. What kind (quality and size) of a labor market would be available to this community to meet the needs of local industrial development?

Subcommittee on Trades and Services

1. List the total number of each of the following types of establishments in this community:

Grocery stores, bakeries, department stores, variety stores, women's clothing stores, men's clothing stores, children's clothing stores, shoe stores, furniture stores, electrical appliances stores, automobile dealers, filling stations, automobile repair shops, machinery repair shops, electrical and radio repair shops, general fix-it shops, plumbing shops, stationery stores, book stores, hardware and farm implement stores, feed stores, lumber and building material dealers, florists, jewelry stores, frozen locker plants, hotels, motels, laundries, cleaning shops, theaters, bowling alleys, pool halls, taverns and bars, barber shops, beauty shops, insurance agencies, real estate agencies, taxi companies, hauling services, photographic shops, others not herein mentioned.

A. List any improvement which may be needed in any of these services.

B. Make a list of all opportunities that exist in this community for the development of new establishments in any of these lines.

2. Total number of people engaged or employed in these local businesses, and state the approximate total annual payroll involved.

3. Give information concerning the availability of newspaper and printing services, and radio broadcasting stations.

4. Merchandising practices.

A. Is the local shopping center in need of improvement on any of the following points?
(1) Appearance and attractiveness.
(2) Up-to-date merchandise of the type local people prefer.
(3) Variety of goods.
(4) Prices.
(5) Parking space.
(6) Clean, convenient rest rooms.
(7) Parcel checking service.
(8) Good, reasonably priced lunches.
(9) Club luncheon facilities.
(10) Hours of business.
(11) Special sales events.
(12) Better business practices.
(13) Cooperation among merchants for purposes of making a desirable shopping center.
(14) Cooperation of merchants in community activities.
(15) Quality of service and friendliness.
(16) Overnight accommodations.

B. The Trades and Services Subcommittee should make a special survey of consumer buying habits to find out why people buy where they do, what they buy, and what would cause them to do more shopping at home. The suggested procedure for this survey is set forth at the end of this outline.

C. Would a practical course of study in modern merchandising and salesmanship be of value in this community? If so, should one be established? Assistance for purposes of giving such a course could be obtained from the state university extension service or division of adult education.

5. Tourist and recreation trade.

A. Make a list of all tourist attractions and outdoor sports possibilities in this community, or in the surrounding area, that might cause people to visit here.

B. State what has been done, if anything, to develop these attractions. Have these efforts been enough?

C. List and describe all historic sites in this community. Describe present condition, showing whether they are maintained in an attractive condition and well marked.

D. List and describe all places in the community for tourists and other travelers to find overnight accommodations, and state whether or not these places are adequate.

E. List any need, or profitable openings, for the development of additional tourist facilities.
   (1) What facilities are most needed, if any?
   (2) During what seasons of the year could they be expected to operate?
   (3) From what areas would they draw most of their patrons?

F. State what improvements, if any, are needed in roads and road markings leading into the community.

G. Give information on approximately how many tourists have been coming to this community in recent years. What are the prospects of increasing the number of tourists? What would have to be done in order to bring about such an increase?

6. Professional services.

A. How many of each of the following are in practice in this community:
   Clergymen, teachers, doctors, dentists, nurses, lawyers, accountants, engineers, architects, librarians, social workers, veterinarians, funeral directors, photographers, others not herein mentioned.

B. Are there enough professional people in each of the various groups to adequately meet the needs of this community? If not, list the professions in which more personnel is needed.

General Information for Inclusion in the Final Report of the Economic Development Committee

1. State what relationship exists between a sound program of economic development and such factors as the community's educational system, churches, organizations, health facilities and sanitation, community beautification, community recreation, and community cultural activities.

2. Describe to what extent this community has its "house in order" for purposes of beginning a sound program of new economic development, and indicate what general steps should be taken to help get it in better order.

CONSUMER BUYING HABITS SURVEY [1]

[1] Acknowledgment is given to Edith Dyer Rainboth of the Washington Public

(To be conducted by the Subcommittee on Trades and Services)

1. Assemble a crew of interviewers to make the survey.

2. Make up a questionnaire for use in collecting the information.

3. This questionnaire might include questions that will skim off the principal attitudes of customers which have the greatest influence on their shopping habits.

4. The survey questionnaire may include whatever questions the members of the committee feel it should include, but the main thing is to make it simple to understand and easy to fill out.

5. After the committee has decided what questions should be included in the survey questionnaire and how many copies will be needed, a supply should be mimeographed.

6. Using the map provided by the Boundary Committee, block the community out into districts.

7. It is not necessary to cover every house in this survey. Every third one, or some other sample will be sufficient.

8. Have the interviewers assemble at one place, divide into crews each with a crew leader, and begin the survey together. It should be completed, or at least nearly so, in one day.

9. Each individual questionnaire should be anonymous and confidential. The interviewer should explain the purpose, get the questionnaire filled out, and move on quickly.

10. Tabulate the results, and write the survey up as a special section in the report.

Suggested Questionnaire for Consumer Buying Habits Survey
Introduction

A. What things do you like about the stores in (*name of community*)?

B. What things do you dislike about the stores in (*name of community*)?

C. What are the most important changes you would like to see made in the stores in (*name of community*)?

D. What things do you buy the most of that you cannot get at the present time in (*name of community*)?

E. What kind of stores do you think (*name of community*) is most in need of that we do not have at the present time?

F. When do you most like to shop? (Time of day and day of week.)

Groceries

A. To what extent do you buy groceries in (*name of community*)?

.... Never buy groceries in (*name of community*).

Opinion Laboratory, University of Washington, for special assistance in the preparation of this survey.

_____ Buy some groceries in (*name of community*).

_____ Buy about half our groceries in (*name of community*).

_____ Buy quite a large part of our groceries in (*name of community*).

_____ Always buy our groceries in (*name of community*).

B. About how much do you spend per month for groceries?
Total amount $_____.
About how much of this amount do you spend in (*name of community*) $_____.
About how much of this amount do you spend outside of (*name of community*) $_____.

C. About what percentage of your grocery money is spent each month:

In (*name of community*) _____%

Outside (*name of community*) _____%

Total   100
                              _____%

D. What grocery stores in (*name of community*) do you buy from?
E. What things do you *like* about buying groceries in (*name of community*)?
F. What things do you *dislike* about buying groceries in (*name of community*)?
G. What stores *outside* (*name of community*) do you buy groceries from?

Name of Store _____   Town _____
(List all   _____   _____
stores you   _____   _____
buy from)   _____   _____
                   _____   _____
                   _____   _____
                   _____   _____

H. What things do you *like* about buying groceries from these stores outside (*name of community*)?
I. What things do you *dislike* about buying groceries from these stores outside (*name of community*)?

Other Categories

Select other categories of merchandise for the questionnaire such as clothing (this may be divided into men's clothing, women's clothing, and children's clothing), hardware, drugs and sundries, automobile supplies, etc., and repeat the same questions for each of these categories as are asked above about groceries.

13

For the Beautification Committee

THE BEAUTIFICATION COMMITTEE IS RESPONSIBLE FOR MAKING A DEtailed investigation of the community from the standpoint of physical appearance, reporting the facts on conditions found, and recommending concrete action for improvement. The work of this committee may present the greatest tangible opportunity for immediate community action from the study group.

Below is presented an outline of research which indicates the type of facts and information that should be included in the report. Suggested steps for getting the report of the Beautification Committee completed are as follows:

1. Set a date for the first meeting of the committee.

2. Each member of the committee get prepared for this meeting by reading carefully (a) Section 10, Part III, (b) this committee outline, and (c) all other references to the Beautification Committee indexed in the study guide.

3. At this first meeting review Section 10, Part III. Read the research outline given below.

4. Adopt a plan of operation. Assign jobs to each member of the committee, and set deadlines for completion of assignments.

5. In making the survey outlined below, members of the committee

should drive through all streets and roads in the community and make notes from actual personal inspection of the items outlined.

6. After the survey has been completed, tabulate the information and write up the report of findings and recommendations for action.

7. From its report the committee should also prepare any questions for discussion in the study group which it feels should be brought up for discussion in addition to those given in Section 10, Part III.

8. At least one member of the committee should sit in on each buzz session and be prepared to help keep the discussion moving toward constructive ends.

9. The report is due in the hands of the study group secretary at least one full week in advance of the study group meeting on Section 10, Part III.

Following is a suggested outline for the committee's report.

1. Purpose of the report. Include a statement as to the value of physical appearance to the life of a community.

2. How the information was collected.

3. Findings of the committee.

4. Summary of needs for improvement and problems posed.

5. Recommendations for definite, concrete action necessary to bring about the needed improvements, including a recommended timetable for action projects.

For purposes of these recommendations the committee should draw up a comprehensive plan for community-wide beautification which includes (a) what projects should be undertaken, (b) which projects should be set up for immediate action and which ones should be set for action later on, (c) by whom, and by what means the recommended action might be accomplished, and (d) what preparations will be necessary to make the action successful.

If there are any special points concerning specific local conditions which the committee feels should be covered by general discussion in the study group, written questions for this purpose should be prepared in advance and included under a separate heading in the committee's report.

RESEARCH OUTLINE FOR COMMUNITY BEAUTIFICATION SURVEY

Drive through all streets and roads in the community and make an actual count of the number of buildings. Make notes on conditions found.

For Residential Property

1. What is the total number of homes in this community? In town? Out of town?

2. How many of these homes appear to be in satisfactory condition, i. e., neat, clean, painted, landscaped, etc.?

3. How many of these homes appear to need care?
    A. Paint?
    B. Repairs or fixing up?

4. How many of these homes appear to have had no care at all within the past several years?

5. How many yards in the community need lawn care?
    A. Grass needs planting?
    B. Flowers should be planted?
    C. Landscaping should be done?

For Commercial Property

1. How many commercial buildings are there in this community? In town? Out of town?

2. How many of these buildings appear to be in satisfactory condition, i. e., neat, clean, painted, landscaped, etc.?

3. How many of these buildings appear to need care?
    A. Paint?
    B. Repairs or fixing up?

4. How many of these buildings appear to have had no care at all within the past several years?

5. How many of them should be landscaped or have grass and shrubs planted around them?

For Barns, Sheds, and Other Buildings

1. How many barns and sheds are there in this community?

2. How many of these barns and sheds are in need of beautification?
    A. Paint?
    B. Repairs or fixing up?
    C. Apparently unused and should be removed entirely?

Summary on Buildings

Adding them all together, how many unsightly buildings are there in this community? In the commercial section in town? In the residential section in town? In that part of the community outside of town?

Roads, Streets, Alleys, Vacant Lots, and Sidewalks

1. How many unsightly roads, streets, alleys, and vacant lots are there in this community?

2. Describe each unsightly road, street, alley, and vacant lot, and state what needs to be done to improve it.

3. Are there any streets that need repairs or pavement? If so, which ones are they, how many blocks are involved, and how much would it cost?

4. Is any new sidewalk construction needed in this community? If so, where, what distance is involved, and how much would it cost?

5. Is any sidewalk repair needed in this community? If so, where, what distance is involved, and how much would it cost?

General Eyesores and Other Features Influencing the
Community's Appearance

1. How many dumping places are there in this community that need attention? Give location of each dumping place, state what improvements are needed, and what action would be necessary to bring such improvements about.

2. Is the community in need of additional dumping places? If so, where might such additional dumping places be located, and what action would be necessary to establish them?

3. How many unsanitary spots are there in this community, if any, that might be described as "rat-catchers," "insect breeders," etc.? Where are they? Why are they allowed to exist? What should be done about them?

4. Does this community have attractive waste receptacles at frequent intervals along streets, particularly in the business section and around public buildings? If not, should anything be done to provide them?

5. How many of the public rest rooms in this community are in a clean, neat, and sanitary condition? How many are in a dirty and untidy condition? Are improvements needed? If so, how might such improvements be brought about?

6. Does this community have zoning regulations? If so, what are they? Are they enforced? Are they adequate? If there are no zoning regulations, should such regulations be established? Why? What action would be necessary to establish them?

7. Photograph selected eyesores, ill-kept buildings, barns, vacant lots, dumps, etc., in the community that in the committee's opinion should be cleaned up. Enlarged prints or slides of these photographs should be shown to the study group for discussion at the time the committee's report is submitted.

8. Write out a description of the over-all appearance of the community's business section from the standpoint of civic beauty. If it is deficient in any way explain how it is deficient, and what needs to be done to beautify it. Are green plants and trees needed?

9. Write out a description of the over-all appearance of each entrance into the town from the standpoint of beauty and attractiveness. If im-

provements are needed, state what ought to be done. Photographs may be useful for illustration.

10. Are there any special projects not covered in this outline, such as cemetery beautification, etc., that ought to be covered by the committee and included in the report?

14

For the Education Committee

THE EDUCATION COMMITTEE HAS THE RESPONSIBILITY OF MAKING AN analysis of the educational life of the community with particular emphasis on the public school system, and of writing a report which will present all the facts necessary for the study group to conduct an intelligent discussion of the material given in Section 11, Part III.

It should not be expected that the study group will be able to cover this report in complete detail in its buzz session discussions. To do this would require a disproportionate amount of the study group's time on this one element of community life.

However, the committee should endeavor to make its report as complete as possible in order that the community may have available a document of facts and citizen expression which will be useful for purposes of actual planning and community action after the initial study has been completed. This report should be highly important as a guidepost to the school board, it should be of considerable value for purposes of further and more detailed citizen study, and as a source of program material for other educational meetings and discussions, such as those of the Parent-Teacher Association.

The committee should make a special effort to organize its report in such a manner as to make it an easy reference for facts and information by the study group in discussing the questions for buzz sessions as set forth in Section 11, Part III. Further questions and more detailed discussion along these lines will probably arise in the buzz sessions, but if the committee organizes its report to coincide with the general outline of questions as given in the study guide, the buzz session discussions will be greatly facilitated. Before beginning the research each member of the Education Committee should make a point to study carefully the material in Section 11, Part III.

If the committee feels that special additional questions should be prepared in order to ensure discussion of specific local issues which are set forth in the report, but not covered by the questions in the guide, it should do so. Every effort should be made to stimulate a lively and constructive discussion in the buzz sessions which will come to grips with the vital educational needs and problems that exist in this particular community. The accomplishment of this objective is largely up to the Education Committee. For this reason much will depend on the way the education report is presented, the extent to which the questions for discussion are integrated with the information, and the needs and problems which the report brings out.

Below is presented an outline of research which indicates the type of facts and information which should be included in the report. To assist in the collection of these facts the Education Committee may wish to make up a questionnaire, or a series of separate questionnaires, for purposes of actually surveying the attitudes of parents, teachers, students, members of the P.T.A., and other persons in the community on various points concerning the school and the educational needs of the community. Points to be included in the questions for such a questionnaire, or series of questionnaires, may be taken from the research outline given below, or from any other sources or ideas which the committee may have.

SUMMARY

Suggested steps for getting the work of the Education Committee organized are in summary as follows:

1. Set a date for the first meeting of the committee.
2. Each member of the committee get prepared for this meeting by reading carefully (a) Section 11, Part III, (b) this committee outline, and (c) all other references to the Education Committee indexed in the study guide.

3. Review Section 11, Part III, and the *Research Outline for the Education Committee* given below.

4. At this first meeting adopt a plan of operation. Decide what surveys the committee should make, how they are to be made, what kind of questionnaires will be necessary, and plan the questionnaires.

For purposes of devising questionnaires and planning surveys the committee may get some ideas from the material given in Part IV of the study guide for the Population and other committees. The committee should draw on the advice of the school superintendent and other school personnel for the assistance they have to offer.

5. Assign jobs to each member of the committee and set deadlines for completion of assignments.

6. Conduct the research, tabulate data, and write the report. The report is due in the hands of the study group secretary at least one full week in advance of the first study group meeting on Section 11, Part III.

7. From its report the committee may wish to prepare certain questions for discussion in addition to those given in Section 11, Part III. If so, this should be done, and the questions handed in to the secretary along with the report.

8. At least one member of the Education Committee should sit in with each buzz session and be prepared to help keep the discussion moving toward constructive ends.

Following is a suggested outline for the committee's report:

1. Purpose of the report.
2. How the information was collected.
3. A statement on the role and meaning of education in the life of the community.
4. Findings of the committee.
   A. Purpose and objectives of the public school in this community.
   B. Community's attitude toward the school.
   C. School's attitude toward the community.
   D. School program.
   E. School organization and administration.
   F. School personnel.
   G. School buildings and equipment.
   H. School finance.
5. Summary of conclusions as to community needs and problems posed.
6. Recommendations for action.
   A. Immediate action.
   B. Long range action.

RESEARCH OUTLINE FOR THE EDUCATION COMMITTEE

Purpose and Objectives of the Public School

1. Write out a statement showing what the Education Committee feels should be the broad purpose and objectives of the public schools in this community.

2. If this statement differs in any respect from the actual purpose and objectives of the present school board, administration, and teaching staff, point out wherein it differs. For this purpose the Education Committee should interview separately each member of the school board and school administration, and a sample of the teachers, and find out from them what they feel the purpose and objectives of the public schools in this community actually are.

3. If there are any differences of opinion among the various school officials and personnel on this point, indicate those differences.

4. Does the committee feel that the present educational aims of the public schools in this community are sufficient to meet the total needs for education in this community? Consider family life, marriage and divorce, alertness toward public and civic issues, community responsibility, economic needs, vocational needs, etc. Are any changes needed? If so, in what ways?

Community's Attitude Toward the Schools

1. Consider the extent to which people in this community patronize school events. Check attendance figures and compare with house capacity. Check the kind of events that are given the most support. What does this reflect? Is there any lack of balance in the community interest?

2. Check the attendance of citizens at school board meetings. State what responsibility the community has toward its school board. Is there any good reason why the community should feel a responsibility toward the school board? Is there any assistance that the community can give the school board in the development of a better school system?

3. Indicate whether there is any friction between the schools and the rest of the community. If there is, describe the nature of this friction and the reasons for its existence. Are these reasons valid?

4. State whether there is any lack of close relationship between the school and the rest of the community. If there is, is it because the school is aloof toward the desires and opinions of the community, or is it due simply to a lack of interest on the part of the community? If it is the latter, explain why.

5. Do people in this community as a whole commonly think of the school as a real community educational center where all people in the

community can get help on problems requiring information and educational services? If they don't, why don't they? What connection, if any, might this have with the level of community interest in its schools?

6. Check the record of community support for local school bond elections and special levies. Why is there support for these matters, or why isn't there?

7. Has there been a bond election or special school levy recently? Is another bond election or special school levy needed at the present time? If so, why? Is this popular or unpopular in the community as a whole? Why?

8. Give information to show when the last major school improvements were made due to citizen activity. What were these improvements and what was necessary to bring them about?

9. To what extent do the citizens of this community assist the school in providing supplemental instruction, such as vocational training, wherever they are qualified to do so?

10. What about the relationship between parents and teachers? Do the parents show a vital interest in the school program? Do they really know what goes on at school? Is there anything other than the fact that their child is in school that would cause them to want to exercise an interest in what goes on in the school?

11. To what extent do people in this community make an effort to find part-time employment for students seeking work? What about employment for new graduates?

12. Check the degree of cooperation the schools get from the local press and radio.

13. Information concerning the P.T.A.:
  A. Percentage of parents who belong, and the percentage who do not.
  B. Total P.T.A. membership.
    (1) Average percentage of membership at regular meetings.
    (2) Average percentage not present at regular meetings.
  C. Stated objectives of local P.T.A. organization.
    (1) List concrete accomplishments within the past year which show evidence that these objectives have been realized.
    (2) Has the P.T.A. done as much as it would like to have done during the past year toward the realization of these objectives? If not, what do the P.T.A. leaders and members feel have been the chief reasons?
  D. Describe the current P.T.A. program.
    (1) The extent it could be called constructive, vital, urgent, and concerned with basic issues.

    (2) Improvements needed, if any. If so, list suggested improvements.

E. The extent to which members of the P.T.A. have an opportunity to express themselves at the organization's regular meetings, and in the planning of the organization's program.
    (1) The extent to which members actually do express themselves at P.T.A. meetings.
    (2) In the planning of P.T.A. programs and projects.

F. Ease of getting acquainted in P.T.A., and the extent to which new members are made to feel welcome and a part of the organization.

G. The extent to which P.T.A. members are really informed on basic school problems. On school laws. On school administration, organization, and finance. On the school program.

H. The extent to which the P.T.A. has a mind of its own and actually directs its own affairs, and the extent to which it is a mere pawn of the school administration.

14. Organizations in this community other than the P.T.A. whose stated objectives or programs include support for the local school system, if any.

A. Names of such organizations.

B. Accomplishments within the past year.

C. Degree of coordination between these organizations and the P.T.A.

D. Are there any organizations or groups in this community whose school programs are in conflict? If so, what is the nature of this conflict?

E. Are there any organizations or groups in this community who are hostile to the local school administration or system? If so, describe the reason for such hostility.

15. What specific information can the Education Committee develop on Question VI in Section 11, Part III?

16. After checking these, and other points, what is the opinion of the Education Committee as to the degree of citizen interest in school matters in this community as a whole? Explain reasons for this opinion.

School's Attitude Toward the Community

1. The extent to which the school board and the school administration welcome inquiry, suggestions, and advice from citizens in matters pertaining to school programs and operations.

A. Is improvement needed?

B. If so, in what respect?

2. The extent to which school authorities keep the community as a whole informed on school policy, needs, and activities.

    A. Is improvement needed?

    B. If so, in what respects?

    C. Give specific suggestions as to how improvements could be brought about.

3. The extent to which the school's attitude toward the community is one of honest and sincere cooperation in meeting community needs and problems, and to which it is simply a policy of public relations designed to keep in good with the community.

    A. Is improvement needed?

    B. If so, in what respects?

4. The extent to which the schools endeavor to cooperate with local business in an effort to help solve the businessman's problems.

    A. Give specific ways in which such help is extended.

    B. Is improvement needed?

    C. If so, in what ways?

5. The extent to which the schools seek out and make an effort to use in their programs people in the community who have special information to offer.

6. State in what specific ways the schools cooperate with other public agencies and with civic organizations.

    A. Is improvement needed?

    B. If so, in what ways.

7. Consider the extent to which school buildings and facilities are made available to community groups.

    A. Availability of meeting rooms that are suitable and pleasant for adult groups.

    B. Extent to which the school is a true community center.

8. Consider the extent to which school projects have been created in which parents may become personally involved with their children's activities.

    A. Is improvement needed?

    B. If so, give specific suggestions.

9. After considering these, and other points, what is the opinion of the Education Committee on the extent to which the local school system seeks to serve the total community and actually take part in community affairs? And, to what extent does the community permit the schools to participate in its total life?

School Program

1. Write up for inclusion in the report the entire program of the public school system in this community, showing both curricular and extra-

curricular activities, as it actually is at the present time. This should be arranged by grades or by departments, or in some other breakdown which will make it clear to persons reading the report.

2. Examine the school program in terms of the points raised in each question in Section 11, Part III, beginning with Question XII and continuing through Question XIV. The committee should consult with the school administration and teachers on these points and then write out for inclusion in its report a frank and objective analysis, with explanations for whatever situations are found or conclusions drawn. On the basis of this analysis the committee should state its opinions and recommendations for discussion by the study group buzz sessions as indicated in Question XV, Section 11, Part III.

3. Are there any provisions in the school program for having students visit local industry, business, and public offices of various kinds to learn how they operate and thereby gain practical knowledge of the community in which they live? If so, to what extent are these visits integrated with the lessons which the students are getting in school?

    A. Is improvement needed?

    B. If so, list specific suggestions.

4. Are there any courses in the present school program that the committee feels are not necessary? If so, what are they? Give reasons.

5. Are there any activities or courses not included in the present school program that the committee feels should be included? If so, what are they? Give reasons why.

6. What provision is made to provide students with vocational guidance?

    A. Is improvement needed?

    B. If so, list specific suggestions.

7. What provision is made to provide students with counseling and guidance in connection with personal and emotional problems?

    A. Is improvement needed?

    B. If so, list specific suggestions.

8. Give the rate of student withdrawal from school before graduation.

    A. How does this compare with the rate of withdrawal in other parts of this state?

    B. What are the reasons for these withdrawals?

    C. What specific suggestions can be made for reducing it?

9. Make a list of the programs in this community that offer organized education for adults.

    A. If there are none, so indicate.

    B. Describe what part the public school plays in making these programs possible.

C. Could the school do more in this respect? If so, give specific suggestions. What are the present handicaps? How might these handicaps be overcome?

D. How many people are being reached by these programs? How might this number of people be increased?

10. Do any of the programs of education for adults in this community deal with such matters as . . . (Indicate also on which items the present program is short or inadequate. If it is short or inadequate on all of them, this should be included in the report.)

Information on matters of general community interest, including any local issue on which people need more knowledge in order to make intelligent decisions.

Understanding of world affairs.

Problems concerning international peace.

Current political issues—local, state, national.

Propaganda analysis—how to evaluate propaganda used in political campaigns and for other purposes.

The American heritage—including regional history, folklore, legends, stories, and traditions of this area and of America as a whole; human interest in American history, and American social, political, and economic developments.

Current social and economic problems in this state.

Parent education in the raising of children.

Nutrition and family health.

Courses for expectant parents.

General family life problems.

Emotional and mental hygiene.

Divorce and how to prevent it.

Home planning and design.

Furniture making and upholstery.

Home gardening.

Human relations and how to get along with other people.

Community leadership training to help people learn how to be more effective in organizational affairs.

Group discussion.

Public speaking.

Merchandising and salesmanship courses for businessmen and sales-clerks.

Agricultural practices.

Accounting and bookkeeping.

Typing and shorthand.

Hobbies, including arts and crafts to provide creative outlets for personal enjoyment and relaxation.

Cultural activities to provide creative outlets for personal enjoyment in such things as music groups and music appreciation, folk songs and ballads, creative writing, playwriting and dramatic productions.

Creative dramatics for children.

11. To what extent are people in this community interested in such educational activities as those listed above?

    A. Why is the degree of interest as it is?

    B. How, and under what conditions, might this interest be increased?

    C. Is there any particular reason why it should be increased?

    D. What would an increase in interest in such educational activities mean to the life of the community? To the lives of individuals? To public interest in the schools?

12. To what extent do the schools assist in contributing to the over-all needs of the community in terms of cultural activities such as concerts, dramatic productions, etc.?

    A. Could it do more?

    B. If so, give specific suggestions.

13. To what extent do the schools contribute toward the development of community recreation for all ages in all seasons?

    A. Could it do more?

    B. If so, give specific suggestions.

14. Considering all the points mentioned above, what is the opinion of the Education Committee as to the adequacy of the present school program from the standpoint of meeting the total educational needs of this community as a whole? Or, does this community utilize its schools to the fullest possible advantage?

    A. Are improvements needed?

    B. If so, what improvements? Give specific suggestions.

    C. What might be necessary to bring about such improvements?

    D. How might they be achieved?

15. Again, considering all the points mentioned above, are there any improvements or additions in the present utilization of the schools in this community that would help the community to gain the educational ends of the local school system as described above under *Purposes and Objectives of the Public School?*

    A. If so, give specific suggestions for the improvements needed. (This is simply an elaboration, but an important one, on the information asked for in the previous question.)

B. What effect would such improvements in the utilization of the public schools have on community life, and how might this in turn affect the education and development of the community's young people?

C. What effect might all this have on the vitality of democracy in America, on the leadership of America in the modern world, and in turn on international peace, and the security of the American way of life?

16. The Education Committee should endeavor to include in its report as much information as possible on Questions XXII and XXIII in Section 11, Part III.

17. The committee should also include in its report as much information as it can get on Question XXVIII, Section 11, Part III. For this purpose all possible information should be obtained on what services the tax-supported universities and colleges are prepared to render at the present time.

A. Are these services as much as they should be, or of the kind that they should be, to meet the needs of this community?

B. Are improvements or expansions in these services needed?

C. If so, what changes or additions should be made?

D. How might these improvements be brought about?

18. Describe what part the churches, civic organizations, hobby clubs, farm groups, governmental agencies, and private commercial firms might play in the development of an expanded educational program for the community as a whole. Make a list of the institutions, agencies, groups, or organizations that might help and indicate what each one might do.

School Organization and Administration

1. Draw up an organizational chart showing the governmental structure of the school system in this community. This chart should show all departments and offices, including the school board, administration, etc., and their relationship to each other. It should be accompanied by a written explanation which tells clearly what the chart means and how the school organization functions.

A. Describe the responsibilities and duties of each office in this organization, and indicate to whom each office is responsible.

B. How long has this organizational structure been in effect?

C. Does it present any difficult problems?

D. Is it adequate to meet today's needs?

2. How are persons chosen for the school board?

A. What is their term of office? Is this term too short, too long, or just right?

B. What kind of background and experience should a person have to do an effective job as a member of the school board?

School Personnel

1. Make a list of the institutions in this state that prepare teachers for their profession.
   A. Which of these institutions are represented by the teachers in this community?
   B. Do the teachers feel that these institutions provided them with the kind of training that best fits them for the practical problems of today's teaching in this community?
      (1) If not, in what specific ways do the teachers feel these institutions are deficient?
      (2) What improvements or changes, if any, do the teachers feel should be made in these institutions?
      (3) Does all this warrant any further inquiry by citizens interested in their public school system?
      (4) How might action be initiated to bring about improvements that are found needed in state teacher training institutions?

2. To what extent are the teachers in this community satisfied with present school personnel policies?
   A. Are improvements needed?
   B. If so, list specific suggestions.

3. Does the school system in this community have a definite salary schedule for its teachers?
   A. Is it the same for both sexes?
   B. Is it adequate?

4. What has been the rate of teacher turnover in this community during the past five years?
   A. Is it high enough to cause any serious problems?
   B. What are the causes of this turnover?

5. To what extent do the teachers feel that they are a definite part of the community?
   A. Is improvement needed?
   B. If so, give specific suggestions.

6. Do teachers hold regular conferences with parents regarding each child in school?
   A. If so, what does it accomplish?
   B. If not, would anything be gained by it?

7. What is the situation in regard to student discipline?
   A. Does this present any problems?
   B. If so, what problems? Why?

    C. What can be done about them?
  8. What is the average teaching load per teacher?
    A. Is it too light, too heavy, or about right?
    B. Does this present any problems?
    C. If so, what problems?
    D. What can be done about them?

School Buildings and Equipment

  1. How many school buildings are in use in this community?
  2. Make an inspection tour of each building and state whether it is satisfactory or unsatisfactory on the following points:

Age and over-all condition	Laboratories
Space for today's needs	Vocational shops
(Consider the total community.)	Teachers' lounges
Space for tomorrow's needs	Adult meeting rooms
(See report of Population Commit-	Cafeteria
tee.)	Storage
Heat	Furnishings
Ventilation	Physical beauty
Sanitation	Lavatories
Light	Office space
Safety	Teaching equipment
Wiring	School supplies
Auditorium	Playgrounds
Gymnasium	Outdoor athletic grounds
Health rooms	Landscaping
Libraries	Sidewalks

  3. Make a list of all improvements needed, if any.
    A. Itemize the cost of needed improvement.
    B. What efforts are being made at the present time to bring such improvements about?
    C. Are these efforts enough?
    D. If not, what additional action should be taken?

School Finance

  1. Total valuation of school district.
    A. Present millage.
    B. Tax yield for school purposes.
  2. Give millage limit for school purposes.
    A. Is present millage up to limit?

B. Is there a special levy above this at present?
C. For how long a period may special levies for school purposes be voted? Is this as it should be?
D. Give legal bond limits for school purposes.
E. What is present bonded indebtedness of the local school district? At what rate is it decreasing?
F. How much more could be raised by additional school bonds?
G. Explain how a special levy or bond issue for school purposes is brought about.

3. From what other sources does this school district obtain its funds?

4. Draw up a chart showing the present school budget, showing where the money comes from and how it is spent.

5. Does the Education Committee feel that this community is getting the most return from each dollar that is going into the support of the local schools at the present time?

A. If so, explain reasons for the committee's opinion.
B. If not, explain reasons for the committee's opinion.
   (1) What changes are recommended?
   (2) How might these changes be brought about?

15

For the Health Committee

THE HEALTH COMMITTEE IS RESPONSIBLE FOR MAKING AN ANALYSIS OF the health needs and resources of the community, and for reporting all available facts and information which will be needed by the study group to conduct an intelligent discussion of the questions set forth in Section 12, Part III. Before turning in its report the committee should check each one of these questions to make certain that the basic facts necessary for discussing them have been gathered and are included.

The report of this committee should, however, contain information which goes beyond that needed for the study group discussion in order to make it a document which can be used as the basis for further detailed study and definite planning and community action after the initial study has been completed. Below, an outline of research is provided which suggests some of the points that should be checked in the analysis. The committee should not consider itself limited to these points, but should endeavor to extend its research in whatever direction may be necessary to bring out whatever specific health needs and problems may exist in the community.

If there are any specific health problems in the community not covered by the questions outlined in Section 12, Part III, the committee should add other questions which will ensure discussion on these points, and include in its report whatever facts and information may be needed for this part of the discussion.

SUMMARY

Suggested steps for organizing and completing the work of the Health Committee are in summary as follows:

1. Set a date for the first meeting of the committee.

2. Each member should get prepared for this meeting by reading carefully (a) Section 12, Part III, (b) this committee outline, and (c) all other references to the Health Committee indexed in the study guide. At this meeting review Section 12, Part III, and the material in this outline.

3. Adopt a plan of operation.

4. Assign jobs to each member of the committee and set deadlines for completion of assignments.

5. Assemble collected information and write the report. Write special questions for discussion in the study group if necessary to cover certain specific health problems in this community which may not be covered by the questions set forth in Section 12, Part III.

6. The committee's report is due in the hands of the study group secretary at least one full week in advance of the night the study group begins its discussion of Section 12, Part III.

7. At least one member of the Health Committee should sit in on each study group buzz session and be prepared to help keep the discussion moving toward specific and constructive ends.

Following is a suggested outline for the committee's report:

1. Purpose of the report.

2. A statement on the meaning of good health to the life of the community.

3. How the information was collected.

4. Findings of the committee.

5. Summary of the community needs and problems posed.

6. Recommendations for action.

If there is a need for prepared questions for discussion to ensure coverage of specific local problems not covered by the questions given in Section 12, Part III, these should be added under a separate heading.

The information in the report should be organized in the same order in which the questions for discussion are presented in Section 12, Part III, and in such a manner as to make it an easy reference for the buzz sessions in their discussions of these questions.

RESEARCH OUTLINE FOR THE HEALTH COMMITTEE

Health Personnel

1. Doctors.
   A. Total population of community. (See report of Population Committee.)
   B. Total number of doctors in active practice.
      (1) Ratio of doctors to population.
         (a) Comparison of this ratio with that in other communities of this state.
         (b) Comparison with the optimum ratio as recommended by health authorities.
         (c) Number of practicing doctors in this community who specialize in certain types of cases only.
            (1) Kind of specialists.
      (2) Patient loads of practicing doctors.
         (a) Approximate number of persons who visited a doctor in this community during the past year.
            (1) Approximate total number of visits.
            (2) Average number of patients per doctor.
            (3) Opinion of local doctors as to what constitutes an optimum patient load.
      (3) Hours of practice.
         (a) Ease of getting an appointment with a doctor in this community.
         (b) Availability of doctors in this community twenty-four hours a day, seven days a week.

        (1) Days or hours, if any, during which no doctor is available in this community.

C. Doctors in neighboring communities.

    (1) Approximate percentage of visits to a doctor that go outside the community.

    (2) Reasons for outside visits.

        (a) Personal preference.

        (b) Type of service or specialty sought, but not available locally.

        (c) The extent to which it is because this community does not have enough doctors of its own.

    (3) Extent to which the need to visit doctors outside the community works a hardship on local people.

    (4) Extent to which people in this community delay seeking a doctor's services because such services are difficult to obtain within the community.

    (5) Distance to closest doctors outside this community.

        (a) Kind of roads which must be traveled to reach these doctors.

        (b) Length of time involved in travel.

            (1) Winter

            (2) Spring

            (3) Summer

            (4) Autumn

D. Considering all the above factors, and others which may be pertinent, does this community have all the doctors it needs for optimum service?

    (1) If not, why aren't there more doctors in the community?

    (2) Would this community be attractive to most doctors who are strangers and considering a place to practice?

        (a) Are improvements needed?

        (b) If so, give specific suggestions.

    (3) Is any effort being made at the present time to attract more doctors?

        (a) What results are these efforts getting?

        (b) Are the people who are making these efforts having any particular difficulties? If so, what difficulties? How can these difficulties be overcome?

        (c) What action is recommended to assist these efforts?

        (d) If no efforts are being made at the present time to attract more doctors into the community, should such efforts be made? If so, what action is recommended?

      (e) If a new doctor moved into this community, to what extent would he be patronized?

E. Future doctors.
    (a) Number of young people from this community who have entered school to become doctors within the past fifteen years.
    (b) What is the current need for doctors in the United States as a whole?

2. Dentists.
  A. Check the community's supply of dentists, using the same points listed above for checking doctors.

3. Nurses.
  A. Check the local public health agency, or nearest one serving this community for the following information:
    (1) Total number of professional nurses employed.
    (2) Number of additional nurses needed.
    (3) If more are needed, why aren't they employed?
    (4) Get same information for practical nurses.
  B. Check the local hospital, or nearest one serving this community for the same information asked for on public health nursing under "A" immediately above.
  C. Ratio of active professional nurses to local population.
    (1) Comparison of this ratio with that in other communities of this state.
    (2) Comparison with optimum ratio as recommended by the nursing profession.
  D. Considering all these factors, and others which may be pertinent, does this community have an adequate supply of active nurses?
    (1) If not, why?
    (2) What reasons can be given by the nurses themselves?
    (3) About how many additional nurses are needed?
    (4) What kind? Public health? Hospital staff? Private duty? Doctors' offices? Practical nurses?
    (5) What action is in order to obtain the additional nurses needed?
  E. Include in the report information which is needed to answer and discuss Question IV in Section 12, Part III.
  F. Future nurses.
    (1) Total number of young women graduating from high school in this community in each of the past five years who have entered nurses' training.

(a) What percentage did these young women represent of each high school graduating class?

(2) Total number of girls now in high school who intend to enter nursing.

    (a) Freshmen. Percentage of total class?
    (b) Sophomores.   "   " "   "
    (c) Juniors   "   " "   "
    (d) Seniors   "   " "   "

(3) What is the present need for nurses in the United States as a whole?

(4) What are the principal reasons why young women in this community enter the nursing profession? What are the principal reasons why they do not?

Health Agencies

1. Public.
  A. List all public health agencies that serve this community at the present time.
    (1) Describe what services are rendered by each.
    (2) What do each of these agencies feel are the major health needs of this community? Explain reasons for each need, and what should be done about it.
  B. Is this community in need of the services of any public health agency that it does not now have? If so, explain.

2. Private.
  A. List all private health agencies, including hospitals, nursing homes, other institutions, and professional health organizations that serve this community at the present time.
    (1) Describe what service is rendered by each.
    (2) What does each of these agenices, institutions, or groups, feel are the major health needs of this community? Explain reasons for each need, and what should be done about it.
  B. Is this community in need of any private health agency, institution (such as a hospital or diagnostic clinic), organizations, or groups, that it does not now have?
    (1) If so, explain details of need.
    (2) What should be done about it?
  C. Does this community have a local health council?
    (1) If so, explain in details its objectives.
    (2) Is it active? If not, why isn't it?
    (3) If there is no such council, what are the functions of local health councils?

(4) Could such a council serve a useful purpose in this community? Should one be organized?

Sanitation

1. Water supply.
   A. Source of supply.
   B. State whether community has a public water system.
      (1) If not, is one needed? Give information on cost and the steps that would be necessary to get one.
      (2) If there is a public water system, are improvements needed?
         (a) If so, list specific improvements needed.
         (b) What action would be necessary to bring these improvements about?
   C. State whether samples are taken from local water supplies at regular intervals for testing.
      (1) Record of tests during the past year.
      (2) Have there been any tests that showed unsatisfactory results?
      (3) If so, what action has been taken to effect improvements?
   D. State whether the source of water supplies in this community is regularly inspected by a sanitary engineer.
      (1) Record of engineer's reports.
   E. Indicate the percentage of people in this community who have their water piped into their homes, and the percentage who do not.
      (1) Does this reflect any problems?
      (2) If so, describe problems and state what should be done to correct them.

2. Sewage disposal.
   A. Give information on the public sewer system in this community.
      (1) Are improvements needed?
      (2) If yes, describe needs and problems posed.
      (3) What action is needed to solve these problems?
   B. If there is no public sewer system in this community, the committee should make a detailed investigation of the situation and furnish available facts for discussion by the study group.
      (1) Reasons why no sewer system has been installed to date.
      (2) Describe any specific efforts that have been made to install sewers, and results of these efforts.
      (3) Describe advantages and disadvantages of sewer installation.

(4) Give information on probable total cost, possible methods of financing, and average amount it would cost taxpayers.

(5) Describe chief handicaps that would have to be overcome in order to install system.

(6) Recommendations as to future action.

C. If the community has septic tanks, so state, and describe condition.

   (1) Are improvements needed?

   (2) What specific needs and problems does this pose?

   (3) Recommended action.

D. If the community has cesspools, so state, and describe condition.

   (1) Are improvements needed?

   (2) What specific needs and problems does this pose?

   (3) Recommended action.

E. Does this community have any outdoor toilets?

   (1) If so, are they maintained in a sanitary condition?

   (2) State what improvements, if any, are needed, and how such improvements might be brought about.

F. Is there a sewage disposal plant in this community?

   (1) If yes, is it adequate?

   (2) If no, is such a plant needed?

   (3) What steps would be necessary to obtain such a plant, what would be the advantages and disadvantages, and what would it cost?

G. Where are sewage wastes from this community being disposed of?

   (1) Are these wastes treated or untreated?

   (2) Is there any problem of pollution?

   (3) What should be done about it?

3. Drainage.

A. Does this community have any drainage problems?

   (1) If so, describe problems.

   (2) What corrective action should be taken?

   (3) How much would it cost, and how might such action be brought about?

4. Garbage disposal.

A. Describe methods by which garbage in this community is collected and disposed of.

   (1) Are improvements needed?

   (2) If so, describe needs and problems posed.

   (3) What should be done to bring about such improvements?

5. General nuisances.
   A. See report of Beautification Committee.
      (1) Are there any conditions described in that report that con-
          stitute a general nuisance from a community health stand-
          point?
      (2) If so, what action should be taken to remove or correct
          them?
6. Public food handlers.
   A. Are there any problems in this community with respect to sani-
      tation in restaurants, butchershops, grocery stores, and other
      public places handling food?
   B. If so, what action should be taken to correct them?
7. Summary.
   On the basis of the research suggested above, plus any other
   checking by the committee, make a list of the major problems
   of sanitation in this community.

Communicable Disease

1. Make a list of all agencies or institutions in this community that
provide immunization against communicable disease.
   A. How does a person obtain these services, and at what cost?
   B. Are these services being used to the extent that they should? If
      not, why aren't they? What should be done to cause people to
      make greater use of them? What might community groups, such
      as this one, do about this?
   C. What are the major diseases against which immunization is
      given? Why? To what extent is there a danger of being infected
      by these diseases without immunization?
2. State whether or not the immunization service available to this
community is adequate.
   A. If not, why isn't it?
   B. Describe what action should be taken to make these services
      adequate.
   C. Make a list of the agencies that would be able to give assistance,
      and state what help they are prepared to give.

Child Health

1. Public schools. (Part of the information asked for under this heading may be obtained from the report of the Education Committee.)
   A. Describe the school health program in this community.

(1) Could it be called an integrated health program beginning in the elementary grades and carrying on through high school?

(2) State whether the teachers in the local schools receive systematic health instruction on signs or symptoms as a basis for referring students for medical, dental, or psychiatric examination.

(3) To what extent are the teachers given special in-service training in health education in order to keep them up-to-date for purposes of instructing the students?

(4) To what extent do the schools make use of the county or local health department for purposes of planning and operating the school health program?

(5) Are courses in health and mental hygiene an established part of the school curriculum?
   (a) Do all students take these courses?
   (b) At what level?
   (c) Are they adequate?

(6) Does this community have a school hot lunch program?
   (a) If so, what proportion of the students are reached by this program? Is this satisfactory?
   (b) If not, is such a program needed? If such a program is needed, give reasons why, and specific suggestions as to how it might be established.

B. Health service for school children.

(1) Are regular full-time public health nurses available from the public health department for service to children in school?
   (a) What is the ratio of nurses to children?
   (b) Is this ratio adequate?
   (c) If not, why isn't it?

(2) Describe in detail what services public health nurses render in the schools of this community.
   (a) State whether or not these services are considered adequate.
   (b) What do the nurses themselves feel about this?
   (c) If these services are in any way inadequate, give reasons why.

(3) Describe the program that is now in effect for giving health examinations to children before they enter school. If there is no such program, so state.

    (a) Is this program sufficient?

    (b) If not, in what ways is it deficient? Why?

    (c) What, if anything, should be done to correct the deficiencies?

    (d) Are records of these preschool examinations made available to the nurse and teacher for use in student guidance? If not, should they be?

    (e) Are these records made a part of the student's regular school records so that they will go with him all through school? If not, should they?

    (f) Describe what systematic measures have been taken to follow up with appropriate action the findings of these pre-school examinations.

  (4) Describe the current school practice with regard to regular teacher-nurse conferences on each child.

    (a) Is this practice satisfactory?

    (b) If not, give reasons why and indicate what should be done about it.

C. School environment.

  (1) Check each of the following and indicate whether they are satisfactory or unsatisfactory:

School water supply.

School drinking fountains.

School lavatories.

Hand washing facilities.

Sewage disposal.

School milk.

Yards and grounds.

Refrigeration facilities for food.

Cafeteria and kitchen.

D. In summary, state to what extent the school health program is adequate to meet the needs of all the children. Also indicate to what extent, if any, it is inadequate.

  (1) Make a list of the most important school health problems, if any, in this community, and state what corrective measures should be taken.

2. Infant care.

A. Infant death rates in this community.

B. Infant abnormalities due to improper care.

C. Give all available facts and information needed to answer and discuss Question XIV in Section 12, Part III.

Mental Health

Give all available facts and information needed to answer and discuss Questions XV through XVIII in Section 12, Part III.

The problems of older people

Give all available facts and information needed to answer and discuss Questions XIX through XXIV in Section 12, Part III.

Moral Health

1. Describe conditions in this community as regards vice, crime, delinquency, and other manifestations of social ill-health.
    A. What problems, if any, do these matters present to this community?
    B. What action should the committee recommend?
2. List all agencies whose services are available to this community for purposes of dealing with the type of problems indicated above.
    A. Are these agencies adequate to do the job which is necessary?
    B. If not, what corrective action is indicated?

Conclusions

Make as complete a list as possible describing the major health problems of this community, and give specific recommendations for solution.

16

For the Recreation Committee

THE RECREATION COMMITTEE HAS THE RESPONSIBILITY OF MAKING AN analysis of the recreational and cultural life of the community, and of writing a report which will present all facts necessary for the study group to conduct an intelligent discussion of the material given in Section 13, Part III.

The committee should make certain that the information in its report is arranged in the same order as the questions for the buzz sessions in Section 13, Part III, so that it can be used as an easy reference during the buzz session discussions.

If the committee feels that special additional questions should be prepared in order to ensure discussion of specific local issues which are included in the report, but not covered by the questions in the guide, it should do so. Every effort should be made to stimulate a lively and constructive discussion in the buzz sessions which will come to grips with the vital recreational needs and problems in this particular community. The accomplishment of this objective is largely up to the Recreation Committee. For this reason a great deal will depend upon the way the recreation report is presented, and the extent to which the questions for discussion are integrated with the information and the needs and problems which the report brings out.

Below is presented an outline of research which indicates the type of information that should be included in the report. To assist in the collection of these data two suggested questionnaires are provided. One of these questionnaires is designed to be used in a survey of the community at large, and the other is designed for a special survey of young people in school.

In making the survey of the community at large the committee need not attempt to cover every house in the area, but may divide the community into districts and make a sampling type of survey. Or it may work out some other method of getting enough questionnaires filled out. The main thing is to reveal a cross section of the people's needs and desires.

In making the survey of the students, the committee may simply pass out copies of the questionnaires to all the students in school and get them filled out. It is recommended that the planning and completion of this particular survey be done by the teen-agers themselves. Persons of this age group should also be included in the committee's membership.

SUMMARY

Suggested steps for getting the work of the Recreation Committee organized are in summary as follows:

1. Set a date for the first meeting of the committee.

2. Each member get prepared for this meeting by reading carefully (a) Section 13, Part III, (b) this committee outline, and (c) all other references to the Recreation Committee indexed in the study guide.

3. At the first meeting of the committee review the material in Section 13, Part III, and the *Research Outline for the Recreation Committee* which is given below.

4. At this first meeting adopt a plan of operations.

   A. Decide how the two recreational questionnaire surveys are to be conducted. Check the questionnaires provided in this outline to make certain they include all the questions the committee wants them to include. Decide how many questionnaires will be needed for each survey and make arrangements to have them mimeographed. Organize the survey crew, and arrange for the results to be tabulated for inclusion in the committee's report.

   B. Decide how the other information called for in the research outline is to be collected, and make arrangements for getting it.

5. Assign jobs to each member of the committee and set deadlines for completion of assignments.

6. Conduct the research, tabulate and assemble data, and write the report. The report is due in the hands of the study group secretary at least one full week in advance of the night the study group begins its discussion of Section 13, Part III.

7. From the information disclosed by its investigation the committee may wish to prepare certain questions for discussion in addition to those given in Section 13, Part III. If so, this should be done, and the questions handed in to the secretary along with the report.

8. At least one member of the Recreation Committee should sit in with each buzz session and be prepared to help keep the discussion moving in a lively manner toward constructive ends.

Following is a suggested outline for the committee's report.

1. Purpose of the report.

2. A statement on the role and significance of recreational and cultural activities in the life of the community.

3. How the information was collected.

4. Findings of the committee.

5. Summary of conclusions as to community needs and problems posed.

6. Recommendations for action, including a proposed plan for a complete all-age, all-season, community recreation program.

RESEARCH OUTLINE FOR THE RECREATION COMMITTEE

1. List and describe the recreational programs that are in operation in the community at the present time and check them against Questions I, II, III, IV, and VI in Section 13, Part III.

2. Conduct a sample survey of the community at large to determine the people's personal wishes and needs for recreational and cultural activities. A questionnaire for this purpose is provided below in this outline.

3. Conduct a special survey of the teen-age young people to determine their personal wishes and needs for recreational and cultural activities. A questionnaire for this purpose is provided farther along in this outline.

4. Write up an objective description of the present school athletic and physical education program, and of the present nonathletic extracurricular program in the schools, for inclusion in the report as a factual background for the discussion of Questions IX and X in Section 13, Part III.

5. Make a detailed examination of all committee reports and minutes of meetings of the study group for information that has been brought out in the study thus far which might have a bearing on the community needs for recreational and cultural outlets. From these reports and minutes draw up a summary of points already brought out in the study group for inclusion in the report of the Recreation Committee.

6. In every community there are certain people whose professions have brought them into close personal contact with the social and personality problems of other people. By reason of their everyday work, these professional people are in a special position to observe certain needs of the community for recreational and cultural outlets.

    A. One of the members of the Recreation Committee should assume the job of conducting a personal interview with several of these persons and obtaining from them a written statement of their opinions on the needs of this community for organized recreational and cultural activities. These written statements should be included as a part of the committee's report.

    B. Suggested persons who might have such special knowledge are ministers, social workers and welfare administrators, teachers and school administrators, public health nurses, doctors, police officials, judges, and persons of other occupations which bring them into contact with emotional and social problems.

7. Write out a list, with description as to their use and capacity, of all physical facilities in the community such as buildings and grounds that are in any manner being used for recreational and cultural purposes at the present time. This list should be included in the committee's report.

A. The description of each facility should cover such points as the following:

    (1) Kind of facilities, and capacity.
    (2) Equipment available for use.
    (3) Programs now being conducted.
    (4) Kind and age of groups now being served.
    (5) Hours and frequency of use.
    (6) Type of supervision available.
    (7) Sponsorship.
    (8) Costs of upkeep and operation.
    (9) Problems encountered in the operation, if any.
  (10) Needed improvements, if any.
  (11) Other pertinent matters.

B. State whether each of these facilities is being used to full capacity at the present time.

    (1) If not, what additional recreational or cultural activities might this facility be good for?
    (2) Specifically, what arrangements would have to be made in order to use it for such additional activities?

8. Write out another list of all physical facilities in the community such as buildings and grounds that could be used for recreational or cultural programs, but which are not being used for this purpose at the present time.

A. Describe each facility in terms of the following points:

    (1) Kinds of programs for which suited.
    (2) Age groups that might be served.
    (3) Hours they could be made available. Also frequency of availability.
    (4) Supervision, sponsorship, and specific arrangements that would be necessary in order to use this facility for recreational or cultural purposes.
    (5) Cost.
    (6) Any other specific points that should be taken into consideration.

9. Describe what facilities are available in this community at the present time for swimming and water sports.

A. Is improvement needed?
B. If so, describe what specific improvements are needed and indicate what problems are involved in bringing about such improvements.
C. Give suggestions for overcoming these problems.

10. Write out a list of all recreational resources for inclusion in the report, such as mountains, forests, lakes, beaches, etc.

A. Describe each of these resources in terms of the following points:

(1) Recreational activities for which these resources offer an opportunity.

(2) Extent to which these resources have been developed for the opportunities they offer.

(3) If these resources are under-developed, or under-utilized, describe what might be done to make them more available for use.

(a) Costs involved.

(b) Action necessary.

(4) Are organized programs with competent supervision a need in connection with the use of these resources?

11. Write out for inclusion in the report, a list of all organizations and institutions in this community that are sponsoring or conducting recreational or cultural activities at the present time.

A. Describe each organization or institution listed in terms of the following points:

(1) Type of programs being conducted.

(2) Age and type of groups served.

(3) Number of people being served.

(4) Hours and days of actual operation of the programs.

(5) Are there any conflicts between the programs of one organization or institution, and those of another, from the standpoint of time, dates, and groups being served?

(6) Are there any problems involved in the operation of these programs that are in need of solution?

(7) Would it be possible for this institution or organization to open up its recreational programs to more people or more groups in the community?

(8) Would the institution or organization be willing to take such action as that indicated immediately above?

(a) Under what conditions?

(b) Would this involve any additional costs, supervision, equipment, or facilities? If so, how might such additional needs be met?

12. Inquire through federal, state, county, and local agencies in this area to obtain information as to what interests they might have in recreational and cultural activities for this community.

A. Would any of these agencies be prepared to offer assistance? If so, describe what assistance would be offered.

13. Make up a directory of all persons in this community whose names can be obtained, who would be willing to act as leaders, or who have

special skills which they would be willing to teach others if an all-age, all-season community recreation program were developed.

These might be skills in group organization and leadership, skills in arts and crafts, in nature and other outdoor activities, in sports, drama, music, local history and folklore, storytelling, writing, sewing, designing, or in any one of many other activities that could be mentioned. Persons do not need to be highly trained in these skills to help out in a community recreation program, but need have no more than a personal interest and aptitude.

The people listed in this directory might well form the nucleus of leadership around which a well-planned community recreation program could be developed. They might also wish to participate in training courses which could be brought in from outside the community by such institutons as the state university or college for purposes of helping to get the program started.

14. On the basis of the information obtained from the research suggested in this outline, plus any other research conducted by the committee, draw up a tentative plan for an all-age, all-season recreational and cultural program for this community.

    A. List in summary all needed improvements, new facilities, equipment, cost estimates, and proposed plan of action, necessary to bring this program into being.

RECREATION SURVEY FOR COMMUNITY AT LARGE

NOTE: The purpose of this survey is to help find out what people in this community would like most to do for recreation if their favorite recreational activities were available to them. No one's name should be given.

1. Age .... Male ...., or Female ....

2. What are your favorite recreational activities in the:

Spring: ....

Summer: ....

Fall: ....

Winter: ....

3. What activities are there that you like, but seldom do because they are not available to you in this community? ....

....

....

4. What are the favorite recreational activities that you and your whole family like to do together in the:

Spring: ....

Summer: ....

Fall: ....

Winter: ....

5. What activities are there that your family likes to do together, but seldom does because they are not available to you in this community?

....

6. Which of the following activities would you, or your family, take part in if they were included in a recreation program in our community?

.... Archery
.... Baseball
.... Softball
.... Basketball
.... Football
.... Billiards
.... Bowling
.... Handball
.... Volley ball
.... Horseshoes
.... Ping pong
.... Tennis
.... Swimming
.... Water sports
.... Boating and canoeing
.... Playground activities
.... Rifle range and gun clubs
.... Skeet shooting
.... Skiing
.... Fishing
.... Fly casting groups
.... Fly tying groups
.... Hunting
.... Horseback riding
.... Community forum
.... Community barbecues and picnics
.... Community stunt nights
.... Harmonica club
.... Square dancing and folk dancing
.... Modern dancing
.... Tap dancing

.... Jewelry making groups
.... Leather craft groups
.... Millinery (hat making) groups
.... Ice skating
.... Ice hockey
.... Photography groups
.... Weaving groups
.... Sewing groups
.... Quilting groups
.... Basketry groups
.... Woodworking groups
.... Furniture making groups
.... Hiking parties
.... Nature photography
.... Amateur botany (wild plant collection and identification)
.... Croquet
.... Chess playing groups
.... Checker playing groups
.... Card playing groups
.... Puppet making
.... Puppet shows
.... Community chorus
.... Community band
.... Community orchestra
.... Community drama (pageants, plays, etc.)
.... Community folklore groups (collecting local history, traditions, legends, folk songs, etc.)

.... Writing groups (creative writing in fiction or non-fiction)
.... Poetry groups
.... Story telling groups
.... Discussion groups
.... Interior designing groups
.... Soap carving groups
.... Drawing and painting groups
.... Ceramics groups
.... Stone cutting and polishing groups
.... Arts and crafts exhibits
.... Flower shows
.... Rock and mineral collecting groups
.... Gardening
.... Backyard playground contests
.... Pet shows
.... Book clubs
.... Other activities not listed above

....

....

....

....

7. What is your opinion of the present school athletic and physical education program in this community from the point of view of serving all of the young people in school? ....

8. Do you think the extra-curricular activities in our schools such as drama, music, and other programs of this nature adequately serve all of the young people in school? ....

9. In this community as a whole, do you think that the recreational and cultural needs of the people are being met as well as they should? Check for each group listed below.
Pre-school children: Yes .... No............ If answer is "no," what do you think is most needed? ....

Grade school children: Yes .... No .... If answer is "no," what do you think is most needed? ....

High school age: Yes .... No .... If answer is "no," what do you think is most needed? ....

Young adults: Yes .... No .... If answer is "no," what do you think is most needed? ....

Adults: Yes .... No .... If answer is "no," what do you think is most needed? ....

Family groups: Yes .... No .... If answer is "no," what do you think is most needed? ....

10. What would you be willing to do to help make a better recreation program possible in our community? ....
....

RECREATIONAL SURVEY FOR STUDENTS

(Please answer the questions asked below.)

1. Age .... Check whether: Boy .... Girl ....
2. What do you usually do for fun after school? ....

On week-ends? ....

On other days? ....

In the summer? ....

3. What sports do you like most to take part in? ....

4. Are there enough programs in this community for you to take part in these sports as much as you would like: Yes .... No .... If answer is "no," what things do you think are most needed? ....

5. What are your favorite hobbies? ....

6. Are there enough programs in this community for you to take part in these hobbies as much as you would like: Yes .... No .... If answer is "no," what things do you think are most needed? ....

7. Do you think the athletic and physical education programs in your school are adequately serving the needs of all the students in school: Yes .... No .... If answer is "no," give reasons why ....

8. Do you think that the nonathletic extracurricular activities programs in your school are adequately serving the needs of all the students in school: Yes .... No .... If answer is "no," give reasons why

9. In your opinion, are there enough things to do for recreation in this community: Yes .... No .... If answer is "no," what new things

would you like most to see added? ....

10. Which of the following activities would you take part in if they were available in this community:

NOTE TO RECREATION COMMITTEE: Select from Question 6 in the questionnaire for the community at large a list of activities for the students to check, and insert at this point.

11. Give the names of any people you think could help you plan, learn, and do any of the activities listed in the last question above.

Name of Person	Name of Activity

12. What would *you* be willing to do *yourself* to help plan and make possible any of the activities listed above so that you could take part in them?

17

For the History Committee

THE HISTORY COMMITTEE HAS THE RESPONSIBILITY OF MAKING AN analysis of the history and development of life in this community from the point of view of its human interest and the influence it has had on life in the community today.

History is much more than a mere listing of dates, names, and places. From the events and thoughts and life of yesterday have come the communities of today. Virtually all the problems of today had their origins in the past, either in the long-ago or in recent times. The basic job of the History Committee, then, is not merely a listing of certain dates and events, but an interpretation and narration of the events, the people, the feelings, the thoughts, the situations, the social and economic problems, the cultural content that has gone into making this community what it is, or what it might become.

The committee should make certain that the information in its report is arranged in the same order as the questions for the buzz sessions in Section 13, Part III, so that it can be used as an easy reference during the buzz session discussions.

If the committee feels that special additional questions should be prepared in order to ensure discussion of specific local issues which are included in the report, but not covered by the questions in the guide, it should do so. Every effort should be made by the committee to stimulate a lively and constructive discussion in the buzz sessions which will come to grips with the real meat that is to be gained from a review of the community's history.

SUMMARY

Suggested steps for getting the work of the History Committee organized are in summary as follows:

1. Set a date for the first meeting of the committee.
2. Each member get prepared for this meeting by reading carefully (a) Section 14, Part III, (b) this committee outline, and (c) all other references in the guide that bear on the community's history.
3. At the first committee meeting review the material in Section 14, Part III, and the *Research Outline for the History Committee* given below.
4. Adopt a plan of operation, assign jobs to each member of the committee and set deadlines for completion of assignments.
5. Conduct the research and write the report. The report is due in the hands of the study group secretary at least two full weeks in advance of the night the study group begins its discussion of Section 14, Part III.
6. At least one member of the History Committee should sit in with each buzz session and be prepared to help keep the discussion moving in a lively manner toward constructive ends.

Following is a suggested outline for the committee's report:

1. Purpose of the report.
2. A statement on the significance of the past to the present life of the community.
3. How the information was collected.

4. Findings of the committee.

5. Summary of conclusions as to problems posed, and the lessons for today that may be learned from the past.

6. Recommendations for action with specific attention to Questions IV and VI in Section 14, Part III.

RESEARCH OUTLINE FOR THE HISTORY COMMITTEE

1. First settlement of the community.
   A. When, why, by whom, how and under what conditions was the community settled?
   B. Factors that caused the community to grow.
   C. Describe the kind of people who lived here and the kind of community life they had.
   D. Early problems of the community and how the people solved them.
   E. Influence of these early days on the life of the community as it progressed up to the present time.

2. Beginning with the date of the first settlement and coming up to the present time, describe each period or era in the history of the community.
   A. Factors that brought each of these periods into being.
   B. Factors that caused each to decline and grow into the next period.
   C. If there were periods in which the community seemed to be in a state of decline, describe the conditions and give reasons and causes.
   D. Present community problems, if any, and cause, that had their origins in any of these periods of history, either early or recent, and the effect of these problems on today's community life.

3. A brief description of selected phases of the community life.
   A. Economy.
   B. Education and school system.
   C. Churches.
   D. Community organizations.
   E. Cultural development.
   F. Other phases selected by the History Committee.

4. Influence of the developments described under "3" above on the community life today.
   A. Problems created for today, if any.
   B. What changes in circumstances might have prevented these problems?

5. Interesting anecdotes, incidents, events, and personalities in the history of the community.

    A. What recommendations, if any, does the committee feel that it can make with respect to parts "A" and "B" of Question IV, Section 14, Part III?

6. Legends and folklore from the community's history, and significance to community life today.

    A. What recommendations can the History Committee make with respect to Question VI, Section 14, Part III?

18

For the Publicity Committee

REGARDLESS OF HOW MUCH PEOPLE ARE URGED TO TAKE PART, IT CAN- not be expected that more than a small percentage of the total population will become active in the community development program from the time the study actually begins. The percentage of total community participation will grow only as the program moves forward toward action. Therefore, it is of utmost importance that every possible effort be made to inform the entire community on the purpose of the program, and the findings and conclusions of the study as they are developed.

This is the job of the Publicity Committee. Actually it is a public information committee, designed to keep the entire community informed of what is happening and why. The prime objective is not so much to inform people that the study group is meeting, but to inform them of how the meetings are conducted, of the facts and information that are being brought out in the meetings, of the community problems that are being revealed, of the recommendations for the solution of these problems, and the work and findings of the various committees.

In summary, then, the chief items to be publicized are:

1. The purpose and objectives of the community study group.

2. The form of organization of the group, and the fact that everyone in the community is asked to join in the program.

3. The thinking, the ideas, the facts and information, the community problems, and the recommendations for action that are brought out in each of the meetings.

4. The significance of these meetings and their findings to the future of the community.

5. The work of the committees. Each survey that is to be conducted by the various committees should receive sufficient advance publicity to place the entire community on notice that the survey is to be made, when it is to start, the reasons for making it, the possible use of the information to be gained from it, and the potential value of the survey to the community. Then, as the survey and other committee work develops, the community should be informed of the progress, with special attention to the final results. The same principles apply to the discussions and work of the study group as a whole.

Population Survey

Publicizing the population survey and alerting the entire community to the plans for doing it, is one of the first major jobs of the Publicity Committee. For this purpose read the special outline in Part IV for the Population Committee.

Plan Campaign

If the work of the Publicity Committee is really effective it will not be done in a piecemeal fashion, but instead each move and act will be done as a part of an over-all campaign that is worked out in advance from the first week the study group is organized. The campaign should be well planned, yet fluid enough to take advantage of special opportunities as they arise. If certain activities and methods of the committee prove to be of little avail, they should be dropped and substituted with other efforts that will yield results.

The first step in building the committee's campaign is to list the various items about the study that are to be publicized. Next, list the media that are available for publicizing each item and work out the best way of making use of the available media for the items to be publicized. The next step is to divide up the work load and assign specific jobs to each of the various members of the committee.

Among the various media that may be available for use are the following:

1. Regular publications.
    A. Newspapers.
    B. Papers and newsletters published by various community organizations.
    C. Church news bulletins.
    D. Papers published by schools located in the community.
2. Radio stations.
    A. Items in the regular local newscasts.
    B. Special interviews with persons active in the community study.
    C. Radio forums and group discussions.
    D. Special shows dramatizing the work of the study group. For example, experiences of the committees, experiences of committee interviewers making special surveys, experiences in the buzz sessions, street conversations, etc.
3. Community bulletin boards.
4. Posters telling in an eye-catching manner special facts about the findings of the study.
5. Direct mail.
    A. Mimeographed bulletins explaining various aspects of the study and telling about specific findings and problems that are of general concern to the community.
    B. Copies of the study group secretary's report. These might be mailed out to each person who misses a meeting to cover the meeting missed.
    C. Reminders of meetings.
6. Word-of-mouth.
    A. Street and home conversation.
    B. Telephone calls to remind people of specific meetings and urge their attendance.
    C. Talks at the meetings of various community organizations.
    D. Brief personal progress reports with previews of things to come, given at meetings of various community organizations.
    E. Announcements made by ministers in the local churches.

A good publicity campaign will be built up to fit the items to be publicized and the media available for publicizing them. It should tell what has already happened, what is in the process of happening, and include interest-catching previews of things that are to happen the following week. Each project of the Publicity Committee should carry definite news value, human interest, and contain reader or listener appeal. Publicity for the mere sake of publicity is of little use. To be successful it must inform people, and it must be provocative. The study group, as such, is of little value. The true value can be measured and told only in terms of what the study group is doing, what it is discovering, what it is recommending, and what it is planning to do next.

Definite arrangements should be made for designated members of the Publicity Committee to act as reporters for gathering the news to be publicized. These reporters should make regular contact with all committee chairmen for information on each committee meeting, for advance information on special surveys and other activities being planned, and for previews on reports that are about to be released. Arrangements need also to be made for obtaining the secretary's report in advance of each meeting, and one or more members of the Publicity Committee should keep notes on interesting incidents and provocative discussions that are brought out in the study group meeting each week.

These are merely a few suggestions. In the final analysis the success of the Publicity Committee will depend upon the initiative and imagination of its members.

STUDY THE STUDY GUIDE

No one can adequately inform people on something about which he is not well informed himself. Each member of the Publicity Committee should read immediately the entire study guide and become an expert on the purpose and objectives, the workings and operations, and the nature and scope of the program.

BIBLIOGRAPHY

BOOKS

BROWNELL, BAKER. *The Human Community: Its Philosophy and Practice for a Time of Crisis.* Harper & Brothers, New York, 1950.

——. *The College & the Community: a Critical Study of Higher Education.* Harper & Brothers, New York, 1950.

——. HOWARD, JOSEPH KINSEY; and MEADOWS, PAUL. *Life in Montana: as seen in Lonepine, a Small Community.* The Montana Study, University of Montana Press, Missoula, 1945.

CANTOR, NATHANIEL. *Learning Through Discussion.* Human Relations for Industry, Buffalo, New York, 1951.

Cooperative Study of Secondary School Standards. *Evaluative Criteria & Educational Temperatures.* Washington, D.C., 1940.

CURRAN, JEAN A., and BUNGE, HELEN L. *Better Nursing: a Study of Nursing Care and Education.* University of Washington Press, Seattle, 1951.

DAHIR, JAMES. *Communities for Better Living.* Harper & Brothers, New York, 1950.

DAVIDSON, LEVETTE J. *A Guide to American Folklore.* University of Denver Press, Denver, 1951.

GOLDEN, CLINTON S., and RUTTENBERG, HAROLD J. *The Dynamics of Industrial Democracy.* Harper & Brothers, New York, 1942.

HAYES, WAYLAND J., and NETBOY, ANTHONY. *The Small Community Looks Ahead.* Harcourt, Brace & Company, New York, 1947.

HITCH, EARLE. *Rebuilding Rural America.* Harper & Brothers, New York, 1950.

McCORMICK, CHARLES P. *The Power of the People.* Harper & Brothers, New York, 1950.

MILBANK MEMORIAL FUND. *Epidemiology of Mental Disorders.* New York, 1950.

OGDEN, JEAN CARTER, and JESS. *Small Communities in Action.* Harper & Brothers, New York, 1946.

OGDEN, JEAN CARTER, and JESS. *These Things We Tried.* University of Virginia Extension, Charlottesville, 1947.

PEARSE, INNES H., and CROCKER, LUCY H. *The Peckham Experiment, a Study of the Living Structure of Society.* George Allen & Unwin, Ltd., London, 1943.

305

PETERSON, ELMER T. *Cities Are Abnormal.* University of Oklahoma Press, Norman, 1946.

POSTON, RICHARD WAVERLY. *Small Town Renaissance: a Story of The Montana Study.* Harper & Brothers, New York, 1950.

QUILLEN, I. JAMES, and KRUG, EDWARD. *Living in Our America.* Scott, Foresman & Company, New York, 1951.

SAARINEN, ELILL. *The City, Its Growth, Its Decay, Its Future.* Reinhold Publishing Corporation, New York, 1943.

SANDERS, IRWIN T. *Making Good Communities Better.* University of Kentucky Press, Lexington, 1950.

SCHACTER, HARRY W. *Kentucky on the March.* Harper & Brothers, New York, 1949.

YAUCH, WILBUR A. *How Good Is Your School?* Harper & Brothers, New York, 1951.

ARTICLES AND OTHER DOCUMENTS

BRADFORD, LELAND P. "Group Dynamics and Education," from a series of articles from *The Journal of the National Association of Education,* 1948–1949.

Bringing Modern Medicine to the People. Long Island College of Medicine, Brooklyn, 1947.

Community Development in the South. Workshop Proceedings, Annual Convention of the Association of Southern Agricultural Workers, Memphis, February 5, 1951.

DIEHL, DANIEL L., MILLMAN, HAROLD C., and WYAND, C. S. *Local Action for Community Development,* Pennsylvania State Chamber of Commerce, Harrisburg, 1948.

GILLAN, RUTH I. *A Report of Washington Nursing Study,* United States Public Health Service, Washington, D.C., 1950.

HOOK, SIDNEY, "The Dangers in Cultural Vigilantism," *The New York Times Magazine,* September 30, 1951.

Reports and Publications of the Bureau of Public Administration, University of Alabama, University.

Reports and Publications of the Bureau of Community Service, University of Kentucky, Lexington.

Reports and Publications of the Bureau of Community Development, University of Wisconsin, Madison.

Reports and Publications of the United States Government, Washington, D.C.

ROSECRANCE, FRANCIS CHASE. *The Individual Sense of Community in Industrial Civilization,* New York University, New York, an unpublished manuscript.

SAMPSON, DONALD C. *Handbook for Municipal Officials of Fourth Class Towns.* Bureau of Governmental Research and Services, University of Washington, Seattle, 1947.

TEAD, ORDWAY. *The Community College Looks Ahead,* an address delivered at American International College, November 9, 1950.

———. *The Fruits of Scholarship,* an address delivered at the University of Michigan, April 27, 1951.

———. *Higher Education as a Public Trust,* an address delivered at Hollins College, April 16, 1951.

Index